'THE NORTH-WESTERN FLANK'

LEGEND:

SOVIET AIR BASES

N.A.T.O. AIR BASES

NATO
AIR POWER

NATO
AIR POWER

ROBERT JACKSON

★
PRESIDIO

Library of Congress Cataloging-in-Publication Data

Jackson, Robert, 19841—
    NATO air power.

    1. Air forces—Europe.   2. North Atlantic Treaty
Organization—Armed Forces.   3. Europe—Defenses.
I. Title.
UG635.E85J33   1987   358.4'03'091821   86-30346
ISBN 0-89141-294-8

Published 1987 by Presidio Press
31 Pamaron Way, Novato CA 94947

First published in England in 1987 by
Airlife Publishing Ltd.

Printed in England by Livesey Ltd., Shrewsbury.

Contents

Acknowledgements

I am indebted, first and foremost, to British Aerospace PLC for permission to use photographs and other material in the preparation of this book. Special thanks are due to John Godden of B.Ae Kingston and Mandy Penistone of B.Ae Warton. My thanks also to Alan Todd for certain photographs, and to Dr Bob McManners for the maps. Valuable information was provided by Captain James H. Fuld, Chief of Public Affairs, 32nd Tactical Fighter Squadron, USAFE; the Information and Press Service of the Federal German Defence Ministry; and HQ Defence Command Norway, Royal Norwegian Air Force. My acknowledgements to the Editor of *NATO Review* for permission to draw on material that has appeared in that publication over the past decade, and to Bill Gunston for assistance with the F-111 details. Valuable photo sources were provided by Ann Harington and by Mike Roberts of TRH Pictures.

Finally, my sincere thanks to Angela Tunstall, who took on the task of proof-reading, indexing — and in parts typing — this work with her customary efficiency.

Note: Since this book was completed in mid-1986 some of the units mentioned have undergone changes, either in equipment or location. For example, the Tornados of No 9 Squadron RAF, formerly at Honington, are now at Bruggen in Germany, while the 86th TFW (USAFE) at Ramstein has exchanged its F-4Es for F-16s. Other details were correct at January 1987.

Introduction

In April 1949, four years after the end of the Second World War, the North Atlantic Treaty was signed in Washington, DC, by twelve nations: Belgium, Canada, Denmark, France, Iceland, Italy, Luxembourg, the Netherlands, Norway, Portugal, the United Kingdom and the United States. The alliance was aimed specifically at containing communist expansion into western Europe and, by organising the collective defence of the member nations, at ensuring the maintenance of peace. In the first post-war years a widening gulf had appeared between the manpower and equipment levels of the Soviet and satellite armed forces and those of the western nations, a critical deficiency made apparent when, in 1948, the Russians imposed the Berlin blockade. Prompt reinforcement of Europe by the United States, together with the biggest airlift in history, prevented what might have become a political disaster — and perhaps something far worse — befalling the west, and provoked a determination that the Soviet Union should never again be left in a position where she could hold the western nations to ransom.

The concerted front presented by the new North Atlantic Treaty Organisation brought a halt to further Soviet expansion in Europe. This was achieved largely because the comparatively small forces of the western world were able to form a front-line defence which could shelter under the cover of America's massive nuclear strength; the Russians realised that any incursion against any NATO nation would provoke a response which they were quite unable either to match or contain.

NATO strategy has changed radically since those formative years. The earlier policy of total reliance on nuclear deterrence has been brought into question and replaced by a strategy of flexible response. This requires that there be adequate conventional reaction to any initial emergency, in order that there may be time for negotiation, while efforts are being made to limit the actual or potential conflict before the point of final committal to nuclear weapons. NATO therefore maintains the principle of forward defence — 'forward' meaning the actual frontier with the countries of the Warsaw Pact. Emergencies must be dealt with as far forward as possible to ensure an adequate defence of the territory concerned, as well as allowing for a degree of mobile defence which, in turn, predicates depth in the battlefield. A principal objective must be to gain time before battlefield nuclear weapons have to be used; in all circumstances, a potential aggressor must realise that, against any attack which he may make at the conventional level, there exists an immediate and effective response.

The underlying theme of this book is to assess how well NATO's air forces are equipped to fulfil this primary mission. It examines the combat squadrons available, the aircraft and weaponry at their disposal, their tactics and training — and also those of the other side. It also seeks to pinpoint the areas of maximum danger in the event of an armed conflict in Europe, from Norway to the Black Sea, and begins with what may turn out to be the most dangerous area of all: the seas that surround Europe's coasts, the biggest simulated battleground of all between the forces of NATO and the Warsaw Pact. For in concentrating on the forces that oppose one another on the land-locked central front, it is too easily forgotten that the nations of western Europe could be brought to their knees by a non-nuclear war fought on the high seas.

CHAPTER ONE
The Northern Flank: The Soviet maritime threat

The 1960s witnessed a marked development in Soviet maritime activities involving new construction and an increasingly bold fleet policy. Previously, in accordance with Soviet military policy, the Navy was little more than an extension of the Red Army and naval strategy was consequently based on the defence of the homeland. The sight of Soviet warships on the high seas was extremely rare, except for occasional transfers of units between the Baltic and Northern Fleets. These transfers were always carried out in great haste and gave the impression that the Russians felt somewhat uncomfortable outside the waters of their own fleet areas.

Things began to change in 1961. In July of that year the first significant Soviet out-of-area exercise took place, with eight surface combatant units, associated support vessels and four submarines exercising in the Norwegian Sea. This was followed, in 1962, by the first transfer between the Black Sea and Northern Fleets, and an exercise in July

included four surface units plus support ships and more than twenty submarines, operating within an exercise area that extended from the Iceland-Faeroes Gap to North Cape. Soviet maritime aircraft also took part in strength. The Cuban Crisis of late October 1962 taught the Russians a stern lesson in the importance of sea power, and future Soviet naval policies were amended accordingly.

A pattern of bi-annual exercises was established in 1963. In March and April seven surface units plus support ships exercised near the Lofotens, and in August a similar force conducted exercises in the Iceland-Faeroes Gap. Part of this group circumnavigated the British Isles before returning to the Baltic. Inter-fleet transfers between Northern, Baltic and Black Sea Fleets continued and intensified. The exercises of 1964 saw the introduction of the latest missile-carrying warships; fleet strengths were increased and the scope and type of exercises in areas between North Cape and the Faeroes Gap revealed more imagination and expertise. The Soviet Mediterranean Squadron was also established on a continuing basis — although small numbers of submarines had been in the Mediterranean since 1958 — and there was a transfer of ships to Cuba.

Production Tornado ADV in its pale grey camouflage, carrying 4 × Sky Flash missiles, 2 × Sidewinder short-range missiles and 2 × long-range fuel tanks.

C-130 Hercules of the Royal Norwegian Air Force in UN markings.

Close-up of the cockpit of a Tornado F.2.

The spring work-up of 1965 involved only a small force near North Cape. In the summer, however, a full-scale manoeuvre ranging from the Iceland approaches through the Iceland-Faeroes Gap to North Cape took place, involving about thirty combatant units plus support ships and a large number of submarines. In the Mediterranean, the Soviet squadron increased its presence but remained in the eastern half with little activity. In 1966, referring to the growth and presence of Soviet

sea power during 1965, Admiral V. A. Kasatonov, First Deputy C-in-C of the Soviet Navy, commented: 'The USSR Navy flag can be seen in all parts of the world's oceans. The aim of these trips is to support the national interests of the Soviet Union. At present, our ships are undergoing naval training in parts of the world's oceans which earlier used to be considered the traditional preserve of the British and American navies.' Activity in 1966 consisted mainly of patrol and surveillance duties in the North Sea, off the Shetland Islands and in the Norwegian Sea. Again there was an exercise near North Cape, and for the first time the basic work-up exercise was conducted in the Iceland-Faeroes Gap. Meanwhile, the Mediterranean Squadron continued a slow build-up.

The May exercise of 1967 involved a large number of surface units and submarines operating in the Norwegian Sea, with isolated ASW exercises taking place in the Iceland-Faeroes Gap and off North Cape. The dramatic event of 1967 was the Arab-Israeli Six-Day War; Soviet reaction included port visits to Syria, Egypt, Yugoslavia and Algeria. At the same time unit deployments were increased and lengthened, with Soviet warships venturing as far south as the Canary Islands and passing through the English Channel en route to and from the Mediterranean. Summing up the year's activities, Admiral Kasatonov stated: 'The Central Committee has precisely defined the Soviet Navy's place in the defence of the country and has shown the way for the building of a modern ocean-going nuclear rocket fleet which is capable of solving strategic tasks of offensive character in modern warfare'.

In 1968, a small exercise in the Iceland-Faeroes Gap in May and surveillance of a NATO exercise off the Lofoten Islands prefaced the largest Soviet out-of-area exercise ever held. Exercise 'Sever' (North), which was held in the Norwegian Sea, was a multi-phased, multi-areas operation involving a very large number of surface units, submarines and aircraft. Later, from October to December, a small

Victor K.2 tanker refuelling a Phantom FGR.2 of No. 56 Squadron.

force patrolled an area off north-east Scotland and a single vessel patrolled north of the Faeroes in August. In the Mediterranean, force levels were maintained and deployments lengthened. The new 'Moskva' Class helicopter carrier entered the Mediterranean for the first time in September.

The spring exercise of 1969 began in the Iceland-Faeroes Gap during March and involved a large number of ships. During this period, the first large-scale relief of Mediterranean forces by the Northern Fleet took place, and an ASW exercise was conducted in the Norwegian Sea. Other exercises took place in the North Sea and in the area of Jan Mayen Island.

On 14 April 1970 the Soviet Ministry of Defence announced that a naval exercise, named 'Okean', was to be conducted in the Atlantic and Pacific Oceans. The exercise started rather badly when a Soviet nuclear submarine sank in the Atlantic on 12

April. That same week a Soviet replenishment auxiliary convoy of nine ships appeared north of North Cape and proceeded to an exercise area at approximately 72°N 02°E; it was followed two days later by two surface task groups from the Northern Fleet, bringing the total deployed strength to 26 ships. Anti-submarine warfare exercises were conducted west of the Lofoten Islands from 13 to 18 April, and on 21 April an exercise with forces from the Mediterranean and the Northern Fleet battle group was scheduled in an area centred on approximately 57°N 20°W in the Atlantic, with replenishment of the two major groups taking place between the Faeroes and Shetlands. Two groups of surface vessels also moved out of the Baltic and operated off south-west Norway, while a landing exercise was held off North Cape.

Two production Tornado F.2s of No. 229 Operational Conversion Unit, RAF Coningsby.

In late June 1971 the Soviet Northern Fleet conducted an exercise that followed the traditional 'defence of the homeland' theme evident on 'Okean 70'. However, in a significant departure from former practice in the Norwegian Sea, the Soviet forces conducted extensive anti-submarine warfare operations in the area north-east of Jan Mayen Island. Additionally, an exercise apparently aimed at establishing a defence against a carrier task force was conducted further south, around 70°N, while an amphibious exercise was carried out in local waters north of the Kola Peninsula.

There were no major Soviet naval exercises in 1972; the Soviet Navy appeared to be more interested in practising the lessons learned from the 1970 and 1971 exercises. The Russians also used the NATO naval exercise 'Strong Express' to sharpen their surveillance and targeting procedures. April 1973 saw exercise 'Springex 73', with activities concentrated in the Norwegian Sea and the Iceland-UK Gap. The theme was mainly anti-submarine

warfare, and surface units, submarines and ASW aircraft took part in the operations. Heavy concentrations of submarines in the well-defined choke points of the exercise area were detected. These submarines, if allowed to take up similar positions in time of conflict, would considerably threaten any NATO attempt to reinforce the northern flank of the Alliance.

'Springex 74', conducted in late May, was held over a considerably shorter time frame than previous Soviet exercises witnessed in the Norwegian Sea, but it was no less significant than its predecessors. Although no obvious scenario presented itself, air, surface and subsurface units operated in two main areas between Jan Mayen Island and Iceland and between Iceland and the UK. The theme of the exercise seemed to be one of surveillance and quick reaction, and this pattern of activity was again repeated during the NATO exercises 'Quick Shave' and 'Swift Move', conducted later in the year. The Russians used both these NATO exercises to enhance their own monitoring and surveillance capabilities.

In April 1975 the Russians conducted the largest maritime exercise ever witnessed. Over 200 ships and submarines and large numbers of aircraft participated in a centrally co-ordinated world-wide operation. The exercise areas included the Norwegian Sea, the North and Central Atlantic, the Baltic and Mediterranean Seas and the Indian and Pacific Oceans. Submarine activity in the Atlantic was concentrated in the gap between Iceland and Jan Mayen Island and off the west coast of Ireland. All phases and methods of modern naval warfare were practised, including the deployment of strategic nuclear submarines. The exercise was also significant in that it included the participation of merchant shipping in a convoy role, and a simulated convoy off North Cape was the subject of intensive air attacks. Soviet aircraft were also observed operating with surface units north of the Azores.

In late June 1976 the Russians conducted an exercise which began in the North Sea and continued into the Baltic. It was the first marshalling of Soviet naval forces that had occurred in the North Sea area as the work-up to an exercise. The maritime event of the year was the emergence of the Soviet capital ship *Kiev* from the Black Sea in July. This ship, designated by NATO as a missile-equipped anti-submarine warfare carrier, deployed into the Atlantic after a moderate amount of exercise and training in the Mediterranean. While in the Mediterranean, the Russians took the opportunity to demonstrate their new Yak-38 Forger V/STOL strike aircraft, as well as Hormone ASW helicopters. The *Kiev* entered the Soviet Northern Fleet area early in August.

In 1977, the Soviet exercise 'Springex I' began during mid-April, with activities concentrated on anti-submarine warfare operations conducted north of North Cape and in the central Norwegian Sea. The exercise included air, surface and subsurface units which carried out operations on a broader scale, although with less co-ordination between the surface attack groups than in previous years. The exercise, with a larger format and more independent operations, was on the scale of 'Okean 75' but lacked the world-wide structure of 'Okean 70'. Subsequently, 'Springex II' was conducted in mid-June in the Atlantic and Barents Sea, with 27 surface units and 160 aircraft carrying out an air-to-surface strike exercise.

Yakovlev Yak-38 Forger V/STOL attack aircraft at the hover over *Kiev's* flight deck.

The Soviet exercise 'Springex 1978' was conducted in mid-April in association with the transit of a 'Kiev' Class vessel, the *Minsk,* from the Mediterranean to the Northern Fleet. The most interesting aspect of this exercise was the area in which the Russians began operations, a locale which had never been used before in an exercise. The area was south of the Iceland-Faeroes Gap, in proximity to major NATO bases. On the whole, the exercise was brief and greatly reduced in composition compared to previous years, although demonstrating a certain flexibility and vigour in execution. In the following year, exercise 'Springex 1979' was conducted in two phases, the first involving the transit of a 'Kiev' Class vessel from the Mediterranean to the Northern Fleet, and all participants conducted anti-carrier warfare operations. The exercise included 25 surface ships, eleven submarines and 250 aircraft sorties, the first reconnaissance flight being conducted west-south-west of the British Isles. The theme of the second phase was anti-submarine warfare; it involved all units that had participated in phase one and was conducted from the vicinity of Rockall to the north of North Cape.

Mya-4 Bison Elint aircraft pictured over the Norwegian Sea during a Soviet fleet exercise.

In April 1980, a Soviet naval exercise was conducted as a 'Kiev' Class ship left the Mediterranean en route for the Northern Fleet. Three 'Krivak' Class frigates departed the Baltic and joined the 'Kiev' group west of Land's End. The units conducted anti-submarine warfare operations west of Ireland with three submarines located in the area. Air activity was conducted south-west over the Norwegian Sea, through the Greenland-UK Gap to an area west of Rockall. The 'Krivaks' entered the Mediterranean and the 'Kiev' group continued north and carried out two days of simulated air-to-surface strikes while continuing en route for the Northern Fleet.

A Soviet Northern Fleet exercise was conducted early in July 1981, activities being concentrated north-west of North Cape and east of 30 degrees. The theme was mainly anti-submarine warfare conducted with surface ships, submarines and ASW aircraft. The surface units formed three different groups (two groups from the Northern Fleet and one joining the Northern Fleet from the Baltic). A heavier concentration of aircraft throughout the complete exercise formed a major difference from previous years, in that aircraft sorties were hitherto active for only one or two days.

There were no major Soviet naval exercises in 1982, but in September 1983 a large multi-facet exercise was conducted with surface, subsurface, aircraft, merchant and fishing fleet participation. It was worldwide and demonstrated the Soviet ability to conduct and control large-scale naval operations in all the major ocean areas during the same period. This was the largest observed co-ordination of merchant and fishing vessels to date, particularly in worldwide participation. The exercise provided tactical strike operations against a threat along with resupply/amphibious convoy, and escort ships in open-ocean ASW operations.

During Springex '84, which was held between 26 March and 21 April, the Northern Fleet conducted a large-scale deployment to the Norwegian Sea, with about half of the Northern Fleet's major surface combatants and a high proportion of the submarine order of battle participating. This was the largest exercise of its type yet seen. Two aggressor groups, consisting mainly of 'Krivak' Class ships simulating NATO forces, carried out an incursion into northern waters, one group deploying from the Northern Fleet and one from the Baltic. Defending forces included a large task force consisting of the new 25,000-ton cruiser *Kirov;* medium anti-surface-vessel destroyers of the 'Sovremenny' Class; anti-submarine destroyers of the 'Udaloy' Class and other older classes of warship. It is believed that protective submarine barriers were also deployed in the Norwegian Sea. Air activity during the exercise was substantial and included attacks by Backfire bombers against the 'Kirov' group and air strikes directed against the Kola Peninsula.

The ability of the Russians to deploy so many warships and supporting units at one time and with speed came as a surprise to NATO. The lesson was clear; if the Soviet Navy could achieve similar surprise at the outset of a real conflict it would be able to secure the northern part of the Norwegian Sea and so prevent the deployment of NATO reinforcements to northern Norway in the event of

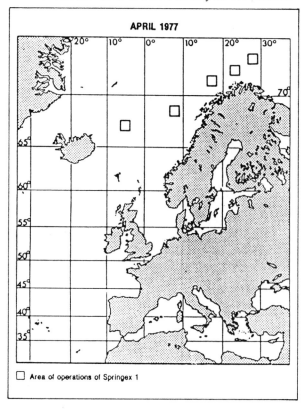

APRIL 1977

☐ Area of operations of Springex 1

The Soviet aircraft carrier *Kiev,* first of its Class, seen in passage through the Mediterranean to join the Northern Fleet, August 1976.

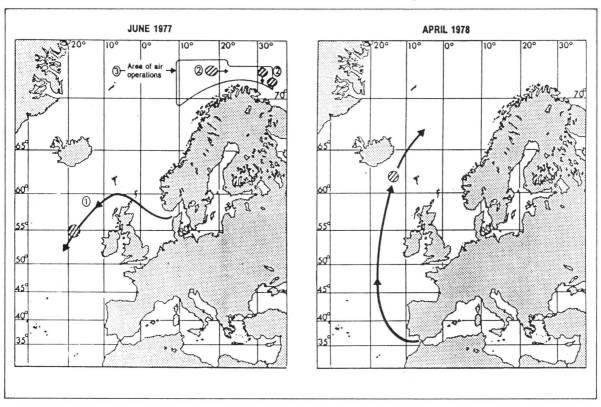

Buccaneers of the Scottish-based No. 208 Squadron form a powerful anti-shipping strike force within No. 18 (Maritime) Group, RAF.

a Soviet offensive. The exercise was repeated in July 1985, when at least fifty surface units, supported by submarines and aircraft, manoeuvred for three weeks in the Norwegian Sea area while other naval forces — albeit smaller — put to sea elsewhere around the periphery of the USSR.

Before considering the maritime roles of the various NATO air forces, and their ability to counter the Soviet naval threat in conjunction with Allied surface vessels and submarines, the threat itself must be examined in some detail. The factor that is of major concern to the Supreme Allied Commander Atlantic (SACLANT) is not the current Warsaw Pact force levels, but the adverse trends. While the Warsaw Pact has launched a massive ship construction programme, NATO nations, despite their capability to do so, are not building enough to keep pace and are no longer numerically equal to the potential adversary. Another trend, even more disquieting, is the closing of the quality gap that SACLANT once enjoyed over the Warsaw Pact. This is due partly to the tremendous transfer of military technology that flows freely from the west to the Warsaw Pact, but also to the vast amount of resources which they commit to improving the capability of their naval forces. Each of their naval platforms has far greater capability than its predecessor in terms of improved weapons, electronics and an increased durability for sustained operations. Almost every unit in their maritime inventory has a missile of some sort, including very effective, sea-skimming anti-ship weapons. Significant improvements have also been made in anti-submarine warfare, electronic warfare and counter command, control and communication (C3) capabilities.

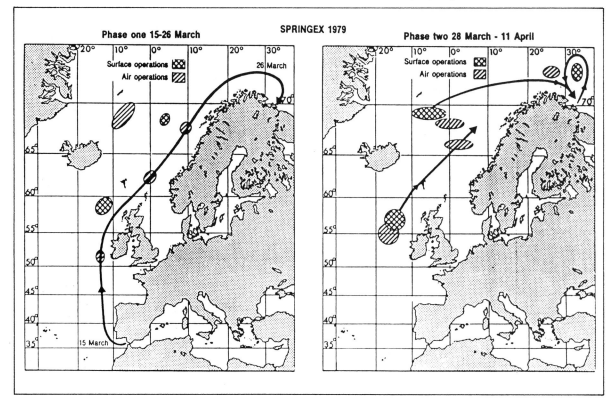

Soviet 'Foxtrot' Class submarine pictured by a
Nimrod while travelling at speed on the surface in the
Iceland-UK Gap.

Developments in the Soviet submarine inventory in recent years have been impressive. Ten classes are currently under construction and two conversion programmes under way. The 'Alfa' Class attack submarine is faster and, with its titanium hull, deeper-diving than anything in the west. The 'Oscar', an anti-ship cruise missile submarine, is revolutionary both in size and in the number of missiles it carries. The displacement of the huge new 'Typhoon' Class ballistic missile submarine is 35 per cent greater than the comparable US 'Ohio' Class, and it is the quietest submarine the Russians have ever built. It carries twenty SSN-20 missiles. Newer still is the 'Akula' Class nuclear submarine, armed with torpedoes and anti-ship missiles, which completed its operational trials in 1985. Neither have the Russians neglected their diesel fleet; in addition to the 'Foxtrot', which is still being produced for export, the 'Kilo' Class and a possible new class of diesel are being constructed.

A lot of progress has been made in the development of diesel-electric submarines since Germany's U-boats caused such havoc in the Atlantic during the Second World War. Then, a submarine's storage batteries had to be recharged for eight hours out of 24, which until the advent of the Schnorkel meant that a boat had to remain on the surface for that length of time. New technology has cut the re-charging time to as little as twenty minutes in every 24 hours, which helps to make the diesel-electric boat a very cost-effective means of patrolling shallow coastal waters. The nuclear-powered submarine, on the other hand, is best employed on missions requiring long range and endurance where it can take tactical advantage of natural deep-water features such as trenches and holes.

Sonar is still the best method of locating a submarine; it provides the basic information which is then confirmed by other sensing equipment. Electronic surveillance measures (ESM) provide information on transmissions on electromagnetic frequencies, but are more useful in locating and identifying surface vessels than submarines, which tend to use radar to scan a narrow arc from which sonar returns are received for only two or three seconds when, say, the submarine is closing for a torpedo attack. The magnetic anomaly detector (MAD), which is usually mounted in a long tail boom to keep any interference from the patrol aircraft carrying it to a minimum, picks up local variations in the earth's magnetic field such as are caused by the transit of a large body of metal; MAD, however, is a short-range sensor and is effective only when the search aircraft is on top of its target.

Generally, then, sonar is the key weapon in the anti-submarine war; the other systems are there to back it up. It comes in two varieties, passive and active. Passive sonar detects underwater noises, amplifies them and transmits the resulting signals to the sonar operator; a passive sonobuoy of the kind dropped by ASW aircraft does not transmit any kind of signal through the water, so it cannot be

Northrop F-5A of the Royal Norwegian Air Force.

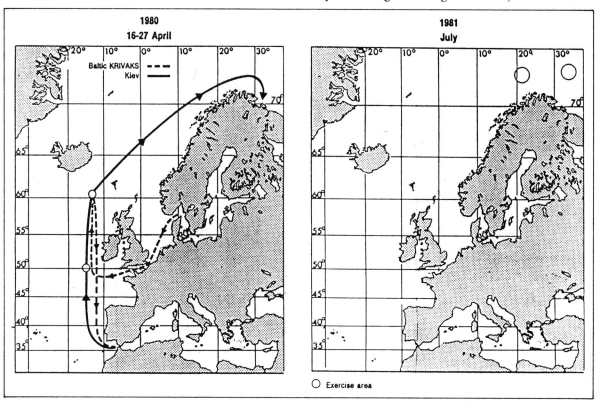

detected by a submarine. It provides the operator with both an aural signal and a visual display, giving a target bearing. The information is processed by computer, which searches its library of sonic data to come up with the required facts. The computer compares stored information on engine and machinery noise, propeller noise and the sounds made by the hull of the submarine as it passes through the water. This not only produces a sonic picture that enables the operator to identify the type of target with considerable accuracy, but often tells him whether the submarine is setting out on, or returning from, patrol. After a long time at sea the build-up of marine growth on a submarine's hull produces more turbulence and consequently more noise.

Active sonobuoys emit a pulse of energy and transmit returned echoes to the search aircraft, producing data on both range and bearing. Their disadvantage is that they alert the submarine to the presence of a threat, so they are most often used in the closing stages of an attack to provide a continuous and accurate update on the submarine's position. Doppler information indicating the target speed is also passed to the aircraft's tactical computer.

To obtain information on prevailing sea conditions in the search area, an ASW aircraft's sonics operator calls for the dropping of a device called a bathythermobuoy, which deploys a sinker. This descends at the rate of just over three feet per second down to about 1000 feet, taking salinity and temperature readings which are passed to the aircraft via the buoy. This is a necessary preliminary, because different temperature layers in the sea, called thermoclines, can either hide a target or interfere with the passage of sonar signals.

With this data established, sonobuoys — which can vary in length from one to four feet and can be dropped from heights varying between 40,000 feet and 150 feet, at speeds of between 60 and 400 mph — are positioned to cover the various depth strata where a submarine might be hiding. The sonobuoy, which is stabilised by either a parachute or ballonet, must enter the water cleanly to reduce the impact and also eliminate any undue noise that might be detected by the target submarine. When it enters the sea the drogue is released and a sea-water battery is activated; at the same time a CO_2 cylinder inflates a flotation bag housing the antenna and the hydrophone sinks on its lead to the required depth. After its operation is completed, the sonobuoy scuttles itself to prevent itself being recovered by the enemy or presenting a shipping hazard.

Modern submarines, with their extremely tough pressure hulls of hardened steel or titanium, are not easy to destroy, and to inflict lethal damage with a conventional depth bomb a direct hit in shallow water or a very near miss in deep water is usually required. Consequently, the homing torpedo is the principal ASW weapon; travelling at up to forty knots, with the ability to manoeuvre rapidly, it seeks out its target in much the same way as an infra-red homing missile. The torpedo homes on the submarine's noise, which increases as it tries to take evasive action. If the class of submarine has been established prior to the attack, the torpedo can be programmed to strike the target's hull at a specified distance from the propeller noise source — for example, in the reactor compartment of a nuclear-powered craft. Tactical warheads in the lower kiloton range form part of the ASW armoury, but these would in general only be used against deep-diving ballistic missile submarines.

Buccaneer S2 at low level.

In the build-up to any war between NATO and the Warsaw Pact, Soviet submarines bound for the Atlantic and Pacific would slip out of their ports at Murmansk and Vladivostok, while others would enter the Mediterranean and North Sea from the Black Sea and the Baltic, all well in advance of hostilities. Ballistics missile submarines would reach their war stations and then go deep and silent — although it is impossible for a nuclear boat to be completely silent, as its reactor cooling pump must be kept running all the time. Attack submarines would transmit to their patrol lines in the Atlantic and lie in wait to intercept convoys in passage from the United States to Europe, in much the same way as their U-boat ancestors did. Before any of these craft could reach their war stations, however, they would have to penetrate some very sophisticated lines of defence, the first of which would consist of NATO hunter-killer submarines operating close to the Soviet ports.

If he succeeds in evading the hunter-killers, the Russian submarine commander next has to contend with the second line of defence: the P-3B Orions of the Royal Norwegian Air Force. The RNoAF has seven of these aircraft, equipping No 333 Squadron at Andoya. Allowing for three hours on patrol at 1500 feet, the Orion has a typical mission radius of 1675 nautical miles, giving it the capability to patrol areas of the Arctic Ocean if required. Over its more usual patrol area of the northern Norwegian Sea its time on station is greatly increased. The Orion's 154-foot weapons bay can accommodate a 2000 lb mine, three 1000 lb mines, three Mk 57 depth bombs, eight Mk 54 depth bombs, eight torpedoes or a combination of depth bombs and torpedoes. There are ten underwing pylons for stores; two under the centre-section on each side can carry torpedoes or 2000 lb mines, while three under each outer wing can carry respectively (inboard to outboard) a torpedo or 2000 lb mine (or a searchlight on the starboard wing), a torpedo or 500 lb mine and rockets. The underwing torpedo stations are used for ferrying only, but mines can be carried and released from underwing pylons. Search equipment includes 87 sonobuoys, 100 underwater sound signals, eighteen marine markers (XI-3A), 42 marine markers (Mk 7), two BT buoys and two parachute flares. ASW equipment includes an ASA-16 tactical display, ASR-3 trail detector, two sonobuoy signal receivers, an AQA-1 sonobuoy indicator, an AQA-5 sonobuoy indicator (Jezebel), an ASA-20A sonobuoy recorder (Julie), an ASQ-10A magnetic anomaly detector, an ECM direction finder for detecting and locating electronic emissions from submarines, and an ECM signal analyser.

The RNoAF Orions would aim to trap Soviet submarines before the latter reach one of two deep trenches which run between Greenland and Iceland and through the Iceland-Faeroes Gap. These trenches run roughly north-east to south-west and permit submarines to dive deep while negotiating the Greenland-Iceland-Faeroes choke points. Soviet submarine commanders would aim to reach these natural features as quickly as possible; in the case of a nuclear boat, this means that the reactor cooling pump would have to be kept running at full speed with a consequent increase in the submarine's tell-tale noise and radiation signatures.

P-3C Orion of No. 320 Squadron, Royal Netherlands Navy.

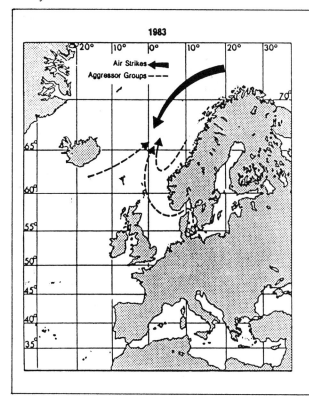

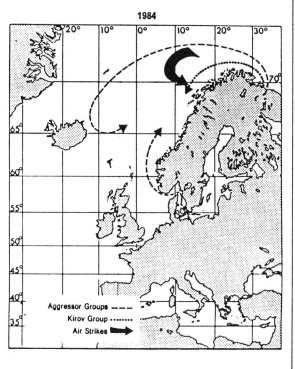

As they approached the trenches, the submarines would have to run the gauntlet of other Orions — P-3Cs, in this case — operated by the United States Navy and the Royal Netherlands Navy Fleet Air Arm. The RNethN has thirteen P-3Cs, based at Naval Air Station Valkenburg, and operates detachments of these aircraft from Keflavik in Iceland in close co-operation with the USN, which rotates its P-3C ASW squadrons to the Icelandic base on a regular basis. In all, the USN has 24 active and thirteen reserve P-3C squadrons; the first unit to be deployed to Keflavik with this version of the Orion was VP-49, in July 1970. The Dutch crews of No 320 Squadron are enthusiastic about the Orion, which has proved very successful against submarines during NATO exercises under operational conditions and which is also far more reliable from the safety aspect than is the Breguet Atlantic, which it replaced. Some of the Orions at Valkenburg are operated by No 2 Squadron, which acts as a maritime operational training unit.

Anti-submarine warfare operations over the Western Atlantic are the responsibility of NATO's Western Atlantic Command, which comprises a Submarine Force Western Atlantic Area; an Ocean Sub-Area; a Canadian Atlantic Sub-Area; and the Bermuda, Azores and Greenland Island Commands. The share of the Canadian Armed Forces' Maritime Air Group in these operations is to conduct surveillance flights over the sea approaches to Canada, over coastal waters and over the Arctic archipelago, and also to provide an airborne anti-submarine force in support of North American and NATO defence commitments. For long-range maritime patrol work the Maritime Air Group employs eighteen CP-140 Aurora aircraft, which is a redesign of the P-3C Orion with increased

Tornado F.2 A03 in pale grey camouflage. This was a trials aircraft used to test the Foxhunter AI radar.

Nimrod of No. 236 OCU, RAF St. Mawgan, photographed over the Eastern Atlantic from the cockpit of a sister aircraft.

internal space and a sensor fit which is mainly an updated version of that in the US Navy's S-3A Viking. The eighteen CP-140s are divided between four squadrons — Nos 404, 405, 407 and 415; fourteen are based at Greenwood, Nova Scotia, and the other four at CFB Comox, on the west coast. Canadian CP-140s, together with other NATO maritime aircraft, occasionally make detachments to RAF Macrihanish, a NATO standby base close to the tip of the Mull of Kintyre.

Shackleton AEW 2 of No. 8 Squadron, RAF. Operating out of Lossiemouth in Scotland, these ageing aircraft provide the RAF's sole AEW force until more advanced equipment enters service.

For short-range patrols and coastal surveillance the Canadian Maritime Air Group uses the de Havilland Canada DHC CS2F-3 Tracker, eighteen of which serve with No 880 Squadron and No 406 Operational Training Squadron on the east coast at Shearwater, and VU-33 at Comox.

The NATO Western Atlantic Command with its HQ at Norfolk, Virginia, is subordinate to the Supreme Allied Commander, Atlantic (SACLANT), as is its counterpart the Eastern Atlantic Command. This comprises Maritime Air Eastern Atlantic Area; Northern Sub-Area; Maritime Air Northern Sub-Area; Central Sub-Area; Submarine Force Eastern Atlantic Area; and the Island Commands of Iceland and the Faeroes. Responsibility for maritime surveillance operations within the Eastern Atlantic area falls primarily on No 18 (Maritime) Group, Royal Air Force Strike Command, with its four squadrons of Nimrod MR 2 aircraft. Three of these — Nos 120, 210 and 206 — are based at Kinloss in Scotland, while the fourth, No 42, is at St. Mawgan in Cornwall, together with No 236 Operational Conversion Unit, which also has a wartime role. Powered by four Rolls-Royce RB 168-20 Spey turbofans, the Nimrod has a typical endurance of twelve hours, patrolling the search area with two engines shut down. Among other advanced surveillance equipment, the Nimrod MR 2 carries the GEC AQS-901 acoustic processor which can receive and analyse data from all NATO sonobuoys, the EMI Searchwater radar and GEC 920 ATC digital central computer. In addition to a formidable array of internal anti-submarine weaponry, the MR 2 can also carry Harpoon anti-ship missiles, AIM-9L Sidewinders or cannon packs on underwing pylons.

The Air Officer Commanding (AOC) No 18 Group holds the NATO posts of Maritime Air Commander Channel Command (COMMAIRCHAN) and Maritime Air Commander Eastern Atlantic (COMMAIREASTLANT). The naval commander, who is both C-in-C Channel and C-in-C Eastern Atlantic, delegates control of all land-based maritime aircraft assigned to him to the Maritime Air Commander. No 18 Group controls Northern Maritime Air Region at Pitreavie Castle, Fife, and Southern Maritime Air Region at Mount Batten, Devon. Units within the Group include the Maritime Reconnaissance Force; the Search and Rescue Organisation; and the RAF element of the Joint Maritime Operational Training Staff, where naval and air force personnel train together.

High over northern Scotland a pair of Jaguar GR.1s from 226 OCU, Lossiemouth. This photograph shows a typical combat spacing.

A Jaguar GR.1 from No. 6 Squadron, based at RAF Coltishall, carrying 6 × 1000lb bombs.

No 18 Group and HQ Eastern Atlantic Command at Northwood, in Middlesex, co-operate closely with NATO's Iberian Atlantic Command (IBERLANT) which, with its HQ near Lisbon, Portugal, covers an area comprising some 600,000 square miles of ocean extending from the Tropic of Cancer to Portugal's northern border and stretching 700 nautical miles westward from the Straits of Gibraltar into the Atlantic. Portugal's contribution to the ocean surveillance task is limited to five Lockheed C-130H Hercules based at BA-6 Montijo (the Portuguese Air Force uses base designations rather than squadron numbers) but in 1986 there was talk of these being replaced by ex-USN Orions. As it is, the Hercules perform a number of other tasks.

Spain's entry into NATO has enhanced the maritime patrol capability in the IBERLANT area; the Spanish Air Force's No 221 Squadron at La Parra operates six ex-USN P-3As, and in 1986 six P-3Cs were on order as part of a general modernisation programme. In addition to these national units, United States Navy patrol squadrons rotate to Lajes in the Azores and to bases in Portugal and Spain, while British Nimrods of No 42 Squadron and No 236 OCU detach to Gibraltar to work with IBERLANT forces. France also has a part to play, and her full role within the Atlantic Alliance — although she remains outside the NATO command structure — will be discussed in another chapter.

In addition to the fixed-wing, shore-based maritime patrol aircraft already assigned to NATO surveillance, the major Allied fleets also have a formidable shipborne anti-submarine capability. In the case of the Royal Navy this is now exclusively rotary-wing, but United States Navy carrier groups in the Atlantic and Mediterranean — which would switch to direct NATO control during a critical build up of east-west tension — operate the S-3A/B Viking fixed-wing carrier aircraft and the SH-3H Sea King helicopter in the anti-submarine role.

A Jaguar GR.1 from No. 54 Squadron, based at RAF Coltishall, carrying 2 × 1200 litre fuel tanks and 4 × 1000 lb bombs.

The Handley Page Victor K 2, together with the VC10, is the backbone of the RAF's tanker force. Victors are seen here refuelling Buccaneer maritime strike aircraft.

The Viking, which can loiter on patrol for eight hours at 184 mph, is responsible for locating and attacking submarines at up to 300 nautical miles from its parent ship, sometimes independently and sometimes in conjunction with Sea Kings. Its main armament is the Mk 44 homing torpedo, with depth bombs and mines as secondary armament. The S-3B differs from the S-3A version in having enhanced acoustic processing, expanded ESM,

improved radar processing, a new sonobuoy reference system and Harpoon anti-ship missile capability. The Sea King helicopters, equipped with dunking sonar and towed MAD, provide an inner ASW screen at up to thirty miles outside the task force's outer destroyer screen, and can be refuelled in flight from destroyers and frigates, the helicopter hovering above the warship's fantail while a fuel line is plugged in by a deck party. Anti-submarine warfare control can be provided by Grumman E-2 Hawkeye early warning aircraft, at least one of which would be airborne all the time over a task force under war conditions.

So much for NATO's anti-submarine forces. But how effective would NATO air power be in dealing with a real threat from a Soviet surface battle group making an incursion into the Norwegian Sea? Before we can answer that, we must first of all take a look at the extent of the air cover the Russians would be able to provide over their warships, and how that cover might be utilised. It must be sufficient not only to establish superiority over the battle group, but to maintain superiority throughout operations. Otherwise, as one senior NATO commander put it, 'Once the Soviet Northern Fleet has sailed down into the north Norwegian Sea, it's a hell of a long way back to Murmansk'.

NATO has a number of highly sophisticated systems available for detecting and tracking Soviet fleet movements, both surface and subsurface. The US Navy has orbited a series of super-secret satellites, code-named 'Whitecloud', specifically for this purpose. Developed by Martin Marietta, they are placed in 700-mile-high orbits, where they release three smaller spacecraft that fan out to cover a wide area. The spacecraft follow the movements of ships and submarines by tracking their radar and communications.

One of the older US Navy Fleet Ballistic Missile Submarines, the USS *Robert E. Lee* (SSBN (601) travelling at speed on the surface.

The secret enemy: a Soviet intelligence-gathering trawler caught in the act off Orkney by an RAF Nimrod.

Long-range airborne surveillance of Soviet fleet movements, and the gathering of associated electronic intelligence, is undertaken to a great extent by NATO's own AEW force, comprising eighteen Boeing E-3A Sentry advanced warning and control (AWACS) aircraft. Carrying the insignia of NATO and Luxembourg, in accordance with international law, these aircraft are based at Geilenkirchen in West Germany and deploy to forward operating locations in Greece, Turkey, Italy and Norway. The AWACS' operating base in Northern European Command is at Orland, on the west coast of Norway. It was originally intended that the NATO E-3As would form an integrated early warning system with the Nimrod AEW Mk 3, eleven of which were to have assumed a major part of the surveillance and warning task over northern European waters by the mid-1980s, but in 1986 continuing problems with the Nimrod's radar were jeopardising the aircraft's future, and it was becoming increasingly likely that the E-3A would be more suited to the RAF's requirements. In the meantime, the early warning role continued to be fulfilled, albeit to a limited extent, by six ageing Shackleton AEW Mk 2s of No 8 Squadron, operating from RAF Lossiemouth. Also engaged in long-range surveillance, under the control of No 18 (Maritime) Group, is No 1 Photographic Reconnaissance Unit with five Canberra PR 9s and No 51 Squadron with three Nimrod R 1s, both based at RAF Wyton near Huntingdon.

The NATO surveillance task is also assisted by USAF E-3As of the 552nd Airborne Warning and Control Wing at Tinker Air Force Base, Oklahoma, which deploys aircraft periodically to RAF Mildenhall in Suffolk and to Keflavik in Iceland. Also operating out of Mildenhall, under Strategic Air Command control, are Lockheed U-

2s and SR-71s of the 9th Strategic Reconnaissance Wing. The SR-71 Blackbird can hold a speed of Mach 3 at 78,000 feet for an hour and a half, during which time it can cover a distance of nearly 3000 miles. It carries a crew of two, the pilot and reconnaissance systems officer, the latter being responsible for operating a mass of highly classified equipment ranging from simple battlefield surveillance devices to multiple-sensor high-performance systems that can survey 60,000 square miles of the earth's surface in one hour from an altitude of 80,000 feet. A unique aircraft, the SR-71 incorporates design technology that is not known to have been equalled or surpassed since.

A Soviet 'Charlie' class nuclear-powered cruise missile submarine photographed surfacing.

Panavia Tornado of the Federal German Navy armed with Kormoran anti-ship missiles.

McDonnell Douglas F-15A Eagle of the 36th Tactical Fighter Wing, Bitburg.

Completing the line-up of USAF surveillance aircraft is the Lockheed TR-1, which is also under the control of Strategic Air Command and is operated out of RAF Alconbury, Huntingdonshire, by pilots of the 95th Reconnaissance Squadron, 17th Reconnaissance Wing. Although intended primarily for battlefield surveillance and control, the TR-1 also has a maritime role in that it can track multiple warship targets at long range and direct strike aircraft on to them.

One of the first offensive uses of Soviet air power in the northern area, in conjunction with anti-satellite operations, would almost certainly be against the surveillance and early warning aircraft and the tanker aircraft that would be essential to the effective provision of NATO air cover and reinforcement. NATO air-to-air refuelling facilities are provided primarily by the Boeing KC-135s of Detachment One, European Tanker Task Force, which forms part of Strategic Air Command's 306th Strategic Wing and is based at RAF Mildenhall; KC-135s and KC-10As of the 11th Strategic Group, which deploys elements of the 34th and 922nd Strategic Squadrons to Fairford in Gloucestershire as well as to Zaragoza in Spain and Hellenikon in Greece; and RAF Strike Command's tanker force, which comprises the Victor K 2s of Nos 55 and 57 Squadrons and No 232 OCU at RAF Marham, the VC10 K 2s and K 3s of No 101 Squadron and the TriStars of No 216 Squadron at Brize Norton (the latter aircraft also performing a long-range transport role).

The principal threat to the surveillance and tanker aircraft is the Sukhoi Su-24 Fencer which — although its primary roles are strike and interdiction — would almost certainly be used in the air-to-air role because of its substantial combat radius of nearly 1000 nautical miles, which would enable it to engage targets in the north Norwegian Sea while operating from bases on the Kola Peninsula. The Tupolev Tu-22M/Tu-26 Backfire A/Backfire B could also conceivably be used in the air-to-air role, equipped with AAMs on its underwing pylons. Without adequate air-to-air refuelling facilities — which in 1986 were limited to a fairly primitive probe-and-drogue system used by Mya-4 Bison and Tu-16 Badger aircraft — effective air cover over the Northern Fleet breaking out into the Norwegian Sea would depend on the rapid seizure of forward bases; the Fencer and Backfire combination could hardly sustain operations, particularly since the latter would bring them in range of NATO interceptors.

The provision of fighter cover for the NATO surveillance and tanker aircraft would be an early task for the fighters of No 11 Group, RAF Strike Command, operating from Scottish bases. The United Kingdom Air Defence Region covers the Norwegian Sea and most of the Iceland-Faeroes Gap, so the RAF's responsibility in this area is considerable — so much so, in fact, that some senior NATO advisors advocate a British decision to place the defence of the British Isles under NATO's Northern European Command. As it is, UK air defence, although dedicated to NATO, remains autonomous.

In 1986, the mainstay of No 11 Group's interceptor squadrons was still the McDonnell Douglas FG 1 and FGR 2 Phantom, equipping Nos 43 and 111 Squadrons at RAF Leuchars, No 29 Squadron and 228 OCU at Coningsby, and No 56 Squadron at Wattisham. No 74 Squadron was also at Wattisham with fifteen ex-USN F-4J Phantoms, allocated to fill the gap left by the departure of No 23 Squadron for air defence duties in the Falklands. Two further squadrons, Nos 5 and 11, were at RAF Binbrook with Lightning F 3s and F 6s. The future key to UK air defence, however, is the Tornado F 2/F 3, which at the time of writing equipped No 229 OCU at RAF Coningsby and which will replace the Phantom in the primary air defence role — although two Phantom squadrons will be retained, possibly replacing the Lightnings of Nos 5 and 11 Squadrons. Developed from the basic Panavia Tornado design specifically to meet the threat from a new generation of Soviet bombers, the F2/3 will be able to provide coverage not only from Iceland to the English Channel, but also of the vital Western Approaches to the United Kingdom.

The Tornado F 2 — 165 of which were on order for the RAF at the time of writing — is probably the world's most formidable long-range interceptor. It is designed to remain on combat air patrol for lengthy periods, and patrol loiter time can be extended to several hours with in-flight refuelling. Its mission is to detect, identify and destroy enemy aircraft approaching the UK ADR at all speeds and altitudes, using its snap up/snap down AAMs. Its

Tupolev Tu-95 Bear maritime reconnaissance and Elint aircraft, photographed over the North Sea by RAF interceptors. The Bear serves in numerous versions, the latest of which has been adapted to carry cruise missiles.

The Tu-16 Badger still plays an important part in Soviet maritime aviation, although it is gradually being phased out of service.

fire control system is able to engage multiple targets in rapid succession; its weapons systems are highly resistant to enemy ECM; and its good short-field performance enables it to operate, if necessary, from damaged airfields. In carrying out its task the Tornado F 2 operates in conjunction with the United Kingdom Air Defence Environment radar system, AEW aircraft and certain radar warning vessels, all linked on a secure and ECM-resistant data and voice command and control net. Such is the F 2's potency that it is able to operate more than 350 nautical miles from its base at night, in bad weather, in heavy ECM conditions, against multiple targets coming in at low level; this means that Tornado F 2s operating from RAF Leuchars, in Scotland, under such conditions are capable of engaging targets at up to 64 degrees N which is about the latitude of the Faeroes.

The Tornado F 2's GEC Avionics AI-24 Foxhunter pulse-Doppler radar uses a technique known as frequency modulated interrupted continuous wave (FMICW), with which is integrated a Cossor IFF-3500 interrogator and a radar signal processor to suppress ground clutter. The radar's high pulse repetition frequency (PRF) enables it to detect targets at an initial range of about 100 nautical miles, while FMICW allows the range of the target to be determined from the frequency changes between transmission and reception. Targets are stored in the aircraft's main computer as they are detected and the system rejects unwanted signals, leaving only real targets which then pass through the radar data processor before

The Beriev Be-12 Chaika (NATO code-name MAIL) is still used extensively for patrol and ASW duties along the extensive coastline of north Russia.

An Il-38 is caught in the act of releasing a sonobuoy over the North Norwegian Sea.

being displayed to the aircraft's crew. While this is happening the AI-24 radar continues to scan normally, so that targets are unaware that they are the subject of detailed analysis. Once target priority has been established, the Tornado's crew can plan their approach to engage the maximum number of targets with the weapons available to them. Long-range targets can be engaged at up to thirty miles with the F 2's principal armament of four British Aerospace Dynamics Sky Flash semi-active homing AAMs, while for closer-range interceptions the aircraft carries four AIM-9L Sidewinders on underwing stations. The aircraft also carries a 27 mm Mauser cannon for close-in combat.

With 67 degrees of sweep and maximum reheat, the Tornado F 2 accelerates quickly to 920 mph at low level and Mach 2.0 at high altitude. It is an extremely agile aircraft, being capable of pulling a 4-g turn at 288 mph and a 6-g turn at a little over 345 mph, giving it a turning radius of about 1500 feet. The only aircraft that might outfly it in combat would be a fighter designed for the limited role of air superiority, which it is not likely to encounter in its operating areas.

Apart from Backfire and Fencer, the aircraft most likely to be engaged by the Tornado F 2 in time of war — and, because of the Russian aircraft's role, a very important target — would be the Tupolev Tu-95 Bear. About 36 of these long-range maritime reconnaissance, ECM and ASW aircraft are operated by an air regiment of the 206th (Naval) Air Division, which forms part of the Fleet Air Force of the Northern Fleet and is based on airfields in the Murmansk area. Each of the four Soviet fleets — the Northern, Black Sea, Baltic and Far Eastern — has its associated naval air force, with air divisions organised into three air regiments, each with three squadrons.

The turboprop-powered Tu-95, which first flew in prototype form in 1954, has received the NATO classifications of Bear A, B, C, D, E, F, G and H, according to its operational status. The original Bear A was a strategic bomber; the B was a maritime reconnaissance variant and the first of the type to enter service in 1961 with the Soviet Naval Aviation; the C and D had an ECM capability; the E and F were conversions of earlier models with a higher standard of equipment and avionics; the G version was modified to carry the AS-4 supersonic air-to-surface missile; and the latest version, the Bear H — also known as the Tu-95/142 — carries four AS-15 cruise missiles. From the maritime point of view the most important version is the Bear F, which is now dedicated to the maritime patrol role and has a substantial ASW capability. The Bear is still in production, five each of the F and H versions being built every year.

Any major incursion by the Soviet Northern Fleet into the north Norwegian Sea would be supported by Tu-26 Backfires, Su-24 Fencers, Tu-95 Bears and also by the Il-38 May maritime reconnaissance and ASW aircraft, which also equips two squadrons of the 206th Air Division and is a version of the Il-18 civil airliner. AWACS would be provided by the Tu-126 Moss, which will eventually be replaced by the Il-76 Mainstay. The Tu-16 Badger, which can carry anti-shipping missiles and perform other roles including ECM, would also have a part to play, although this aircraft is gradually being phased out of first-line service. None of these types, however, could provide the Northern Fleet with adequate air cover. Once outside the range of shore bases, air cover for the fleet would depend entirely on the presence of a 'Kiev' Class carrier and its complement of Yak-38 Forger V/STOL aircraft, twelve of which are carried by each of the four vessels in service, and on long-range naval SAM systems backed up with AAA. What chance, then, would NATO's anti-shipping strike squadrons have of inflicting lethal damage on the Soviet task groups — enough, at any rate, to prevent them securing control of the northern Norwegian Sea?

A Royal Norwegian Air Force F-16 streaming its brake parachute on landing at Bodo.

The initial anti-shipping response would almost certainly come from the Buccaneer S 2 strike force of No 18 Group, RAF. Based on Lossiemouth, in northern Scotland, this comprises Nos 12 and 208 Squadrons and No 237 OCU. The primary anti-shipping weapon of the Buccaneer S 2 is the British Aerospace Dynamics Sea Eagle, a very advanced sea-skimming missile. A Buccaneer can carry four of these weapons, which — before an attack is initiated — are supplied with target range and bearing data from the aircraft's nav/attack system, together with launch airspeed, wind speed and direction, and other information such as target selection criteria and ECM information. If such data are not available, the missile can be launched on a pre-set heading, which it follows until its own radar seeker detects the target. Because of the need to maintain radar silence, Sea Eagle's J-band pulse radar seeker is not activated until the missile's flight

F-5 of the Royal Norwegian Air Force at Rygge. As re-equipment with the F-16 progresses, the remaining F-5s will be concentrated in No. 336 Squadron.

computer determines that it is nearing the target; the large scan angle and long range of the seeker ensures that the target will be detected, even if fast-moving and taking evasive action. The seeker is also designed to cope with the severest weather conditions.

Once lock-on has been obtained, Sea Eagle descends to its final sea-skimming height until impact. Details of the high-explosive warhead are classified, but it is sufficient to disable even the largest warships. During evaluation by the Joint Services Trials Unit, Boscombe Down, late in 1985, Buccaneers and Sea Harriers — which also carry the missile operationally in the anti-shipping role — fired eleven Sea Eagles, singly and in salvoes, from different altitudes against stationary and moving targets at ranges up to the missile's maximum. (This is classified, but may be up to fifty nautical miles.) The targets ranged from moored rafts to converted trawlers and decommissioned warships; some of them were protected by sophisticated electronic and other countermeasures as the trials progressed. These tests were highly successful.

Another highly-effective airborne anti-ship missile is the American AGM-84A Harpoon, which gives No 18 Group's Nimrods a strike capability in addition to their primary roles of maritime reconnaissance and ASW. The weapon, which also has a range of about fifty nautical miles, has a 500 lb warhead. Two squadrons of SAC B-52Gs tasked with the maritime reconnaissance/anti-shipping role, as well as the F/A-18 Hornet and the S-3 Viking, carry Harpoon as well.

In the build-up to possible hostilities, and with a major breakout of the Soviet fleet expected, it is likely that a proportion of No 18 Group's Buccaneer force would be deployed to one of the Norwegian bases inside the Arctic Circle — Banak,

Guardian of NATO's skies: an F-16A Fighting Falcon flies high over Western Europe.

Tromsö, Bardufos, Andoya or Bodo — in order to extend the area of operations without the need to flight-refuel. One of the RAF's home-based Tornado GR 1 strike squadrons — No 617 from Marham, for example — may also operate in the anti-shipping role, together with some F-111Es of the USAF's 20th Tactical Fighter Wing from Upper Heyford (whose primary task is discussed elsewhere). The use of the bases in northern Norway would also bring the Soviet Naval Aviation's eighteen airfields on the Kola Peninsula within range of NATO strike aircraft.

Arguably the world's most versatile naval combat aircraft, the Royal Navy's Sea Harriers have given creditable performances in NATO exercises against Mach 2-plus aircraft. There are three RN Sea Harrier squadrons. Top photograph shows the aircraft armed with the BAe Sea Eagle anti-ship missile.

Rapid elimination of the northern Norwegian airfields would therefore be likely to assume high priority for the Russians in the event of an outbreak of hostilities, particularly as those airfields are essential to the rapid deployment of NATO reinforcements. No foreign troops are allowed to be stationed in Norway on a permanent basis in peacetime, so the security of the northern flank of the Alliance depends on the swift action of the ACE (Allied Command Europe) Mobile Force, which carries out regular deployment exercises in the area.

Air reinforcements are critical, for the Royal Norwegian Air Force's modern combat element consists of only 58 General Dynamics F-16A fighter-bombers and ten two-seat F-16Bs, in addition to two squadrons of Northrop F-5A Freedom Fighters. The F-16s are operated by four squadrons, Nos 331 and 334 at Bodo and 332 and 336 at Rygge. Although optimised for the interceptor role these aircraft were, in 1986, being modified for fighter interceptor-attack (FXA), the attack role being primarily anti-shipping operations with the Penguin Mk 3 ASM. Developed by the Kongsberg Vaapenfabrikk, the Penguin Mk 3 cruises at high subsonic speed and has a 270 lb warhead with a delayed impact fuze; range is in the order of 25 miles. In the air-to-air role, the Norwegian F-16s carry the AIM-9L Sidewinder. The F-5As are operated by No 336 Squadron at Rygge (nine F-5As and fifteen RF-5As) and No 338 Squadron at Orland (34 F-5As and ten F-5Bs). As No 338 Squadron re-equips with the F-16, the remaining F-5s will be concentrated in No 336 Squadron.

Sea Harrier FRS.1s of No. 800 Squadron, Royal Navy.

NATO air reinforcements to Norway would include US Marine Corps and Canadian Armed Forces F-18 Hornets, USAF F-15 Eagles and RAF Jaguars and Harriers. The USMC Hornets would be assigned from Fighter/Attack Squadrons VMFA-314, VMFA-323, VMFA-531 or VMFA-115, while the CAF Hornets (known as CF-188s in Canadian service) would be assigned from the NATO-dedicated Nos 433 and 434 Squadrons. The RAF's Jaguars would be drawn from Nos 6 and 54 Squadrons at Coltishall, with tactical reconnaissance provided by aircraft of No 41 Squadron, while the Harriers would come from the two UK-based V/STOL units, No 1 Squadron and

No 233 OCU at RAF Wittering. All these aircraft would operate in support of the ACE Mobile Force; the bulk of this would be provided by the US Marine Corps, but first on the ground would be the three specialist units of the Royal Marines — the Special Boat Squadron, the Mountain & Arctic Warfare Cadre and 3 Commando Brigade Air Squadron (3 CBAS) — and elements of the Royal Netherlands Marine Corps. Their task, alongside the Norwegian forces, would be to hold the line until the arrival of the USMC, which would take about a week.

Westland Sea King Mk 43 helicopters of No. 330
Squadron, Royal Norwegian Air Force, which carry
out ASR duties along Norway's rugged coast.

In planning an assault on northern Norway, the
Russians have very few options open to them. The
first is a direct assault over the Soviet-Norwegian
frontier in the Kirkenes area, but the difficulty of
the terrain, which is best described as an Arctic
desert and is in darkness for much of the year,
together with the fact that the front narrows down
to a 94-mile bottleneck between the Finnish border
and the sea, makes such a manoeuvre unlikely. The
second option is to violate Finnish neutrality and
attack across the top of the Finnish plateau,
followed by a rapid advance along the so-called
'Finnish Finger' which runs across the top of
Sweden's northern frontier towards Tromsö, where
the Northern European Command's base complex
is mainly concentrated. The distance from the tip of
the 'Finnish Finger' to Tromsö is less than 62 miles,
and it has been calculated that three elite Soviet
divisions might make rapid progress along that
axis, although again the nature of the terrain —
long and deep fjords, separated by steep mountain
spurs — would make it extremely difficult to exploit
any gains. The only real advantage would be that
the seizure of Finnish air bases would permit the

Soviet Air Force to provide continual air cover, but
seizing the bases in the first place might not be easy.
The Russians have bitter historical experience of
how the Finns, outnumbered though they are, will
fight in the defence of their homeland.

The Russians have three divisions permanently
stationed on the Kola Peninsula together with a
Naval Infantry Brigade that includes Spetsnaz
(Special Forces) units, and these could be rapidly
reinforced from the Leningrad Military District. In
terms of manpower and equipment, the threat faced
by Northern European Command amounts to
100,000 men and 440 aircraft of all types. Apart
from the naval aircraft, these are under the control
of the 13th Air Army, which is responsible for the
defence of the Kola-Murmansk region. Combat

Opposite:
The Westland Lynx helicopter — seen here in Royal
Norwegian Navy service — is used by several NATO
air arms in both the utility and ASW roles.

units assigned to this formation have included the 2nd Guards Fighter Air Regiment, the 11th Guards Fighter Air Regiment, the 26th Guards Fighter Air Regiment, the 159th Fighter Regiment, the 275th, 276th and 277th (Ground-Attack) Air Divisions and the 334th (Bomber) Air Division. The aircraft employed by the 13th Air Army include the MiG-21 Fishbed, MiG-23/27 Flogger, MiG-25 Foxbat, MiG-31 Foxhound and possibly the MiG-29 Fulcrum, which is replacing the MiG-21 and is roughly an F-16 equivalent. The Su-17 Fitter, Su-24 Fencer and Su-25 Frogfoot are employed in the ground-attack roles.

Apart from a land assault, the other alternative open to the Russians is a large-scale amphibious landing, but the success of this would depend on full naval control of the Arctic Ocean and the north Norwegian Sea. To accomplish this the Soviet Northern Fleet possesses 140 submarines (not counting forty or so ballistic missile submarines), a 'Kiev' Class carrier with its ASW helicopters and fourteen Yak-38 Forgers (the other carriers in the class are the *Novorossiisk, Minsk* and *Kharkov)* and eighty major surface combatant units including the nuclear-powered battle cruiser *Kirov,* the 12,000-ton cruiser *Slava,* surface attack destroyers of the 'Sovremenny' Class and ASW destroyers of the 'Udaloy' Class, all supported by the maritime aircraft mentioned earlier in this chapter.

Given the fact that any Russian bid to control the sea areas above and below the Arctic Circle would be quickly opposed by the United States Atlantic Fleet, backed up by the Royal Navy and other NATO naval forces with their associated air power, the Northern Fleet would have a difficult, if not impossible task on its hands. Each Carrier Air Wing of the US Navy has 90-95 aircraft, composed

of F-14 Tomcats, F-18 Hornets, A-7E Corsairs and A-6E Intruders, backed up by KA-6D tankers, AEW E-2Cs, and an ASR squadron with S-3As/Bs and ASW/SAR SH-3H helicopters. In 1986 the US Navy had thirteen such CAWs afloat with carrier battle groups throughout the world, and could probably deploy four or five carrier attack groups in the North Atlantic at short notice — and as many as eight with adequate warning. Also taking part in operations in the critical north-eastern Atlantic area would be two or more of the Royal Navy's carriers — HMS *Invincible, Illustrious* and *Ark Royal* — each with nineteen Sea King helicopters and up to eight Sea Harrier FRS 1s. The Royal Navy has two first-line Sea Harrier squadrons, Nos 800 and 801, and a Headquarters and Training Squadron, No 899. In 1986 a total of 57 Sea Harriers was either in service or on order, plus four T 4 two-seat trainers.

As the Falklands conflict showed, the Sea Harrier is not an aircraft to be taken lightly, and it has earned the respect of the NATO air forces with which it comes into contact during exercises. One exercise, code-named 'Ocean Venture' and consisting of two opposing forces operating across the Atlantic through the Iceland-Faeroes Gap and up to Norway, saw HMS *Invincible,* with nineteen Sea Kings and five Sea Harriers (of No 801 Squadron), tasked with defending the 90,000-ton US carrier *Dwight D. Eisenhower* against simulated attacks by surface vessels, submarines and aircraft. In addition, the opposition had the support of another large US carrier, the USS *Forrestal,* with her Carrier Air Group. HMS *Invincible*'s performance as a unit was summed up by Rear-Admiral Jerry Tuttle, USN, the battle group's commander, as 'the finest anti-submarine protection I have ever seen in my entire career. Cox [Rear-Admiral John Cox, the British commander] made those goddam aircraft do things that surprised me. I was impressed.'

Lockheed P-3B Orion of the Royal Norwegian Air Force.

Captain Edward Clexton of the *Dwight D. Eisenhower* echoed these sentiments when he said: 'In the whole exercise there was not a single submarine from my nation (nor any Russians, if they were around) who got near enough to have taken a shot at us'. And the submarine attacks were not made singly, either; at one point during the exercise HMS *Invincible* was tracking at least three nuclear-powered submarines and a number of conventional ones as she swept ahead of the larger carrier. While the ship was occupied in her ASW role, the Sea Harriers were also fully occupied in their air defence role against F-14s from the *Forrestal.* To add a touch of realism, Tu-95 Bear aircraft attempting to shadow the battle group were frequently intercepted by No 801 Squadron. During the peak of operations, No 801 Squadron maintained continuous air patrols for a total of ninety hours; this involved one aircraft on patrol, one on readiness with the pilot in the cockpit and the third aircraft on standby at all times.

The defence of the Baltic area presents NATO's Northern European Command with a different set of problems. Here the threat is much closer than in the far north, and although Warsaw Pact forces would still have to be brought forward to support an offensive in this area, they would not need to move to anything like the same extent as in the Kola region. The Soviet Baltic Fleet is numerically the smallest of the USSR's four fleets, with less than twenty submarines and about fifty surface vessels; the latter make regular excursions to participate in exercises with the Northern Fleet, but in time of war they would find it extremely difficult to get through the narrow Danish-controlled, 150-mile-long Skagerrak. The Baltic Fleet's primary task is therefore to secure control of the Baltic Sea and

Westland Sea King Mk.48 helicopter of No. 40 Squadron which is jointly operated by the Belgian Air Force and Belgian Navy in the search and rescue role.

support the northern flank of the Warsaw Pact forces. Its area includes four large naval bases — Leningrad, Kronstadt, Riga and Tallin — all commanded by Rear Admirals except the enormous Leningrad complex, which is commanded by a Vice-Admiral.

Air power in the Baltic Military District is provided by the 30th Air Army, with around 300 aircraft: much the same mixture of types as those in the Kola-Murmansk area. NATO maintains a standing force of surface warships and submarines in the Baltic; submarines are preponderant, because it would be almost impossible to provide adequate air cover for surface vessels operating close to hostile Warsaw Pact shores. Air defence of the Skagerrak area is the responsibility of the Royal Danish Air Force (Kongelige Danske Flyvevaben), which, like the Royal Norwegian Air Force, operates the F-16 Fighting Falcon as its principal combat aircraft. Forty-six single-seat F-16As and twelve two-seat F-16Bs equip Nos 723, 727 and 730 Squadrons at Skrydstrup, while eleven more Falcons are operated by No 726 Squadron at Aalborg. At Karup, Nos 725 and 729 Squadrons operate a total of 43 Saab F 35, RF 35 and TF 35 Drakens; about half of these aircraft are used in the reconnaissance role. In 1986, all RDAF F 35s were being modified with head-up displays, new weapon aiming computers, radar warning receivers and inertial navigation systems.

The Royal Danish Air Force could therefore put up quite a formidable opposition against both enemy aircraft and surface naval forces which

A Royal Navy Sea King helicopter at the hover, with sonobuoy deployed.

might attempt an amphibious landing on Danish territory. Its F-16s and Drakens could both be used in the anti-shipping role. However, the main NATO anti-shipping task in the Baltic falls to the Marineflieger, the Naval Air Arm of Federal Germany, and in particular to four squadrons of Tornados equipped with the MBB Kormoran anti-ship missile; this weapon has a speed of Mach 0.9, a range of around twenty miles and a 500 lb warhead. The first German Navy Tornado wing, Marinefliegergeschwader 1 (MFG 1) was formed in July 1982 and declared operational in the anti-shipping strike role towards the end of the following year, and the second wing, MFG 2, became operational in 1986. In all, 112 Tornados are either in service with the two Geschwader or on order for the Navy; the principal Tornado operating base is Jagel, sixty miles south of the Danish border near Schleswig, which is the home of MFG 1, and Eggebeck, between Schleswig and Flensburg, where MFG 2 is based. The Federal German Navy also has a considerable ASW strength in the Baltic area; Marinefliegergeschwader 3 at Nordholz is equipped with nineteen Breguet Br 1151 Atlantic maritime patrol aircraft, which are capable of carrying all NATO standard bombs, US or French 385 lb depth charges, HVAR rockets, homing torpedoes, or four underwing air-to-surface missiles with either nuclear or conventional warheads. Electronic equipment includes a retractable CSF radar installation, a MAD tail-boom and an ECM pod mounted on the tail fin. The Atlantic, which cruises at 345 mph and has a patrol endurance of eighteen hours at 195 mph, is powered by two Hispano-built Rolls-Royce Tyne Mk 21 turboprop engines and carries a normal crew of twelve.

At Kiel, Marinefliegergeschwader 5 is equipped with 21 Westland Sea King Mk 41 helicopters in the ASW and ASR roles, while fourteen Westland Lynx Mk 88s are employed in the reconnaissance and anti-shipping roles. The unit also operates twenty Dornier Do 28 Skyservants for communications and light transport.

The ability to secure the exit from the Baltic against the passage of Soviet warships is vital to the security of another NATO command: the Allied Command Channel, which covers the area from the western limits of the English Channel through the Dover Straits and the southern part of the North Sea. The Channel area is vital to the re-supply of NATO in the event of war, when SACEUR would require reinforcements from the UK of some 130,000 men, 22,000 vehicles and about a ton of supplies per man, together with about one million men and a million tons of supplies from the United States. Enemy mining activity is the principal threat in this area, but if the Warsaw Pact were to succeed in establishing air bases in Denmark or northern Germany the Channel would also be threatened by heavy air attack.

Northern Command — Transport and other air units
Denmark No 721 Squadron at Vaerlose has three Lockheed C-130H Hercules, three Grumman Gulfstream IIIs and four Saab T 17 Supporters for transport and communications, and No 722 Squadron at Vaerlose operates seven Westland Lynx Mk 80 and eight Westland Sea King S 61As in the SAR and Coast Guard roles.

Norway No 330 Squadron (HQ Bodo) operates ten Westland Sea King Mk 43 helicopters in the SAR role, with flights at Bodo, Banak, Orland and Stavanger-Sola; No 335 Squadron at Gardermoen has six Lockheed C-130H Hercules and three Dassault-Breguet Falcon 20s in the transport and VIP roles; and No 718 Squadron with three de Havilland Canada Twin Otters for communications.

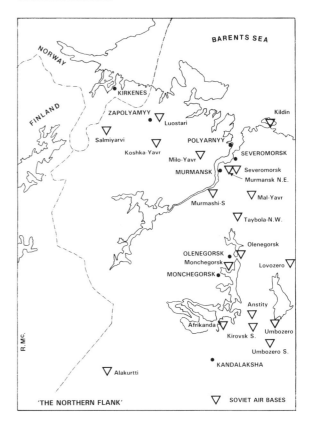

CHAPTER TWO
The Central Front: 2nd Allied Tactical Air Force

Nowhere in the world is there a denser concentration of manpower, artillery, armour and aircraft than on NATO's Central Front, where the frontier of Federal Germany joins those of the German Democratic Republic and Czechoslovakia. For both tactical and geographical reasons, the Allied Forces Central Europe (AFCENT), the most important of the NATO commands, is divided into two Army Group areas, Northern and Central. The northernmost part, consisting of Jutland and Schleswig-Holstein, is actually part of Allied Forces Northern Europe and comprises three Danish brigades and the Bundeswehr's 6th Panzergrenadier mechanised infantry division under the Commander Land Forces Jutland (COMLANDJUT), but for tactical purposes it is included in AFCENT's order of battle.

The Northern Army Group consists of four corps, I Dutch, I German, I British and I Belgian. Further south, the Central Army Group (CENTAG) comprises another four corps, III German, V and VII United States, and II German in that order from north to south. The two Army Groups are supported, respectively, by the 2nd and 4th Allied Tactical Air Forces (2 and 4 ATAF).

Warsaw Pact air strength
The main Warsaw Pact forces facing the NATO Central Front are the Soviet divisions stationed in the East European satellites and designated 'Groups of Forces'. The Group of Forces in Germany (GSFG) has twenty divisions, ten armoured and ten mechanised infantry; they are all Category One divisions and are armed with the latest equipment. Two armoured divisions in the Northern Group (Poland), two armoured and three mechanised infantry divisions in the Central Group (Czechoslovakia), and two armoured and two mechanised infantry divisions in the Southern Group (Hungary) make a total of sixteen armoured and fifteen mechanised infantry divisions in the Groups of Forces.

In the event of war, the Groups of Forces would be supported by the divisions located in the seven military districts (MDs) in European Russia nearest the NATO centre. From north to south, these are the Leningrad, the Baltic, the Byelorussian, the Moscow, the Carpathian, the Kiev and the Odessa MDs. In these areas there are 63 divisions — 35 mechanised infantry, 23 armoured and five airborne — so the total that could be mustered to

fight a war against NATO in the north and centre comes to 94. Not all these divisions, however, are Category One; many are in Categories Two and Three and are badly understrength, so they would take some time to mobilise.

Of the Soviet air armies supporting these MDs, the 13th and 30th have been dealt with in the previous chapter. The largest of all the air armies is the 16th, which supports the GSFG and musters some 1000 combat aircraft together with 200 transports and helicopters. Units known to have served with the 16th Air Army include the 1st, 2nd, 3rd, 6th and 11th Guards Air Divisions, the 198th, 265th, 278th, 299th, 301st and 402nd Air Divisions, and the 15th, 43rd, 127th and 515th Air Regiments, all in the tactical role.

Also under the control of the 16th Air Army is the Luftstreitkräfte und Luftverteidigung of the GDR (LSK), comprising two air defence divisions. The 3rd ADD, with its HQ at Neubrandenburg in the north, administers the 2nd Fighter Air Regiment with MiG-21s and MiG-23s, the 9th Tactical Air Regiment with Su-7s at Peenemünde, and three surface-to-air missile regiments with SA-2s and SA-3s at Parchim; while the 1st ADD, with its HQ at Cottbus in the south, administers the 1st, 7th and 8th Fighter Air Regiments at Cottbus, Drewitz and Marxwalde, the 3rd Tactical Air Regiment at Preschen with Su-7s, and two SAM missile regiments with SA-2s and SA-3s at Steurgrabchen and Ladeburg. Each flying air regiment consists of three squadrons, each with a theoretical establishment of sixteen aircraft.

Warsaw Pact air strength in Czechoslovakia is partially administered by the Soviet 57th Air Army in the Carpathian Military District, which has some 350 combat aircraft. The Czech Air Force (Ceskoslovenske Letectvo) itself has two air armies, the 7th (HQ Prague) and the 10th (HQ Tabor). The 7th Air Army, which is responsible for national defence and therefore to the Czech government, has three fighter regiments with 200 MiG-21s and MiG-23s, together with supporting AA missile sites; the 10th Air Army, which is tasked with supporting the Warsaw Pact Central Group of Forces and is under Soviet control, has four fighter-bomber regiments, each with three squadrons, operating MiG-21s, Su-7s, Su-20s, MiG-23s and Su-25s. There are also two tactical reconnaissance air regiments with about forty MiG-21RFs, and a Soviet fighter air division is based in Czechoslovakia on a rotational basis.

Poland hosts the Soviet 37th Air Army, which musters about 300 combat aircraft and supports the Northern Group of Forces. The Polish Air Force (Polskie Wojska Lotnicze) has some 900 aircraft and is the largest of the Warsaw Pact satellite air forces, although much of its equipment is outmoded. There are about 350 MiG-21s in the air defence role, although these are gradually being phased out in favour of MiG-23s, and a gradual modernisation programme is replacing the MiG-17 with the Su-20 and MiG-27 in the ground attack role. There is a strong SAM force, with nine regiments operating 400 SA-2 and SA-3 missiles at some fifty sites. In addition, the land-based Polish Naval Air Arm operates a mixture of MiG-17Fs and Su-20s in the ground attack role, together with an air regiment of MiG-21s and a small number of Il-28 Beagles, the latter equipped for reconnaissance, torpedo attack and minelaying. In time of war, much of the 37th Air Army and the Polish Air Force's ground attack regiments would be deployed forward into Germany and Czechoslovakia.

To the east of Poland, in Byelorussia — White Russia, the great expanse of flatland centred on the ancient city of Minsk — is the 1st Air Army with some 300 combat aircraft. Units known to have been deployed under 1st Air Army command at one time or another include the 1st Guards Air Division, 6th Guards Air Division, the 277th and

Tornado IDS of the Federal German Luftwaffe.

303rd Air Divisions, and the 9th, 75th and 124th Guards Air Regiments.

On the south of the Warsaw Pact line stands Hungary, hosting the Soviet 24th Air Army which, with 250 aircraft, supports the Southern Group of Forces. Its headquarters are at Tokolnis. The combat element of the small Hungarian Air Force comprises one fighter regiment with sixty MiG-23 interceptors, two fighter regiments with 110 MiG-21s, and one ground attack air regiment with Su-7Bs, which is reportedly converting to MiG-23s.

All the Soviet air armies mentioned above belong to the Frontal Aviation, which is roughly the equivalent of the USAF's Tactical Air Command and is tasked with the direct support of the Warsaw Pact ground forces. Even without taking the contribution of the Warsaw Pact satellites into account, the Soviet Frontal Aviation can muster some 2,500 combat aircraft for operations on the Central Front. Each tactical air army is subordinate to the ground forces commander of the group or district to which it is assigned; the General in command of the air army is a deputy commander on the staff of his ground forces superior, but all air operations are scheduled through him. The air army has its organic services and staff personnel, its own communications and maintenance equipment, and its own transport, both ground and air. In other words, it is equipped to operate as an independent force, and has the ability to move rapidly to forward areas in support of a ground offensive.

Opposite: Dassault-Breguet Alpha jets of the Luftwaffe.

Harrier T.4 of No. 4 Squadron, RAF Gutersloh.

Any NATO response to a surprise Warsaw Pact offensive depends very much on quick reaction, because the territory of Federal Germany is

Tornado F.2s could replace 2 ATAF's air defences in war.

vulnerable from a geographical point of view — at least in parts. The main problem is that it lacks depth. Although the Central Front is 560 miles long, the vital port of Hamburg lies only 25 miles from the East German border, the Ruhr is 94 miles away and Frankfurt-am-Main, the main US base complex, 62 miles. Given the element of surprise, elite Warsaw Pact formations might slice their way through to the rear areas within 48 to 72 hours of the offensive starting, isolating and encircling substantial AFCENT forces.

Some analysts envisage a surprise attack by 54 Warsaw Pact divisions, 27 of them Soviet. Another scenario assumes that the Pact would mobilise all its forces near the West German border and then launch a full-scale attack with about ninety divisions. According to up-to-date assessments, the Pact would need thirty days to prepare such a massive assault; it would take a week for NATO to discern what was happening and decide to respond, leaving 23 days for the Allies to mobilise. This, however, does not mean that NATO would be totally unprepared for up to a month following the Pact's first offensive moves. NATO has a number of insurances against sudden attack, including the maintenance of certain units at extremely high states of readiness. Moreover, routine operational planning always envisages the worst case of a surprise attack, when M-Day — the day mobilisation begins — equals D-Day, the day conflict starts.

In recent years, the idea has become current that NATO is vastly outnumbered across the board in men and equipment. The reality is somewhat different. In fact, NATO spends more on defence than does the Warsaw Pact. The combined populations and Gross National Products of the NATO nations also greatly exceed those of the Warsaw Pact countries. In addition, NATO maintains roughly equivalent amounts of most equipment, although there are some exceptions. For example, the Pact has more tanks in central Europe, while NATO has more anti-tank missile systems. Overall, however, the balance is not unacceptable, despite surveys which purport to show that the Pact enjoys massive superiority. This is particularly apparent in terms of air power. Figures which claim that the Warsaw Pact has a superiority of nearly eighty per cent in available combat aircraft are wrong; in fact, both the Pact and NATO could muster about 3,000 aircraft for use at short notice on the Central Front, and NATO could deploy roughly the same amount of tactical aircraft at every stage in the process of mobilisation. What is alarming is not that the Warsaw Pact has a preponderance of equipment, but that the quality of its equipment is fast achieving parity with that of NATO.

Mirage 5-BR of No. 42 Squadron, Belgian Air Force.

Dramatic take-off shot of a Tornado GR.1 of the Tri-National Tornado Training Establishment, RAF Cottesmore.

2 ATAF — Interdiction

NATO air power in the 2nd and 4th Allied Tactical Air Forces is concentrated in areas from which it can rapidly engage Warsaw Pact forces advancing rapidly into the Federal Republic along the various available axes. There are five — possibly six — approach routes over which Warsaw Pact armour might be expected to make a rapid advance; three lie within the responsibility of 2 ATAF. The first crosses the Baltic coastal zone, where a motorway running westwards across the GDR from a starting point north of Berlin connects with the West German road complex around Hamburg; the second runs due west from Berlin via Magdeburg to Braunschweig and Hannover; and the third, passing Jena and Erfurt, is aligned with the Kassel-Dortmund autobahn.

The northernmost approach into the North German Plain between Hannover and the Baltic is one of the better options open to the Warsaw Pact because it is excellent tank country, although it is constricted in parts by the Elbe Estuary and the Luneburger Heath. Much of the Warsaw Pact's air strength in the GDR is concentrated in the north, between Berlin and the Baltic, and the elimination of the Pact's air bases in this area, together with

Panavia Tornado IDS of Jagdbombergeschwader 31 'Boelcke', Nörvenich. The Federal German Luftwaffe operates eighty Tornados in 2 ATAF's area.

strategic bridges and other key points, would be an early and vital concern of 2 ATAF. It is not difficult to see why the bulk of NATO's Tornado IDS force on the Central Front is concentrated in north-west Germany.

The Tornado IDS (Tornado GR 1 in RAF service) is the aircraft that would, in time of war, be tasked with penetrating the Warsaw Pact's rear areas and inflicting as much damage as possible on airfields and other important targets. Two of the Federal German Luftwaffe's Tornado units are based in the north; they are Jagdbombergeschwader (JaboG) 31 'Boelcke' at Nörvenich, a few miles south-west of Cologne, and JaboG 38 at Jever, west of Wilhelmshaven. JaboG 38 was formed in 1984 from Waffenschule 10, which was responsible for Tornado weapons conversion training in the Luftwaffe; operational training remains the unit's main concern, but it assumes a fully operational role when necessary. Each JaboG has two squadrons, with a combined strength of forty aircraft.

Sharing the interdiction task with the Luftwaffe's eighty-strong Tornado force in 2 ATAF are six Royal Air Force Tornado GR 1 squadrons with 96 aircraft: Nos 15 and 16 at Laarbruch and Nos 14, 17, 20 and 31 Squadrons at Bruggen. (At the time of writing, in the spring of 1986, Nos 14 and 20 Squadrons were in the process of converting from Jaguars, with the possibility of moving to another location.)

All operational conversion to the Tornado takes place at the Tri-national Tornado Training Establishment (TTTE), RAF Cottesmore, so there is a very high degree of co-ordination and standardisation between RAF and Luftwaffe Tornado crews. The TTTE has an establishment of fifty aircraft (21 RAF, 22 Luftwaffe and seven Italian Air Force) and is responsible for training Tornado crews of all three nations in preparing and planning sorties to include simulated weapons aiming and release; navigating to, and carrying out low-level simulated attacks on, one or more targets; carrying out simulated low-level attacks against mobile radar bomb score units; instructing crews in the recognition of electronic warfare threats; planning and executing escape manoeuvres after an attack; and taking evasive action against an air attack without detracting from the main operational task.

All Tornados serving in Germany are modified to carry tactical nuclear weapons, but their primary function is to deliver heavy loads of conventional weapons with great accuracy on targets deep inside enemy territory. Because the Tornado is vital to NATO's air striking power its bases are situated well back to minimise the risk of their being knocked out by surprise attack, and each aircraft is housed in a purpose-built Hardened Aircraft Shelter (HAS) whose three-foot thick walls of reinforced concrete are capable of withstanding all but a direct hit by a conventional weapon.

The Tornado IDS can carry a formidable amount of conventional weaponry. Depending on

Royal Air Force Jaguars display typical weapons loads.

operational requirements, this can consist of the JP233 low altitude airfield attack munitions dispenser, Paveway laser-guided bomb, AS-30, Maverick, GBU-15, Sea Eagle and Kormoran ASMs, napalm, BL-755 Mks I and II 600 lb cluster bombs, MW-1 munitions dispenser, Mk 83 1000 lb bombs, 'smart' or retarded bombs, BLU-1B 750 lb fire bombs, Matra 500 lb ballistic and retarded bombs, Lepus flare bombs, LAU-51A and LR-25 rocket launchers, active or passive ECM pods, Pave Spike pods, datalink pods and chaff/flare dispensers. This array is controlled by the Stores Management System, which before a sortie is programmed by the armourers with data about what weapons are loaded, and on which pylons. Before take-off the SMS is interrogated by the navigator, who allocates the weapons into packages consisting of the type and number of stores to be released at a given time, with appropriate fuze selection. When the release signal is received by the SMS from the aircraft's main computer, the correct weapons are dropped automatically from their hardpoints. All armament is controlled by the navigator with the exception of Tornado's two fixed IWKA-Mauser 27 mm cannon and air-to-air missiles, which are the pilot's responsibility.

The Central Digital Computer is both the heart and mind of Tornado. All data pertaining to the flight are programmed into it via a cassette prepared by the crew before take-off, and

Phantom armed with two Shrike anti-radar missiles and Sparrow AAMs.

throughout the sortie it constantly updates the aircraft's position from four sources: a three-axis digital inertial navigation system (DINS), which provides primary heading, attitude and velocity, a twin-gyro platform (SAHR) giving secondary heading and attitude, a Doppler radar system providing secondary velocity, and an air data computer (ADC) which supplies information such as true airspeed and Mach number. All this information is processed by the main computer and presented to the crew in a variety of ways. In the front cockpit, the pilot has the benefit of an electronic head-up display (HUD), an autopilot and flight director, a command stability augmentation system, a terrain-following display, a terrain-following radar (TFR) and a horizontal situation indicator; in the rear seat the navigator has a TV tabular display, a combined radar and projected map display, a navigation mode panel, ground mapping radar, stores management system, weapon-aiming mode selector, laser ranger and marked target seeker, passive radar warning receiver and active ECM system.

Tornado has excellent handling qualities at very low level and will ride smoothly through turbulence, enabling it to get right down 'on the deck'. During peacetime low-level training Tornado crews may not descend lower than 250 feet or fly faster than 550 mph, but under combat conditions they would come down much lower and pass through the target area at very high speed. Staying low under the contours of the terrain — known as terrain masking — is the best possible insurance against radar detection and most types of SAM, which will not lock-on if the target is below a certain height; in fact, the biggest threat to the low-level crew comes from concentrated small-arms fire and radar-directed anti-aircraft artillery (AAA) such as the Soviet Army's mobile, multiple-barrel ZSU-23/4 Shilka.

Apart from its low-level qualities, Tornado's survival in a hostile environment is enhanced by one of the most advanced — possibly *the* most advanced — active ECM pods in the western world. The MSDS/Plessey/Decca Sky Shadow contains monitoring receivers, signal processing facilities and jamming transmitters capable of operating in noise or deception modes. It can counter ground and airborne surveillance radars, using its receivers to 'look through' its own jamming signals to assess the effectiveness of the current operating mode and if necessary automatically alter the jamming for optimum effect. Because it is software-controlled, it can be re-programmed to cope with advances in enemy equipment and tactics.

There can be no doubt that Soviet air defence systems, although still in some respects unwieldy in terms of command and control, are becoming more advanced by the year. The Warsaw Pact forces on the Central Front have a formidable array of mobile, quick-reaction SAMs at their disposal, some of them — like the SA-11 — capable of engaging targets flying as low as 150 feet. Interceptor capability has also increased with the deployment of aircraft such as the MiG-29 Fulcrum single-seat, twin-engined air superiority fighter which was being deployed with the Soviet Frontal Aviation in 1986. Similar in size to the F-16, the Fulcrum is assessed by NATO Intelligence to have a true look-down/shoot-down capability with a 25-mile-range pulse-Doppler radar and up to six AA-10 active radar-homing AAMs. Similarly, the Su-27 Flanker, which was about to become operational in the spring of 1986, carries eight AAMs of which four are AA-10s, capable of engaging low-flying targets.

Nevertheless, Tornado's chances of survival against these advanced systems are good, and 170-odd Tornados could inflict a great deal of damage on their objectives. For airfield attacks the principal weapon would be the Hunting JP-233 sub-munitions dispenser; Tornado carries two canisters under the fuselage, each dispenser containing both runway-cratering bomblets and area-denial minelets. The aircraft would fly along

Tornado GR1 of No. 31 Squadron, RAF Bruggen, flies low over the West German landscape.

the runway dispensing a mix of bomblets and mines, then jettison the empty canisters. Luftwaffe Tornados similarly use the MW-1 multi-purpose munitions dispenser, which ejects mines, runway-cratering bomblets and anti-shelter sub-munitions. According to Luftwaffe estimates, up to sixteen hardened aircraft shelters could be destroyed in a single pass, and two Tornados could knock out an airfield.

From 1987, Tornado's chances of survival during the critical seconds of its low-level pass over an enemy airfield will be further enhanced by the British-Aerospace ALARM anti-radar missile, which is designed to be lethal against radar-directed AAA and SAM defences, both fixed and mobile. ALARM is intended for use in pre-planned attacks on targets with known defences and operates more or less independently of its parent aircraft. Before take-off, it is programmed with a library of radar signatures against which its computer compares signals picked up by the seeker, and with a list of radar targets arranged in order of priority according to the threats most likely to be encountered during the mission.

Tactically, ALARM can be used in three different ways. In its primary mode, it is launched as the attacking aircraft approaches the target area;

it then climbs very rapidly to 40,000 feet where it deploys a parachute and loiters while it searches for radar emissions. Once an emission has been detected and identified as a threat, the parachute is released and the missile makes a fast unpowered dive on the target. If the radar ceases to transmit, an on-board inertial navigation system keeps the missile on course. Alternatively, the missile can be used in the direct attack mode whereby it is fired towards the target with or without lock-on. If a relevant target is not acquired within a certain distance, ALARM climbs to altitude, deploys its parachute and searches a wider area.

ALARM weighs 450 lb and is slightly larger than a Sky Flash AAM. Up to seven missiles can be carried by a Tornado, whose crew can if necessary re-programme the threat data if they receive a change of target in the course of a sortie.

The elimination of enemy airfields would be an essential preliminary to the establishment of battlefield air superiority, without which AFCENT's ground-attack squadrons could not hope to stem any Warsaw Pact armoured thrust. The attendant problems are compounded by the fact that the Warsaw Pact air forces would almost certainly get in the first strike against NATO's front-line airfields, so the defence of these goes hand-in-hand with the early, interdiction phase of any air battle.

2 ATAF — Air defence

In 2 ATAF's area, the air defence responsibility is shared by F-15s of the USAF, F-16s of the Belgian and Royal Netherlands Air Forces, F-4 Phantoms of the Luftwaffe and Phantom FGR 2s of RAF Germany. The key to the whole air defence system is NADGE — the NATO Air Defence Ground Environment of radar stations which provide an unbroken chain of coverage stretching from Norway to Turkey. There are 85 such stations, ranging from simple monitoring posts responsible for detecting enemy aircraft and reporting their presence to the control centres which, with their tactical electronic processers, are responsible for

General Dynamics F-16B of No. 322 Squadron, Royal Netherlands Air Force, Leeuwarden. The bird on the tail is a parrot, which formed the badge on the RAF crest awarded to the squadron when it was formed in the UK on Spitfires in 1943. No. 322 Squadron's motto is 'Niet praten maar doen' — Actions, not Words.

interception, to the 35 hardened, purpose-built main stations. The latter are equipped with Thomson-CSF tri-dimensional radars showing azimuth, distance and altitude, and Hughes H3118 computers which pick up at supersonic speed, process and simultaneously feed to the controller the data he requires on the aircraft detected, and submit at his request specific information regarding its altitude, course, speed and IFF (identification friend or foe). The computer then selects the most suitable weapon system — missile or aircraft type — and works out the best course and angle of attack for the interceptor, together with its flight and attack plan. Finally it guides the pilot back to his base, or to an alternate if he is low on fuel. All the operations are calculated in micro-seconds.

The most potent interceptor within 2 ATAF's sphere of operations is the McDonnell Douglas F-15C Eagle, which — together with some two-seat F-15Ds — serves with the 32nd Tactical Fighter Squadron USAFE at Camp New Amsterdam, Soesterberg, in the Netherlands. The 32nd TFS is part of the 17th Air Force but is assigned to 2 ATAF, and is the only US Air Force flying unit in that command. It is also the only USAF unit that falls under the operational control of a foreign country, as the Soesterberg Wing is an element of the Dutch Air Defence Command and is commanded by a Royal Netherlands Air Force Officer.

The direct operational chain of command that governs the activities of the 32nd TFS begins at 2 ATAF's Air Defence Sector 1, which has its HQ at Brockzetel in the German Federal Republic and is commanded by an Air Commodore of the Royal Air Force. He in turn is responsible to 2 ATAF (HQ Rheindahlen) which is commanded by a RAF Air Marshal. Operational orders for the 32nd TFS are relayed from Sector 1 to the Combat Reporting Centre (CRC) at Nieuw Milligen in Holland and then to the Soesterberg Wing. The peacetime mission of the 32nd TFS is to intercept unidentified aircraft which penetrate the northern border of the Federal Republic of Germany, and its wartime mission is to establish and maintain air superiority within the 2 ATAF area of responsibility. The unit maintains two aircraft on Quick Reaction Alert/Interceptor (QRA-I) status to fulfil its primary mission, and additional aircraft can quickly be brought to QRA-I status as required.

Simply stated, the F-15 Eagle, which originated in a 1965 USAF requirement for an air superiority fighter to replace the F-4 Phantom, was designed to out-perform, outfly and outfight any enemy aircraft in the foreseeable future. It has a wing loading of only 54 lb per square foot (compared with the Phantom's 85 lb) and this, together with two 25,000 lb st Pratt & Whitney F-100 advanced technology turbofans, gives it an extraordinary turning ability and the combat thrust-to-weight ratio (1.3:1) necessary to retain the initiative in a fight. The high thrust-to-weight ratio permits a scramble time of only six seconds, using 600 feet of runway, and a maximum speed of more than Mach 2.5 gives the pilot the margin he needs if he has to break off an engagement and run for it.

The F-15's wing is a very neat piece of aerodynamic design, with a conical camber and an airfoil section optimised to reduce wave drag at high speed. The last twenty per cent of the chord is thickened to delay boundary layer separation and so reduce drag. Manoeuvre performance is also enhanced by the slab tailplanes, which operate differentially, in concert with the ailerons, in the rolling plane and together for pitch control. They compensate to a great extent for loss of aileron effectiveness at extreme angles of attack, a vital factor in tight air combat. To increase the Eagle's survivability, redundancy is incorporated in its structure; for example, one vertical fin, or one of three wing spars, can be severed without causing the loss of the aircraft. Redundancy is also inherent in the F-15's twin engines, and its fuel system incorporates self-sealing features and foam to inhibit fires and explosions.

Primary armament of the F-15 is the AIM-7F Sparrow radar-guided AAM, with a range of up to 35 miles. The Eagle carries four of these, backed up by four AIM-9L Sidewinders for shorter-range interceptions and a General Electric 20 mm M61 rotating-barrel cannon for close-in combat. The gun is mounted in the starboard wing root and is fed by a fuselage-mounted drum containing 940 rounds. The aircraft's Hughes APG-63 pulse-Doppler air-to-air radar provides a good look-down capability and can be used in a variety of modes; it can pick up Phantom-size targets at around 100 miles range and, in the raid assessment mode, can resolve close formations into individual targets, giving the F-15 pilot an important tactical advantage.

The Luftwaffe maintains two Alpha Jet JaboGs in 2 ATAF, each with 51 aircraft. The Alpha Jet is a very effective light ground-attack machine, and one of its principal roles in wartime would be to destroy Warsaw Pact helicopters.

When the radar detects a target in the basic search mode the pilot directs the APG-63 to lock on and track by putting a bracket over the radar return, using a selector mounted on the control column. The locked-on radar will then show attack information such as target closing speed, range, bearing, altitude separation and parameters governing the F-15's weapons release. When the target enters the kill envelope of the weapon selected, the pilot decides whether to attack using his head-down, vertical situation display (VSD) which gives a synthetic picture of the tactical situation, or go for a visual attack using his head-up display (HUD).

Another useful APG-63 mode is the velocity search. When this is selected the radar shows only target velocities at long range, so if the pilot sees a return that is bowling along at Mach 3 and 70,000 feet, with no IFF, he can be pretty certain that he is dealing with a MiG-25R reconnaissance Foxbat. The radar can also be used to scan the field of view displayed in the HUD for up to ten miles ahead of the F-15; in this mode it automatically locks-on to the nearest target, which is then interrogated. If an IFF response shows it to be friendly, radar lock is broken and the radar continues to search for the next priority target.

The 32nd Tactical Fighter Squadron's air defence role in Holland goes back to November 1954, when part of the 512th Fighter Day Squadron, then operating F-84E Thunderjets from Manston, in Kent, moved to Soesterberg. This formed the core of the 32nd when the unit was re-activated as the 32nd Fighter Day Squadron in September 1955. In 1959, having been successively equipped with F-86F Sabres and F-100C Super Sabres in the meantime, the 32nd was awarded a singular honour when the Royal Netherlands Air Force, in recognition of the contribution made by the squadron to the defence of the Netherlands, offered it the RNethAF crest. The crest, with the crown and wreath of the Royal House of Orange, was blended with the squadron's previous wolfhound insignia, making the 32nd unique in that it is the only USAF unit authorised to use the royal crest of another country.

On 14 September 1960 the 32nd converted to the F-102 Delta Dagger, and in 1969, following a change of name to the 32nd Tactical Fighter Squadron, it became the first unit in Europe to operate the F-4E Phantom. It received its first F-15A Eagles in the autumn of 1978, and these were followed by the more advanced F-15C and -D models in the summer of 1980.

The Royal Netherlands Air Force unit that comes under the control of Air Defence Sector 1 is the Leeuwarden Wing, comprising Nos 322 and 323 Squadrons with General Dynamics F-16 Fighting Falcons. Dutch pilots, like those of other NATO air forces operating the F-16, begin their training at Hill Air Force Base in Utah with the 16th Tactical Fighter Squadron of the 388th TFW, USAF, and complete it at an OCU in Holland. Pilots destined for the interceptor units go direct to the OCU at Leeuwarden, those for the strike units — of which more later — to the OCU at Volkel.

The F-16, which had its origin in a USAF requirement of 1972 for a lightweight fighter and which first flew in February 1974, is an extremely versatile aircraft. In June 1975 it was announced by the four NATO countries of Belgium, Denmark, the Netherlands and Norway that they had selected the type to replace the F-104 Starfighter that had been the mainstay of NATO's European air power since the early 1960s. The initial order was for 348 aircraft — Belgium 116, Denmark 58, the Netherlands 102 and Norway 72 — of which 58 were to be two-seat F-16Bs. A co-production agreement was reached under which F-16 assembly lines were set up in Belgium and Holland, and thirty other European companies became involved in producing components, avionics and equipment.

The F-16 carries an APG-66 pulse-Doppler radar and is fitted with the Marconi HUDWACS (HUD and weapon-aiming computer system) in which target designation cues are shown on the head-up display as well as flight symbols. The HUDWAC computer is used to direct the weapons to the target, as designated on the HUD. The F-16 HUDWAC shows horizontal and vertical speed, altitude, heading, climb and roll bars and range-to-go information for flight reference. There are five ground-attack modes and four air-combat modes. In air combat, the 'snapshoot' mode lets the pilot aim at crossing targets by drawing a continuously computed impact line (CCIL) on the HUD. Lead-computing off sight (LCOS) mode follows a designated target; dogfight mode combines snapshoot and LCOS; and there is also an air-to-air missile mode.

General Dynamics F-16B of the Belgian Air Force's Operational Conversion Flight, No. 10 Wing, Kleine Brogel.

The F-16's built-in armament is a General Electric M61A1 20 mm multi-barrel cannon mounted in the port side wing and fuselage fairing, with provision for 515 rounds of ammunition. An AIM-9L Sidewinder is carried at each wingtip. The aircraft has a combat radius of over 500 nautical miles, a maximum level speed in excess of Mach 2 at 40,000 feet, and a service ceiling of over 50,000 feet. The F-16 is powered by a single Pratt & Whitney F-100 turbofan rated at about 25,000 lb st with afterburning.

Across the border in Germany, the air defence task in Sector 1 is shared by the Luftwaffe's Jagdgeschwader (JG) 71 at Wittmundhafen, not far from the Tornado base at Jever. JG71, which bears the name 'Richthofen', operates McDonnell Douglas F-4F Phantoms. The F-4F has a number of modifications that enhance its air-to-air combat capability, although other Luftwaffe units use it in the ground-attack role. It was the Germans who first applied slats to the Phantom; they are automatically extended at any airspeed, depending on the angle of attack, and immediately enable the aircraft to achieve one more 'g' than the pilot is already pulling.

Phantom FGR 2 of No. 92 Squadron, RAF Wildenrath, bearing the unit's distinctive insignia of striking cobra and maple leaves on its tail.

The F-4F carries a 20 mm M61 cannon in a fairing under the nose and four AIM-9L Sidewinders on rails mounted on the side of the inner underwing weapon pylons. In the air-to-air role, the aircraft is tasked with visual identification flights. A radar approach is made to visual contact, the radar target display appearing in the pilot's gunsight in the form of a target symbol which the pilot flies into coincidence with an aiming symbol, the attitude and closing speed being displayed at the same time. Once the target is locked-on, the pilot can fly an interception using the gunsight alone down to the point where he launches a Sidewinder. In the case of a gun engagement, the sight reverts to a normal gyro lead-computing mode; the cannon is harmonised for 2000 feet, and can be fired electrically at 4000 rounds per minute or hydraulically at 6000 rpm. Burst length can be pre-selected, the slower rate giving better dispersion for air-to-air firing.

In a war situation, the Phantoms would fly combat air patrols at 10,000 feet in pairs, flying an open battle formation with the second aircraft a mile away and 3000 to 6000 feet higher or lower. The aircraft has limited look-down capability and its radar might not be much use below 5000 feet, but a relatively low CAP altitude gives the crews a chance to spot low-flying aircraft visually. On the other hand, the heavy smoke trail left by the

Phantom's twin General Electric J79 turbojets would probably enable an enemy pilot to spot the F-4 first, and take evasive action. Luftwaffe F-4Fs are currently being upgraded for service into the 1990s; before the end of that decade, if all goes well, they will have been replaced by the European Fighter Aircraft (EFA), which will provide the high supersonic agility the Phantom does not possess.

The Royal Air Force's Phantom FGR 2s do not have such a severe smoke problem, as their Rolls-Royce Spey 202 turbojets are considerably more efficient than the J79. Two squadrons of FGR 2s, Nos 19 and 92, are based at RAF Wildenrath near the Dutch/German border and are the only flying squadrons of RAF Germany on permanent NATO call, the others switching from RAF to NATO command in a threat situation.

Nos 19 and 92 Squadrons, which form part of NATO's Sector 2 air defence system together with units of the Belgian Air Force, both have long and proud histories. Both have been fighter units since their formation, fighting in two world wars with great distinction. In November 1962, No 19 Squadron equipped with supersonic BAC Lightning F 2 fighters; No 92 followed suit in April 1963, and in late 1965 both squadrons left their parent base at Leconfield in Yorkshire and took their Lightnings to Germany, No 19 Squadron becoming established at Gutersloh, and No 92 at Geilenkirchen. In January 1968 No 92 also moved up to Gutersloh, from where the two squadrons had the primary task of policing the northern half of the thirty mile wide Air Defence Identification Zone (ADIZ), an invisible 'buffer' zone in the sky running the length of the border with the GDR, to prevent infringements by aircraft from either side.

The positioning of the two squadrons well forward at Gutersloh was dictated not so much by the need for a fast reaction time to investigate suspects, but by the Lightning F 2's strictly limited endurance. The first of the two squadrons to convert to Phantoms was No 19, when 'A' Flight formed on the type at Coningsby in July 1976 and moved to Wildenrath in October. Conversion to type was complete by the end of the year, and in the

spring of 1977 No 92 Squadron also converted to Phantom FGR 2s and moved back to join its sister squadron at Wildenrath. The conversion was progressive, flight by flight, so that the air defence capability of the squadrons was not significantly affected, and in both cases Lightning elements were retained until the units had received their full complement of Phantoms.

The move back to Wildenrath was a logical one. Quite apart from the fact that Gutersloh was needed as a V/STOL Harrier base, the Phantom's lengthy endurance made it quite possible for the two air defence squadrons to operate along the ADIZ without suffering any penalty of reduced patrol time. Apart from the endurance factor, the Phantom is a better weapons system than the Lightning (although it is nowhere near as manoeuvrable). In addition to its 20 mm M61A1 Gatling cannon it can carry four AIM-7 Sparrow and four AIM-9L Sidewinder AAMs, which still make it a formidable opponent at all altitudes. The Phantom FGR 2 is equipped with the Westinghouse AWG-12 radar, which is a derivative of the AWG-10A used by Phantoms of the US and other air forces. Modes available are pulse-Doppler look-down, pulse air-to-air search and tracking, high/low radar mapping, air-to-ground ranging, and illumination for the Sparrow missile. It also has digital computing and built-in testing, plus a servoed optical sight.

One operational advantage of the RAF's Phantom FGR 2s was that they were originally ground-attack aircraft, having been released from that role by the introduction of the Jaguar into RAF service. If necessary they could revert to it with little effort, and the addition of a sensor/camera pod would also enable them to undertake reconnaissance tasks.

The Sector 2 air defence task is shared by two F-16 squadrons of the Belgian Air Force: Nos 349 and 350, which together form No 1 Wing at Beauvechain, south-east of Brussels. No 23 and 31

Northrop NF-5B of No. 314 Squadron, AF, Eindhoven, Netherlands.

Squadrons of No 10 Wing at Kleine Brogel also have an air defence role, but their F-16s are tasked primarily with strike. Nos 349 and 350 Squadrons were both formed during the Second World War under RAF auspices; No 350 was, in fact, the first Belgian-manned fighter unit in the RAF, forming in November 1941 and subsequently flying fighter sweeps over France before becoming part of 2 TAF in preparation for the invasion of Europe. A Spitfire unit throughout, it moved to Belgium in December 1944 and undertook low-level attacks on enemy communications until the end of hostilities. It was transferred to the control of the Belgian authorities in October 1946 as the result of an agreement between the latter and the British Government, who undertook to place aircraft and personnel at Belgium's disposal to form a post-war air force.

No 349 Squadron was formed in November 1942 in Nigeria, for service in the Belgian Congo. However, its pilots were employed in ferrying fighters to the Middle East over the trans-Africa route for several months, and in 1943 the squadron was transferred to the UK to re-form at Wittering as a Spitfire unit. It thereafter flew sweeps over France, moving there in the wake of the Allied invasion, and in April 1945 it went to the Netherlands to join No 132 Wing, flying armed reconnaissance sweeps over Germany for the last few weeks of the war. It, too, was transferred to Belgian control in October 1946. Both squadrons were the first in Europe to convert to the F-16, which replaced their F-104G Starfighters in 1981.

Dassault-Breguet Mirage 5BD of No. 1 Squadron, Belgian Air Force. Nos 1 and 8 Squadrons comprise No. 3 Wing at Bierset.

2 ATAF — The tactical squadrons.

Air defence is a means to an end. Its aim is to establish air superiority over the battlefield and to protect key tactical bases so that strike aircraft can get on relatively unhindered from the air with their primary task of battlefield support. Oddly enough, one of 2 ATAF's most effective close support forces is also one of the smallest. It comprises the British Aerospace Harrier GR 3s of Nos 3 and 4 Squadrons, RAF, based at Gutersloh, only seventy miles from the border with the GDR. Gutersloh lies in the centre of the British NATO defence zone within the Northern Army Group (NORTHAG), which permits the Harrier Force to cover I (Br) Corps as well as the Dutch, German and Belgian Corps in the NORTHAG area. Furthermore, Gutersloh lies on the axis of a possible major thrust area for any Soviet move against AFCENT.

At Gutersloh the Harriers are housed in hardened aircraft shelters originally built for the Lightnings of Nos 19 and 92 Squadrons, but in time of tension they are deployed to sites in the field. At that point, the Group Captain commanding RAF

Gutersloh gives up his role as Station Commander and becomes the Harrier Force Commander. Gutersloh then becomes a major airfield for the receipt and dispatch of reinforcement units, in which role it is capable of handling thousands of troops within a matter of hours, unloading two wide-bodied airliners simultaneously with a turnround time of less than an hour.

From their main base, the Harriers deploy to locations containing six to eight aircraft, with the sites roughly triangulated round the central command post. The whereabouts of the dispersal sites to be used in the event of war are secret, but all are near hard surfaces so that it is not necessary to lay down steel take-off and landing areas. The Harrier Force could either activate old training sites or move into pre-selected rural sites in the vicinity of woods, barns or old farmhouses, and in the event of war the options would be increased to include urban areas. Once in the field, the Harrier Force Headquarters comprise the personnel responsible for air operations, engineering and logistics, ground defence operations and intelligence. The trailers which house the HQ personnel are filtered and pressurised to allow safe operation in the event of a nuclear, biological or chemical attack. The dispersal sites are secured and protected by Nos 1 and 2 Squadrons of the Royal Air Force Regiment; these light armoured squadrons are trained to secure the area on the ground and are equipped with Scorpion and Spartan tracked combat reconnaissance vehicles.

The Harriers themselves are concealed in camouflaged 'hides' scattered along the edge of forests with direct access to hard-surfaced, though not necessarily paved, roads on which they can taxy to their take-off strips. When in their hides and covered with camouflaged netting, they can be seen only at very close range and then only after a close study of their locality; they are virtually invisible to all but infra-red detection. It was, in fact, the Harrier Force that was instrumental in changing the RAF roundel, progressing from the Type D (red, white and blue) to the wartime Type B (red and blue only). The paint scheme was also changed from the original high gloss to a flat matt finish.

From their hidden sites, the Harriers operate using STO (Short Take-Off) launches for increased fuel and weapons payload for the sortie, and Vertical Landing (VL) to reduce taxying and 'push-back' time on return. In the field, each hide is self-contained and the aircraft can be refuelled/re-armed and ready to go again within thirty minutes. To reduce turnround time, pilots remain in their cockpits during this period to receive their briefings for the next sortie by landline. The turnround itself could be further reduced, but is kept to thirty minutes to reduce stress and fatigue among the ground crews. Under combat conditions, with a typical thirty-minute sortie and a thirty-minute turnround, the Harrier Force can perform one sortie per hour per aircraft. As each Squadron has eighteen Harriers, this means 36 hourly sorties, considerably augmented in a war situation when the NATO squadrons would be reinforced by aircraft of No 233 OCU, RAF Wittering. The rate would, of course, be progressively reduced by combat attrition, but nevertheless the Harriers could continue to deliver a considerable weight of weapons on to the enemy for a long time. (During the Falklands conflict of 1982, the aircraft's availability remained at over 95 per cent daily and only one per cent of planned missions were cancelled due to unserviceability.)

F-15 Eagles of the 36th TFW taking off from Bitburg.

The Harrier Force has the benefit of a very secure communications system. When minutes can mean the difference between victory or defeat, commands can be transmitted from the site operations centre direct to the pilot sitting in the cockpit, ready for immediate launch. Direct communication to the pilot is normally via a secure line to the site operations room, and mission assignments are received by the Force HQ direct from the Air Support Operations Centre (ASOC) at HQ I (Br) Corps via a secure communications link. The system gives the Harrier Force a response time of only tens of minutes rather than the hour or so it would normally require, and it is the response time that is the key to successful battlefield support. Experience by the United States Marine Corps during the Vietnam War proved that air support with conventional aircraft flying from a main base many miles from the front line, or from an aircraft carrier some miles off the coastline, could mean an unacceptable reaction delay of forty to sixty minutes or more.

In modern warfare, speed of movement and rapidly changing local tactical fortunes could mean that the aircraft delivers too much ordnance too late. Even worse, the ordnance could fall on a friendly unit that had moved into the area during the reaction delay time. Quite often, between the call for conventional air support and its arrival, even the weather will change over the target and therefore negate the planning and military effort. Both the RAF and the USMC therefore attach great importance to rapid reaction and the degree of fire support provided by their forward-based Harriers.

The Harrier Force would normally be allocated to NORTHAG for tasking, with I (Br) Corps getting the principal share of the sorties. I (Br) Corps ASOC is staffed by RAF and Army officers who are responsible for the tasking of all aircraft allocated by 2 ATAF to support the various corps of the Northern Army Group. The flexibility of the Harriers allows them to be moved anywhere they are needed as a stopgap.

Dramatic shot of the Tornado F.2 prototype taking off from the B.Ae airfield at Warton, Lancashire.

General Dynamics F-16A Fighting Falcon of the
Royal Netherlands Air Force.

As mentioned earlier, in spite of the relatively
lengthy impending hostilities warning time, any
Warsaw Pact invasion of AFCENT territory is
likely to be sudden and massive, with missile and
aircraft attacks designed to eliminate NATO
airfields followed by massed columns of tanks
supported by other armoured fighting vehicles and
infantry. In the event of such attacks, the Harrier
Force's role will lie in mass attacks against large
concentrations of enemy forces — that is to say very
large enemy concentrations, such as a tank column
caught in a bottleneck or crossing a river. Such
attacks would be carried out in concert with other 2
ATAF strike aircraft and, hopefully, under a 2
ATAF fighter umbrella. When not tasked with
mass attacks, the Harrier Force would operate in
small groups, scouting enemy movements, hitting
small convoys and troop concentrations or
supporting ground forces engaging the enemy.

To assist the pilot in carrying out these various
tasks, RAF Harriers are equipped with the Ferranti
Inertial Navigation and Attack System (INAS)
which is totally independent of external radio aids.
The pilot can set the co-ordinates of his own
position and that of the reported target, then use the
INAS to direct him to the ordnance release point. If
a target of opportunity is spotted en route to the
primary target, the pilot can co-ordinate that
position on the INAS. Then, as soon as he has

engaged the primary, he can call up the target of
opportunity on the INAS and receive range and
heading for a secondary engagement, subject of
course to remaining ordnance.

The INAS provides information to the Head-Up
Display, through which the pilot sees the target and
the weapon aiming information needed to attack it.
The principal range sensor is a Laser Ranger and
Marked Target Seeker (LRMTS) which measures
range to the target by laser light for more accurate
weapons delivery. It is also able to search for, and
lock-on to, radiation reflected from a target
illuminated by a similar laser used by ground
forces. During the closing stages of the Falklands
campaign, Harrier GR 3s were tasked with
attacking targets in the vicinity of Port Stanley
using 1000 lb Paveway laser-guided bombs. It was
to be the first operational example of this type of
attack, and it proved very successful.

The bombs were dropped by the Harriers at a
height of about 500 feet in a 'loft' release, similar in
principle to an underarm throw, some three to four
miles away from the target. As the aircraft turned
away, the bombs rose through a trajectory of about
thirty degrees to a peak of 1500 feet to fall in the
general direction of the target. As the bomb
descended, the target was illuminated by a ground
mounted Ferranti Laser Designator and the
weapon locked on to the laser light reflected from
the target, homing in to the signal source to achieve
a direct hit. The aircraft meanwhile was on its way
back to base, safe from retaliatory ground fire.

Other equipment carried by the Harrier includes cameras for air reconnaissance, a cockpit voice recorder and countermeasures such as chaff dispensers and the AR 18223 radar warning receiver. The aircraft is armed primarily with two 30 mm Aden cannon and cluster bomb units which detonate above the ground, spewing small bomblets over an area roughly the size of a football field. The aircraft can also be configured to launch the AIM-9L Sidewinder AAM and the fire-and-forget AIM-120 AMRAAM advanced medium-range air-to-air missile. Alternative payloads include six 68 mm or two-inch Matra Type 116M or 115 multiple rocket launchers, or up to five 1000 lb free-fall or retarded bombs.

Although each 'hide' is self-sufficient for its individual Harrier, the sites are supported by logistical parks (logsparks), with each logspark supporting two sites, or between twelve and sixteen aircraft. A logspark contains sufficient fuel, weapons and maintenance supplies for seven days of operations. All Harrier repairs in the field, short of major battle damage, can be accomplished at the logsparks, including the replacement of a wing. When damage occurs, the ground crew engineers in the hide remove the part and pass it to the logspark repair facility, which provides a replacement.

If a site were compromised for any reason, such as a change in the tactical situation or discovery by enemy reconnaissance aircraft, the Harriers would immediately disperse to other pre-selected secondary sites while the support equipment was moved by road. A site can be totally evacuated in

British Aerospace Harrier GR 3s of No. 3 Squadron, RAF Gutersloh. The Harrier is one of 2 ATAF's vital close-support components and, in combat, would certainly make a contribution to the Allies out of all proportion to the numbers involved.

two and a half hours. If deteriorating military conditions resulted in a serious refugee problem, with its attendant clogging of roads, support equipment would be moved by helicopter.

The efficiency of the Harrier Force's flight operations and logistics system has been frequently tested under realistic scenarios by the multi-national Tactical Evaluation Division of AFCENT. The Harriers have been awarded the highest possible ratings both in mission effectiveness and the ability to survive and continue to provide offensive air support and tactical reconnaissance. Day-to-day training for the Harrier pilots involves standard reconnaissance/attack sorties using targets located throughout north-west Germany, while defensive training is conducted against fellow squadron pilots and aircraft from other units. A new pilot first of all flies Harrier v Harrier, then moves up to Harrier v Phantom and so on. Pilots also train using multiple coverage, the Harriers operating under an umbrella of other aircraft types. The Harrier Force is also involved in up to three major field training exercises a year, in addition to other training exercises in Germany and overseas. These major exercises include 'Maple Flag', which is held bi-annually in Canada.

General Dynamics F-16 Fighting Falcons on patrol.

From 1987 the Harrier Force will be receiving the Harrier GR 5 (Harrier II) produced by British Aerospace and McDonnell Douglas, and the GR 3s will rotate back to the UK as the new aircraft arrive. The GR 5 will give NATO's Harrier Force increased range, greater weapon capacity and improved systems such as stability augmentation, which will allow the pilots to fly and land the aircraft virtually hands-off.

Nos 3 and 4 Squadrons have histories that go back to the very earliest days of military flying, having been formed as two of the original squadrons of the Royal Flying Corps in 1912. Unlike other squadrons from the same era, however, these two have enjoyed virtually uninterrupted careers, with only short disbandment breaks. Until assigned to tactical support duties with the Harrier, No 3 Squadron was always a fighter unit. During World War II, it operated Hurricanes until February 1943 and then flew Typhoons for a year until March 1944, when it became one of the first squadrons to receive the powerful Hawker Tempest. Post-war, it successively flew Vampires, Sabres, Hunters, Javelins and Canberra B(I) 8s before converting to the Harrier in 1972.

No 4 Squadron, in contrast, has always had army co-operation as its primary role. During World War I its tasks were reconnaissance, photography and artillery observation, and between the wars it operated a variety of Army co-operation aircraft such as the Hawker Audax before receiving Lysanders, which it took to France in 1939 in support of the British Expeditionary Force. It later flew Tomahawks and Mustangs before re-equipping with Spitfires and then Mosquitoes, which it continued to use until 1950 as part of the British Forces of Occupation in Germany. It then flew Vampires, Sabres — the latter for a little under two years in the day-fighter role, the only break in the squadron's Army co-operation activities — Hunters and, finally, Harriers, which it began to receive in April 1970.

Joining the Harriers in front-line ground attack operations are two Luftwaffe wings, both equipped with Dassault-Breguet/Dornier Alpha Jets. They are JaboG 41 at Husum, south-east of Flensburg on the 'neck' of Schleswig-Holstein close to the Danish border, and JaboG 43 at Oldenburg, west of Bremen. The Alpha Jet bases are more or less aligned with Gutersloh, and the three are spaced to give maximum air support to Allied forces facing the three possible Warsaw Pact thrust lines in 2 ATAF's area.

The Alpha Jet, which replaced the Fiat G 91 as the Luftwaffe's principal close-support type from 1979, is defined as a subsonic basic/advanced training and light attack aircraft. It is powered by two SNECMA/Turbomeca Larzac 04-C6 turbofans and seats two crew in tandem on Stencel S-III-S3AJ ejection seats, licence-built by MBB. (Alpha Jets in service with other air arms have Martin Baker seats.) An extremely versatile aircraft, it can carry more than 75 different basic weapon configurations to fit the variety of roles it has to perform. For close support, it can be equipped with an under-fuselage detachable pod containing a 30 mm DEFA or 27 mm Mauser cannon with 150 rounds, or an underfuselage pylon for a single 500 lb or 1000 lb bomb. Two hardpoints under each wing can accommodate M155 launchers for eighteen 68 mm rockets, HE and retarded bombs of various sizes up to 1000 lb, or 625 lb cluster dispensers. There is also provision for air-to-air or air-to-surface missiles, or a reconnaissance pod.

Each of the two Alpha Jet JaboGs in 2 ATAF has 51 aircraft, so their combined force represents a formidable contribution to NATO close support power. One of their principal roles in wartime would be to destroy Warsaw Pact battlefield support helicopters. The Alpha Jet has a maximum level speed at sea level of 620 mph, but it manoeuvres well at low speed. Its combat radius on a hi-lo-hi mission, including combat at maximum continuous thrust and a high-speed dash of 54 nautical miles with belly gun pod and underwing weapons is 315 nautical miles; this is increased to 580 nm with underwing tanks as well as weapons. A lo-lo-lo mission with the same configurations produces combat radii of 210 and 340 nm respectively.

A powerful strike element is also committed to 2 ATAF by the Belgian and Royal Netherlands Air Forces, operating from their bases to the rear of RAF Germany and the Luftwaffe. The RNethAF's strike wing at Volkel has two squadrons of F-16s, Nos 311 and 312, together with No 306 Squadron in the tactical reconnaissance role. Each squadron has sixteen F-16As and two F-16B two-seaters. In the strike configuration the F-16 can attack with its M61 gun, rockets, conventional bombs, cluster bombs, air-to-surface missiles, special weapons (ie, nuclear), laser-guided and electro-optical weapons. At the time of writing, the F-16 was also scheduled to re-equip four more RNethAF squadrons — Nos 315, 316, 313 and 314, in that order. Re-equipment of the first, No 315, was due to start in 1986. All four squadrons currently operate the Northrop NF-5 light tactical fighter. No 315 Squadron is located at Twenthe, alongside No 313 which performs the role of operational conversion unit; No 314 is at Eindhoven and No 316 at Gilze Rijen.

The NF-5 is powered by two General Electric J85-GE-13 turbojets which give it a maximum level speed at altitude of Mach 1.4. Its combat radius, hi-lo-hi, with maximum fuel, two 750 lb bombs and five minutes' combat at sea level is in the order of 470 nautical miles; this reduces to about 180 nm with maximum payload. The NF-5 can carry a wide variety of operational warloads on five pylons, one under the fuselage and two under each wing. A bomb of more than 2000 lb or an M61 gun pack can be carried under the centre pylon, while underwing loads can include four AAMs. Bullpup air-to-surface missiles, bombs, up to twenty air-to-surface rockets, gun packs or external fuel tanks. In the interception role, the NF-5 carries two Sidewinder AAMs on wingtip launchers and two 20 mm guns in the fuselage nose.

The Belgian Air Force's primary strike force comprises the F-16As/Bs of Nos 23 and 31 Squadrons, No 10 Wing, at Kleine Brogel. There is, however, a powerful secondary strike force of 46 Dassault-Breguet Mirage 5BA fighter-bombers, equipping No 2 Squadron of No 2 Wing at Florennes and Nos 1 and 8 Squadrons of No 3 Wing at Bierset. Also at Florennes is No 42 Squadron, with the Mirage 5BR reconnaissance variant.

The Mirage 5 tactical fighter-bomber was derived from the well-tried Mirage IIIE, using the same airframe and engine, and was intended primarily for export. Although having the same Mach 2 plus capability of the Mirage IIIE, it can also operate from rudimentary airstrips and its maintenance is simpler. The basic version can carry a wider variety of stores than the IIIE, has simplified avionics and increased fuel capacity. In its ground attack capacity, the Mirage 5 can carry up to 8200 lb of external stores and can also be used as an interceptor, carrying two Sidewinder AAMs. Its built-in armament consists of two 30 mm DEFA cannon.

RF-4E Phantom of Aufklärungsgeschwader AG51, Bremgarten. A recent refit has extended the operational life of the Luftwaffe's reconnaissance Phantoms.

Jaguar T 2 of No. 2 Squadron, RAF Bruggen, RAF Germany's last Jaguar squadron.

Belgium's Tactical Air Force is firmly committed to NATO, with about 144 combat aircraft at the disposal of 2 ATAF, and eighty per cent of the Belgian Air Force's budget is spent on maintaining it. In recent years the BAF has suffered from severe financial restraints, resulting in drastic cutbacks in the number of hours flown annually per pilot, but the air force has generally coped with the situation very well. Even though, to cut costs, the BAF is forced to send everybody except Quick Reaction Alert (QRA) crews home for two weeks at Christmas, it maintains that every base can be fully activated within two hours if the need arises. The fact that the lower ranks are trade unionised does not seem to have created many problems, either. One of the reasons, possibly, is that 78 per cent of the Belgian Air Force's personnel are professionals; the conscripts who make up the other 22 per cent serve for a maximum of ten months, and then only on guard and general duties.

Completing the line-up of offensive air power available to 2 ATAF is a powerful strike force represented by the F-4F Phantoms of JaboG 36 at Rheine-Hopsten, under the administration of the German Air Force Tactical Command (GAFTAC) at Köln. In the air-to-ground role the Luftwaffe Phantoms operate in pairs, flying at about 800 feet and using their radar for navigation. The aircraft are equipped with the ALN-10 radar homing and warning system and the APR-36V threat display to give warning of enemy CAP. Close to the target the Phantoms descend to 250 feet and make their pass over the target at about 630 mph. Retarded and cluster bombs are the most usual weapons employed, and Phantom crews have developed a skip-bombing technique whereby the bombs are

released at 200 feet in level flight and then bounce, reaching a height of thirty feet and a forward distance of 100 feet before exploding. A considerable degree of accuracy has been attained with this method, which is useful against targets such as individual buildings.

In war, the F-4Fs of JaboG 36 would join Luftwaffe and Royal Air Force Tornados in attacks on enemy airfields. In a joint sortie of this kind the Tornados would probably go in first to hit the airfield dispersal areas (which in war would be very crowded) with cluster bombs, while the F-4s, attacking in sections of four, would hit hardened aircraft shelters and runways with retarded bombs. Under a programme known as Peace Rhine, designed to keep the F-4Fs effective until the mid-1990s, the aircraft have been modified to carry the AGM-65 Maverick missile. This electro-optically guided ASM, which carries a 300 lb HE/fragmentation warhead and has a range of about fourteen miles, is specifically designed for close support work and is extremely accurate against a wide range of typical targets such as tanks, fuel dumps, radar vehicles and airfield hangars.

Modifications are also being carried out to the Luftwaffe's RF-4E reconnaissance Phantoms to extend their useful life and operational capability. Work includes a new sensor fit, with infrared linescan plus better cameras, a new self-defence chaff/flare dispenser system and provision for the RF-4Es, which were previously unarmed, to carry a warload of 5000 lb. The Luftwaffe has eighty RF-4Es, divided between two Aufklärungsgeschwader (reconnaissance wings), both in 2 ATAF's area; AG51 at Bremgarten and AG52 at Leck, near Flensburg. They share the reconnaissance task with the Jaguar GR 1s of No 2 Squadron, RAF Bruggen, which will eventually re-equip with Tornado (the last RAF Germany Jaguar squadron to do so).

2 ATAF — Transport and other units

Belgian Air Force Nos 7 and 11 Squadrons at Brustum operate Alpha Jets in the training role, up to OCU level, and have a combined total of 31 aircraft which would be used in the light ground-attack capacity in the event of war. No 9 Squadron, at the same base, has 21 CM 170 Magisters, which are gradually being phased out in favour of the Alpha Jet. No 20 Squadron at Brussels-Melsbroek has twelve Lockheed C-130H Hercules, while No 21 Squadron at the same location has two Boeing 727-29Cs, five Merlin IIIs, two Falcon 20s and three HS 748s. Both units form the BAF's transport/VIP/communications/liaison force and come under the command of No 15 Wing. At Gossoncourt, 28 Marchetti SF 260MBs form the equipment of the Ecole de Pilotage Eleméntaire (Basic Flying School). The BAF and the Belgian Navy jointly operate No 40 Squadron, which is based at Koksijde and operates four Sea King Mk 48 helicopters on SAR duties, a role they have taken over from the squadron's three ageing Sikorsky SH-34Gs. The Sea Kings are also used for communications and VIP transport, and the squadron has three Alouette IIIs for liaison.

The Belgian Army has four squadrons, No 15 (Brasschaat), No 16 (Butzweilerhof), No 17 (Werl) and No 18 (Merzbruck), each equipped with eighteen Alouette II helicopters for scouting and liaison. Nos 15 and 16 Squadrons also operate twelve Britten-Norman BN 2A Islanders between them, and No 15 Squadron has three Puma helicopters which are operated by the Gendarmerie.

Royal Netherlands Air Force The RNethAF has a small transport arm comprising twelve Fokker F 27 Troopships (three of which are used as VIP transports) serving with No 334 Squadron at Soesterberg. The Royal Netherlands Navy has two Westland Lynx-equipped squadrons, Nos 7 and 360 at de Kooij; they provide aircraft to operate from frigates in the ASW role, and also for land-based search and rescue duties. The Dutch Army has three helicopter squadrons, two of which — No 298 at Soesterberg and No 300 at Deelen — are equipped with a combined total of 75 Alouette IIIs; the other unit, No 299 Squadron at Deelen, has 32 Bölkow Bo 105Cs.

Luftwaffe By far the greater part of the Luftwaffe's air transport force is located in the 2 ATAF area, with Lufttransportgeschwader (LTG) 62 and 63 based at Wunstorf, west of Hannover, and Hohn, west of Kiel. Each Geschwader is equipped with 29 Transall C-160D medium-range transports and some Dornier Do 28 Skyservants. The Transall, which is powered by two Rolls-Royce Tyne Mk 22 turboprop engines, has a crew of four and can accommodate 93 troops or up to eighty fully-equipped paratroops; alternative loads can include trucks and armoured fighting vehicles up to a total of sixteen tonnes. With an eight-tonne payload, the Transall has a range of 2459 nautical miles, reducing to 634 nm with maximum payload. Cruising speed is 306-319 mph.

Hubschraubertransportgeschwader (HTG) 64 is based at Ahlhorn and is equipped with 75 Bell UH-1D Iroquois utility helicopters. The unit also provides SAR detachments to Bremgarten, Rheine-Hopsten, Jever, Neuburg, Norvenich and Pferdsfeld. Also operating UH-1Ds are the army's Leichtes (Light) Heeresflieger Transportregiment

The Westland/Aérospatiale Puma general transport helicopter equips No. 230 Squadron at RAF Gutersloh and, in the UK, No. 33 Squadron at RAF Odiham. The latter is tasked with the support of the NATO Mobile Force in Norway.

Alpha Jet of the Belgian Air Force Training Command, Brustem. The BAF's Alpha Jets have a light attack war role.

10 at Fassberg, with 58 aircraft, and the Heeresflieger Waffenschule (Army Aviation Weapons School) at Buckeburg, which has 27 Iroquois. This unit also operates nine Sikorsky CH-53G heavy-lift helicopters. Thirty-seven CH-53Gs form the complement of Mittleres (Medium) Heeresflieger Transportregiment 15 at Rheine-Bentlage.

United Kingdom: Royal Air Force and Army Air Corps The United Kingdom Air Transport Force, which is part of No 1 Group, RAF Strike Command, has the primary task of supplying and reinforcing I (Br) Corps of BAOR, Royal Air Force Germany, the Allied Mobile Force and the UK Mobile Force. The principal responsibility for these operations is assigned to the Hercules Wing at RAF Lyneham, Wiltshire, comprising Nos 24, 30, 47 and 70 Squadrons and No 242 OCU. All the Lyneham units are equipped with Hercules C 1/C 3 aircraft. The Hercules normally carries a crew of six, and the C 1 version can accommodate up to 92 fully-equipped troops. In the para-drop role, 62 paratroops can jump from the side doors or forty over the rear ramp. The Hercules can carry a great variety of payloads, and single loads of up to 14,000 lb can be delivered by the low-level extraction method. This involves making a touch-and-go landing or a low-level run a few feet above the ground with the rear loading ramp open. The aircraft trails a hook which is attached by cable to the cargo pallet. The hook engages a steel cable on the ground and the cargo is extracted from the aircraft and brought to a stop on the ground in about 100 ft using a special energy absorption system. Alternatively, a ribbon parachute can be deployed to drag the pallet from the cabin. Thirty aircraft of the sixty-strong RAF Hercules transport force have been, or are in the process of being, converted to 'stretched' C 3 standard by Marshall of Cambridge, substantially increasing the payload.

No 1 Group's helicopter assault and transport force comprises No 7 Squadron at RAF Odiham with Chinooks, No 33 Squadron at Odiham with Pumas, and No 72 Squadron at Leconfield with Wessex (the latter unit operating detachments in Northern Ireland). Also at Odiham is No 240 OCU, with all three helicopter types. The Boeing-Vertol Chinook HC1 twin-rotor heavy lift helicopter has a considerable lifting capacity that includes two 105 mm light guns and their crews, together with ammunition, and a variety of other loads. In peacetime the number of troops carried is restricted to 44, but the lone Chinook that operated in the Falklands — ZA718 'Bravo November', the sole survivor of the four aircraft that were aboard the *Atlantic Conveyor* — on occasions carried eighty or more and went on flying without serious maintenance problems throughout the campaign.

The Aérospatiale/Westland Puma, another twin-engined helicopter, is used for general transport and can carry up to sixteen fully-equipped troops or underslung loads of up to 5600 lb. The Pumas of No 33 Squadron are tasked for the support of the NATO Mobile Force in northern Norway. In RAF Germany, Pumas form the equipment of No 230 Squadron at RAF Gutersloh, from where they fly in support of I (Br) Corps. Also at Gutersloh are the Chinooks of No 18 Squadron, which operate in support of the Harrier Force and provide the heavy lift capability that is necessary for the rapid deployment of the V/STOL squadrons.

The Army Air Corps (HQ Netheravon) is organised into two operational wings, one in the UK and the other in Germany, each with its assigned aviation regiments, squadrons and flights. In Germany, I (Br) Corps controls No 1 Regiment, AAC, at Hildesheim, with Nos 651, 652 and 661 Squadrons; No 3 Regiment, AAC, at Soest with Nos 653, 662 and 663 Squadrons; and No 4 Regiment, AAC, at Detmold with Nos 654, 659 and 669 Squadrons. Nos 651, 652, 653, 654 and 659 Squadrons all operate the Westland Lynx AH 1 helicopter in the anti-tank and combat support roles, while Nos 661, 662, 663 and 669 Squadrons use the Aérospatiale/Westland Gazelle for liaison and forward air control. The primary weapon of the Lynx, which at all times flies 'nap-of-the-earth' under power lines and using all available cover, is the TOW anti-tank missile.

The protection of the RAF's bases in Germany is the responsibility of the Royal Air Force Regiment, which deploys four air defence squadrons in the Federal Republic: No 16 Squadron at Wildenrath, No 26 Squadron at Laarbruch, No 37 Squadron at Bruggen and No 63 Squadron at Gutersloh. Together, the four squadrons comprise No 4 Wing and are armed with the British Aerospace Rapier low-level air defence missile system. The main

Harrier GR.3s of No. 3 Squadron carrying practice bomb dispensers.

Harrier GR.3 of No. 4 Squadron, RAF Gutersloh.

McDonnell Douglas F-15 Eagles of the 32nd Tactical Fighter Squadron, Soesterberg, Holland.

components of the Towed Rapier system are an optical tracker and the launcher, which houses the surveillance and IFF aerials and which carries four missiles and the command link antenna. During a daylight engagement the operator tracks the target optically, using a miniature 'joystick' to hold an aiming mark on the centre of the target.

Once the missile is launched, a TV system synchronised to the optical system tracks the missile flares. These two systems enable the computer to calculate the angular error between the line-of-sight and the missile's position, and to transmit corrective signals to the missile guidance system via the command link. A DN181 Blindfire radar tracker can be added to the daylight system to provide coverage during the night and in adverse weather conditions. The radar automatically tracks both the target and the missile simultaneously, again enabling the computer to calculate corrective commands for the missile to ensure that it intercepts the target. Blindfire produces a single-shot kill probability approaching ninety per cent, compared with seventy per cent for the optical system.

The Rapier missile was designed from the outset to hit the target, rather than rely on a proximity fuze. This approach was vindicated in the Falklands, where Rapier was able to engage very

low-flying aircraft with considerable success. In such engagements, conventional proximity-fuzed weapons would have detonated over friendly forces. Other system features that proved invaluable in the Falklands conflict included a ten-degree depression capability in the optical tracker, and a tactical control unit that allowed safety lanes to be provided for low-flying friendly aircraft.

A complete Rapier fire unit can be transported in three vehicles of Land Rover size. One carries the optical tracker and four missiles, and tows a trailer with the launcher and generating set. A second vehicle carries nine more missiles, and a third tows the Blindfire radar on a trailer. Three men are needed to bring the fire unit into action, but once established it can be operated by one man. The average time from acquiring a target in the sight to missile impact is six seconds, although in the Falklands — where the system was forced to deal with targets flying at less than 150 feet in valleys shrouded in mist and in poor light — this reaction time was reduced to five seconds.

Rapier units mounted on tracked vehicles — the RCM748 of the American M113 series, which combines armour protection to APC standards, all-terrain mobility and air portability — are also in service with units of I (Br) Corps in Germany. The Rapier has a minimum/maximum range of approximately 0.3/4.3 miles, altitude limits of 0/10,000 feet, a speed of Mach 2 plus and has a 1.12 lb semi-armour-piercing HE warhead.

CHAPTER THREE
The Central Front: 4th Allied Tactical Air Force

In the southern sector of AFCENT, the most critical avenue of a possible Warsaw Pact thrust lies along the axis of the so-called Fulda Gap. Running between the high ground of the Vogelsberg and the Hohe Rhön, this is the route that affords the quickest advance to the vital American base area around Frankfurt. This is the area covered by the 4th Allied Tactical Air Force (4 ATAF) which, with its HQ at Ramstein near Kaiserlautern, comprises USAF, Canadian Armed Forces and Luftwaffe combat air units. Their principal task is to provide air support for the NATO Central Army Group (CENTAG) which, from north to south, is composed of III German, V and VII United States, and II German Corps.

The American contribution to 4 ATAF, which is commanded by a USAF General, comprises a first-line combat force of four tactical fighter wings and one tactical reconnaissance wing under the command of the 17th Air Force, USAFE (HQ Sembach). The reconnaissance wing, which flies RF-4C Phantoms and is based at Zweibrucken, is the 26th TRW. It consists of a single squadron, the 38th TRS with twenty aircraft, although the wing retains the facility to accept a second RF-4C squadron as reinforcement from the continental United States should the need arise.

To perform its reconnaissance mission, the unarmed RF-4C incorporates forward-looking radar, optical, infrared and electronic sensor systems for day or night missions in any kind of weather. The optical sensors include high- and low-altitude panoramic cameras, forward, vertical and side-mounted framing cameras and high-altitude mapping cameras. The infrared sensors produce detailed maps from variable altitudes and in any weather situation.

The reconnaissance data gathered during flight operations, depending on the urgency of its nature, can be disseminated either through air-to-ground high-frequency communication for rapid deployment of response aircraft (direct reconnaissance reporting) and/or captured on film for ground interpretation. In the latter case, as soon as the RF-4C returns to base the film is rushed to the Photographic Processing and Interpretation Facility (PPIF), a self-contained complex on the base. Within thirty minutes of engine shutdown the film must be processed and the imagery interpreter must confirm the mission report (MISREP) made by the aircrew. After the MISREP is dispatched, the interpreter makes a detailed readout of the mission film. No later than four hours after engine shutdown, the completed interpreter reports, negatives, maps and prints must be ready for forwarding to the user. Reports are sent electronically, while the prints and negatives are forwarded by air. The information obtained from the interpreter reports can be used to determine priorities of targets, approaches to targets, bomb damage assessment, enemy resources and battle situations.

The 17th Air Force has two more Phantom Wings, the 52nd and 96th. The 52nd TFW at Spangdahlem has three squadrons, the 23rd and 480th with F-4Es and the 81st with F-4G 'Advanced Wild Weasels', whose mission is specialised defence suppression. The Wild Weasel concept originated in Vietnam, in the electronic war that developed between US tactical aircraft and the North Vietnamese complex of radar-controlled AAA and SAM batteries, along with other defence radars. F-100 Super Sabres and F-105 Thunderchiefs, equipped with electronic countermeasures, would lock on to enemy radar emissions and direct strike aircraft on to the source. The primary target was the North Vietnamese 'Fan Song' tracking radar linked to the SA-2 Guideline SAM system.

As a result of the lessons learned in Vietnam, the provision of airborne equipment to fulfil the defence suppression role, and the modification of aircraft to carry it, assumed top priority in USAF Tactical Air Force planning in 1975. What TAC needed was a self-contained weapon system — an aircraft capable of carrying both the necessary electronics and the weaponry to hit enemy SAM radars effectively — and the Phantom was the best choice available. Wild Weasel trials had already been carried out with two F-4Ds in 1968, but later studies showed that the F-4E variant was easier to modify. USAF funding was consequently obtained to convert some 116 F-4Es to F-4G standard under the Advanced Wild Weasel programme.

An F-4E Phantom carrying a full war load. Despite its age the Phantom remains a viable weapons system and is highly effective in the 'Wild Weasel' defence suppression role.

Modifications included the addition of a torpedo-shaped fairing on top of the fin to house APR-38 radar antennae, which are also carried on the side of the fin and along the upper surface of the fuselage. The F-4E's M61A1 cannon installation was removed to permit the installation of the computer systems associated with the F-4G's sensory radar. With this equipment, the Wild Weasel crew can detect, identify and locate hostile radar emitters and select the appropriate weapons package for use against them. F-4G Wild Weasels can operate independently as 'hunter-killers', but more usually they operate as an integral component of a strike force. In time of war, the 81st TFS's F-4Gs would operate in conjunction not only with the other two Phantom squadrons of the 52nd TFW, but also with the F-4Es of the 86th TFW at Ramstein.

The F-4E was the Phantom variant that introduced the internally-mounted M61A1 cannon, and was intended from the outset as a multi-role aircraft able to carry out air superiority, close-support and interdiction missions. Air superiority is now mainly the preserve of the F-15 Eagle, and much of the interdiction task has been assumed by the Tornado; nevertheless, the F-4E remains a powerful interdictor in its own right, having a combat radius of some 700 miles while still carrying a substantial payload. The aircraft has the leading-edge manoeuvring slats first adopted on the Luftwaffe's F-4Fs and has an effective fire-control system, the AN/APQ-120. It is also fitted with Northrop's target identification system electro-optical (TISEO), which is basically a vidicon TV camera with a zoom lens that aids positive identification of airborne and ground targets at long range. The TISEO is mounted in a cylindrical housing on the leading edge of the F-4E's port wing.

Eventually, the 86th TFW will re-equip with the F-16 Fighting Falcon, but at the time of writing this type equips only one 4 ATAF Wing: the 50th TFW at Hahn, which is situated amid the rolling hills and wooded valleys that are a feature of the terrain between the Rhine and the Moselle. The 50th TFW has three squadrons, the 10th, 33rd and 496th TFS, and operates 77 F-16As and seven two-seat F-16Bs.

The 17th Air Force's primary air superiority fighter is the F-15 Eagle, which equips the 36th Tactical Fighter Wing at Bitburg. The 36th TFW has three squadrons, the 22nd, 53rd and 525th, with 72 F-15Cs and seven two-seat F-15Ds. The wing can, in time of emergency, be rapidly reinforced to bring its complement of F-15s up to thirty aircraft per squadron. To test its operational efficiency, the 36th TFW — and also its 32nd Tactical Fighter Squadron at Soesterberg, in Holland — flies periodic 'sortie surges', usually lasting seven days. The 36th TFW's Eagles have, for example, flown 322 missions in less than 24 hours; the 32nd TFS, with only one-third as many aircraft available, has flown 439 hour-long sorties during a seven-day period, using an average of thirteen aircraft a day.

In its early service days, the F-15 experienced a number of serious maintenance problems which raised grave doubts about the ability of the USAF to reinforce the Europe-based TFWs at short notice. Admittedly, the problem lay not with the aircraft itself but with the maintenance system. In

F-4F Phantom of JaboG 35, Pferdsfeld.

the summer of 1980, for instance, the USAF 1st TFW, based at Langley, Virginia, failed its operational readiness inspection, a no-notice test by a Tactical Air Command team of inspectors to simulate a mobilisation of the wing to deploy, on this occasion, to the Middle East. On this type of test, the first requirement is to generate enough serviceable aircraft, within a given time limit, for a unit to fulfil its war role. The unit is then put through its paces and marks are awarded for role efficiency. At the start of the ORI, Langley could provide only 23 mission-capable F-15s from a total of 66 aircraft. Later in the test a further fourteen Eagles were brought to operational standard. These aircraft, however, missed the deadline set by the ORI team and the wing's efforts then 'collapsed in confusion'. The ORI team gave up after two days of the inspection, which had been scheduled for five days, and returned to TAC HQ. The commander of the 1st TFW claimed that the problem had been caused by a lack of spare parts and experienced ground crews to service the F-15s. Some of his aircraft had been unserviceable for a long time (one for eight months) because of a shortage of spares, and others had been cannibalised to provide spares for other aircraft. It was a valid point; General John Pickett, TAC's commander, admitted that the basic problem was that the spares holding for the F-15 force had never been adequate, and that the F-15 squadrons based overseas had a priority claim. This, coupled with a reduced budget to purchase F-15 spares, had created a major shortfall. There were not enough line-replaceable units (LRU — the quick-change components in the F-15's avionics bay) available to replace an unserviceable item with a serviceable item off the shelf. This meant that the 1st TFW's engineers had to resort to either removing an LRU, repairing it on the base and replacing it, taking a replacement LRU from another unserviceable aircraft, or borrowing LRUs from the wing's war readiness supply kit.

Another problem was the high level of inexperienced personnel — as much as thirty per cent of the 1st TFW's established officers and NCOs. The retention problem is widespread in the USAF, with experienced personnel leaving the

Luftwaffe F.4F Phantoms operate both in the air superiority and ground attack roles.

F-4E Phantom of the 480th Tactical Fighter Squadron, 52nd TFW, Spangdahlem AB.

McDonnell Douglas F-4G Wild Weasel/Phantom of the 81st Tactical Fighter Squadron, Spangdahlem.

F-15 Eagles from the 36th Tactical Fighter Wing, Bitburg AB.

The 'HR' tail code denotes that these USAF F-16 Fighting Falcons belong to the 50th Tactical Fighter Wing, Hahn AFB.

Service for better-paid civilian jobs. According to TAC, about one in five of the LRUs said to be unserviceable at the time of the 1st TFW's inspection were in fact operable, and it was the fault-finding skills of the mechanics which lay at the root of the problem. The 1st TFW's traumas resulted in an urgent recommendation by the Senate Armed Services Committee for the allocation of $1500 million worth of spare parts to bring stocks up to the required level, but although the situation has greatly improved over the past five years the war readiness level of the F-15 force in the continental USA is still lower than desirable.

Nevertheless, there is no doubt about the degree of readiness among the 17th Air Force's F-15 squadrons, and their effectiveness is gradually being enhanced by deliveries of F-15Cs whose systems have been modified under a $360 million multi-stage improvement programme (MSIP) which included a new APG-70 radar, improved mission computer, programmable stores management system, updated electronic warfare equipment, and provisions for the AIM-20 AMRAAM advanced medium-range air-to-air missile. The two-seat F-15E version of the Eagle, of which the first of 392 examples was scheduled for delivery to the USAF at the end of 1986, will replace the F-4 Phantom in the interdictor/strike role; it will carry the Lantirn night nav/attack pod, now under development, and the rear cockpit will have head-down CRTs for radar, forward-looking infrared, digital map and threat warning displays while the front cockpit has a wide-angle HUD for presentation of navigation FLIR and air-to-air display. The F-15E is designed to carry up to 24,000 lb of ordnance, and its air-to-ground stores are carried tangentially on intake-mounted conformal

fuel tanks (CFTs) to reduce drag. The aircraft retains its full air-to-air capability.

The most forward-based element of the Luftwaffe's contribution to 4 ATAF is Jagdgeschwader (JG) 74, which is located at Neuburg, twenty miles north-north-east of Augsburg. JG74 has a complement of 37 F-4F Phantoms and is responsible for the interception and identification of all aircraft approaching the southern sector of the Air Defence Identification Zone, which runs north-west from the Austrian border.

Thirty miles south of Neuburg, close to Munich, is Fürstenfeldbruck, the home base of JaboG 49 Light Attack Wing with fifty Alpha Jets. JaboG 49 would have the responsibility of confronting any Warsaw Pact thrust from Czechoslovakia towards Munich along the southern flank of the Central Front, and would have the task of destroying key bridges on the River Danube as well as attacking enemy columns at various bottlenecks along the road that runs into German territory from the Bohemian Forest, parallel to the River Iser. Targets farther afield would be the responsibility of JaboG 32, which is based at Lechfeld, ten miles south of Augsburg, with its 37 Tornado IDSs. JaboG 32's primary task would be to neutralise Warsaw Pact airfields in Czechoslovakia. As well as the Tornados, the unit also operates a flight of Hansa Jets, fitted out for the electronic countermeasures role.

Also tasked with the defence of the southern flank, and the most southerly of the 4 ATAF combat units, is JaboG 34 at Memmingen, with sixty F-104G and sixteen two-seat TF-104G Starfighters. A second Starfighter wing, JaboG 33, is located at Buchel, north-west of the 50th TFW's

F-15 Eagles formate on a Luftwaffe F-4F Phantom.

The Luftwaffe has two F-104 Starfighter Geschwader, JaboG 33 at Buchel and JaboG 34 at Memmingen. Germany's F-104s have a tactical nuclear role.

Line-up of production Alpha Jets at the Dassault-Breguet factory.

F-16 base at Hahn. Both JaboGs have two basic missions, conventional ground attack and nuclear strike. Details of their nuclear strike role, should they ever be required to carry it out as a desperate last resort, are understandably secret; little can be said except that the weapons themselves are stored at secure sites close to the Starfighter bases and are

RF-4C Phantom of the 26th Tactical Reconnaissance Wing, Zweibrucken AB, 4 ATAF.

under the direct custody and control of the United States. Various types of tactical nuclear weapon would be employed and they would be released from the F-104G on a shallow forward trajectory following release at very low level. Luftwaffe F-104G pilots spend about half their flying training on nuclear systems delivery tactics.

Despite the fact that the F-104G has been in Luftwaffe service for more than two decades, and despite an unfortunate accident rate — although never as unfortunate as the public were led to believe through adverse press coverage — the Starfighter is still a viable weapons system. Most of the Luftwaffe's fleet has been rebuilt, so that the airframes and engines still have plenty of hours left, and although the avionics fit may not be exactly modern the F-104G force enjoys a number of advantages, not the least of which is that its pilots spend years training together in the same Jagdbombergeschwader and are therefore able to operate as a highly experienced team, rather like the crews of the RAF's V-Force in the 1960s and 1970s.

Secondly, its small profile makes it extremely difficult to see by enemy CAP aircraft, and if it is spotted it is fast enough to outrun most of the opposition. Although its best war-load is only 2000 lb, this can be delivered with exceptional accuracy from very low level.

The aircraft's North American NASARR radar is an effective low-level navigation instrument, and can be used by both day and night to detect waypoints and radar-identifiable ground targets and to avoid terrain. A computer system at the JaboG operations centre prepares radar predictions which give the pilot a pre-printed picture of what the radar will display at the run-up to a waypoint. The radar pictures are mounted alongside the topographical strip maps of planned training routes bound in special books which are convenient for use in the cockpit.

Carrying four external tanks, leaving the centreline store free, the F-104G can fly for about two hours at low level at around 500 mph. With two tanks only, the aircraft achieves much the same endurance carrying an internal M61 cannon and four 38-tube 2.75-inch rocket pods. However, the most commonly used weapons in the conventional role would be retarded bombs or cluster bombs, carried in pairs on underwing pylons. The Starfighter also has a limited secondary air-defence role; flying at low level, its pilots have practised visual searches for intruders higher up, and when one is sighted they pop up to engage the target with the M61.

Defensive manoeuvring for the F-104G pilot means going as fast as possible in a straight line; the

A long-range precision bomber able to operate at night and in adverse weather, the McDonnell Douglas F-15 Strike Eagle is shown here in its camouflage colours carrying 10,000 additional pounds of fuel in twin conformal fuel tanks called FAST Packs, plus 22 Mk-82 500 lb bombs. Without sacrificing air-to-air weaponry, the Strike Eagle can carry more than 24,000 pounds of external ordnance. The modified Hughes APG-63 synthetic aperture radar sees, maps and displays in the cockpit mobile tactical targets more than 20 nautical miles away, even at night and during adverse weather conditions.

Starfighter, despite its name, is in no sense a fighter in the true sense of the word. Its main defensive asset is its small size and consequent ability to use terrain masking to good effect; its single General Electric J79-MTU-JIK engine is also relatively smoke-free. If the Starfighter pilot needs to climb, he has plenty of power behind him; acceleration is excellent, and the initial rate of climb is 50,000 feet per minute. Maximum indicated airspeed at low level is Mach 1.3 or 863 mph and the F-104G remains very stable at high speed. This all adds up to the fact that, despite its age, the Starfighter still retains a high survivability factor in a hostile environment; it presents a small radar target for enemy CAP and it operates at altitudes so low that few enemy SAMs could effectively engage it. Intense AAA would probably be its main problem.

The C-160 Transall is the workhorse of the Luftwaffe's transport fleet.

Completing the Luftwaffe's strike contribution to 4 ATAF is JaboG 35 at Pferdsfeld, with 36 F-4F Phantoms. This, together with all other Luftwaffe first-line units, also employs two or three Dornier Do 28 Skyservants for communications work. The task of JaboG 35 is the same as that of its sister unit, JaboG 36 at Rheine-Hopsten, described in the section dealing with 2 ATAF.

Lockheed MC-130E Hercules of the 7th Special Operations Squadron, 7575th Operations Group, Rhein-Main AB.

The Canadian Armed Forces provide an important contribution to 4 ATAF's defence task in the shape of the 1st Canadian Air Group at Sollingen, midway between Strasbourg and Karlsruhe. It comprises three fighter/attack squadrons, Nos 421, 439 and 441, which at the time of writing were in the process of replacing their ageing CF-104 Starfighters with CF-188 Hornets. Orders for the CAF version of the McDonnell Douglas F-18 Hornet total 138, for service in Canada and Europe. The CF-188 carries out the dual roles of interceptor and strike aircraft. For the intercept role the CF-188 carries four fuselage-mounted Sparrow missiles, supplemented by a built-in M61A1 cannon, and for the strike role it has a fuselage-mounted forward-looking infrared and laser spot tracker/strike camera pods. The equipment necessary for the two different tasks can be changed in about an hour.

As the Hornet is a single-seater, much thought has been given to cockpit systems design to reduce the pilot's workload. His primary instrument is the HUD, which forms an integral part of the Kaiser multi-purpose cockpit display. The HUD also provides the pilot with attack steering information once the Hughes AN/APG-65 tracking radar has locked-on to and designated a target. More radar symbology, FLIR and weapon seeker images, stores management, radar warning and engine condition data can be called up on two CRT displays, while the pilot can make keyboard inputs governing communications, navigation, IFF and autopilot on a console immediately below the HUD, removing any necessity to look down in the cockpit.

The de Havilland Canada CC-115 Buffalo is now used primarily for search and rescue duties.

Thanks to progressive refinements in the course of its development the Hornet has exceptional handling qualities. It is fitted with a digital fly-by-wire flight control system; leading- and trailing-edge flaps are computer-programmed for optimum lift and drag in both manoeuvring and cruise configurations, while ailerons and flaps are also deflected differentially for roll. This means that when the pilot initiates a roll with a sideways movement of the stick, all these computerised factors are brought into play to give the aircraft a rate of roll in excess of 220 degrees per second. The flight computers also enable the pilot to retain full control at angles of attack of up to sixty degrees by automatically cancelling aileron deflection, retracting the trailing-edge flaps and selecting the leading-edge flaps fully down.

The Hornet is powered by two General Electric F404-GE-400 turbofan engines that provide enough power to get a fully laden (35,000 lb) Hornet into the air without the use of reheat, to take it up to more than 40,000 feet in about eight minutes and to enable the pilot to perform sustained 5g combat manoeuvres at medium altitude — again, all without reheat, although when the afterburners are cut in during combat manoeuvres the results are spectacular. The Hornet's maximum speed is Mach

1.8, its operational ceiling is 50,300 feet and it carries a maximum warload of 18,300 lb. When re-equipment of the CAF squadrons in 4 ATAF is completed they will have a total of 54 aircraft, lending considerable weight to the Allied strike capability on CENTAG's southern flank.

USAFE (Germany) — Transport and other units
7th Special Operations Squadron, 7575th Operations Group (Rhein-Main AB). This unit has the task of providing support for the US Army's Special Force (Green Berets) and is equipped with four Lockheed MC-130E Hercules aircraft. Clandestine support operations are code-named Combat Talon, and the MC-130E is equipped to infiltrate, supply and recover covert sabotage teams behind enemy lines. The aircraft are fitted with terrain-following radar, INS, headup displays and aerial delivery and pick-up equipment and are finished matt-black overall with radar ablative paint. Combat Talon C-130Es also serve with the 1st Special Operations Squadron at Hurlburt Field, Florida, and the 18th Tactical Fighter Wing, a multi-type unit, at Kadena, Okinawa. Aircraft of this type were used in the abortive attempt to rescue hostages from the US Embassy in Tehran in 1980.

The Bell UH-1H Iroquois, the mainstay of the US Army's battlefield helicopter support units for many years, is now being replaced by the Sikorsky UH-60A Black Hawk.

North American OV-10A Bronco of the 601st Tactical Control Wing, Sembach AB. The 20th and 705th Tactical Air Support Squadrons operate forty of these aircraft in the FAC role.

10th Military Airlift Squadron, Military Airlift Command (Zweibrucken AB). The 10th MAS is equipped with eighteen Shorts C-23A Sherpa light transport aircraft and is responsible for the distribution of spares throughout the 17th Air Force.

435th Tactical Airlift Wing, Military Airlift Command (Rhein-Main AB). The 435th TAW comprises five squadrons, only one of which — the 37th, with Lockheed C-130Es — is actually tasked with tactical airlift. Of the other units, the 7405th Squadron, which also operates C-130Es, has an ELINT role, the 7111th is a VIP transport unit, the 55th Air Ambulance Squadron is responsible for aeromedical evacuation and the 58th Military Airlift Squadron is responsible for transport and support. Both the 55th and 7111th Squadrons use the McDonnell Douglas C-9A Nightingale, the military version of the DC-9 commercial airliner. Among the facilities aboard the ambulance version of the C-9A are refrigeration, a medical supply work area, oxygen systems, a hydraulic folding ramp for efficient loading of stretchers and supplies, a special ventilation system for isolating an intensive care section, and provision for electrical power for cardiac monitors, respirators, incubators and infusion pumps at any location in the cabin. The 58th Military Airlift Squadron operates two CT-39 Sabreliners, basic utility aircraft which are used as four- to seven-passenger executive jets for shuttling small numbers of personnel between bases; six C-12F (Beechcraft Super King); four VC-140 Jetstars; and one Boeing VC-135 transport.

601st Tactical Control Wing (Sembach AB). The function of this unit is to provide forward air control (FAC) and battlefield support for the US ground forces in CENTAG. For this purpose it employs forty OV-10A Broncos in the FAC role with the 20th and 705th Tactical Air Support Squadrons, and seven CH-53C 'Jolly Green Giant' helicopters with the 601st Tactical Air Support Squadron in the heavy lift role. The helicopters are used to support command posts and to re-locate mobile radars as dictated by the tactical situation. The North American OV-10A Bronco, originally designed as a counter-insurgency aircraft, was adopted for use in the FAC role as well as to provide limited quick-response ground support pending the arrival of tactical fighters as a result of the lessons of the Vietnam War. Powered by two AiResearch T76 turboprops, it carries a crew of two seated in tandem, with ejection seats, and has a built-in armament of four 30-inch M6OC machine-guns mounted in sponsons under the wings. The Bronco usually carries an armament of 2.75-inch rockets on four weapon attachment points for target marking. The aircraft's maximum speed at sea level is 280 mph, and its combat radius with maximum weapon load of 3600 lb (no loiter) is 228 miles.

7005th Air Base Group (Stuttgart) and 7350th Air Base Group (Tempelhof, Berlin). These groups operate C-12A, C-21A Lear Jet and CT-39A Sabreliner aircraft on communications duties in support of HQ US European Command (USEUCOM), of which USAFE is a part.

1868th Facility Checking Squadron (Rhein-Main). This is part of USAF Communications Command and operates one North American T-39 Sabreliner on calibration duties. There are also four squadrons of the **USAF Electronic Security Command** in Germany with the task of collecting, analysing and reporting data on potential enemy electronic systems to the central HQ at San Antonio, Texas. They are the 6911th Electronic Security Squadron at Hahn, the 6912th ESS at Tempelhof, the 6913th ESS at Augsburg and the 6918th ESS at Sembach.

The Dornier Do 28 Skyservant is the Luftwaffe's standard light transport and communications aircraft. Each Geschwader has one or two on its inventory.

The Bell AH-1 Cobra is widely used in the anti-tank role by the US Army in Germany.

Boeing-Vertol CH-47 assault support helicopter of the
US Army in Germany loading an AFV.

US Army (Germany) — Battlefield Support Units.
The United States Seventh Army operates a very
large number of helicopters in support of its two
corps in Germany. Each corps maintains a 'ready
force' in the form of one armoured cavalry
regiment, positioned close to the front line and
assigned two helicopter troops, a support troop for
combat support and an air troop for attack.

Further back, each corps has two divisions, one
armoured and one infantry, with their own
helicopter combat aviation battalions for attack,
liaison and support. The armoured divisions also
have a Stand-Off Target Acquisition Systems
Detachment which, equipped with the Bell EH-1H
Iroquois, has the task of electronic reconnaissance.
These units will eventually use the EH-60A Quick
Fix II, a communications jamming variant of the
Black Hawk.

Supporting V US Corps' 3rd Armoured Division
at Hanau is the 503rd Combat Aviation Battalion
with four Aviation Companies, three at Hanau and
one at Budingen. One company is assigned to
combat support, two to attack duties and one to
maintenance. The principal helicopter type used by
all units has hitherto been the UH-1H Iroquois, but
in 1986 this was being progressively replaced by the
Sikorsky UH-60A Black Hawk utility tactical
transport helicopter. Designed to carry eleven fully-
equipped troops plus a crew of three, the Black
Hawk has a large cabin which enables it to be used
without modification for medical evacuation,
reconnaissance, command and control purposes or
troop resupply. It can also lift an external load of up
to 8000 lb and is itself readily air-transportable; one
Black Hawk can be carried in a C-130 Hercules, two
in a C-141 Starlifter and six in a C-5 Galaxy. The
Black Hawk is powered by two General Electric
T700-GE-700 turboshaft engines which give it a
maximum sea level speed of 184 mph. Its range with
external fuel tanks is over 1000 miles, and in an
offensive role it can carry sixteen Hellfire missiles,
one or two side-firing M60 machine-guns in the
forward area of the cabin, rockets, mine dispensers,
infrared jamming flares and a chaff dispenser.

The other principal helicopter types operated by
the US Army aviation in Germany are the Bell OH-
58A Kiowa, the military version of the JetRanger,
and the Bell AH-1 HueyCobra. The OH-58A is
used for liaison and scout duties, while the AH-1 is
used for attack. The AH-1S is the main version
used, and is equipped with a 30 mm cannon and up
to eight TOW anti-tank missiles. The US Army's
anti-tank capability in Europe is gradually being
enhanced by the introduction of the Hughes AH-
64A Apache, which has advanced sensor systems
for day and night operations and is equipped with a
Hughes M230 30 mm chain gun with 440 rounds
plus sixteen Hellfire missiles in the anti-tank role, or
1200 rounds of 30 mm and 38 2.75-inch folding-fin
rockets in the airmobile escort role.

The versatile Hercules C-130 transport aircraft makes rush deliveries a routine operation. Using the Low Altitude Parachute Extraction System (LAPES), the Hercules can pinpoint aerial drops of heavy duty equipment.

The Alpha Jet would be effective in the light strike and anti-helicopter roles.

Sikorsky CH-53G Stallion heavy assault transport helicopter of Mittleres Heeresflieger Transportregiment 35, Mendig.

Within V US Corps, these helicopter types are also used by the 8th Combat Aviation Battalion, which supports the 8th Infantry Division at Bad Kreuznach; a Support Troop and an Air Troop with the 11th Armoured Cavalry Regiment at Fulda; the 205th Aviation Company at Mainz-Finthen (which uses the UH-1H and also the Boeing-Vertol CH-47C Chinook for assault support); the 11th Aviation Battalion at Hanau; and the 205th Transportation Battalion at Hanau. The VII US Corps' 1st Armoured Division is supported by the 501st Combat Aviation Battalion at Ansbach, with companies and detachments at Ansbach, Bamberg, Furth and Illesheim; the 3rd Infantry Division is supported by the 3rd Combat Aviation Battalion at Kitzingen, with companies and detachments at Kitzingen, Aschaffenburg, Giebelstadt and Schweinfurt; and the 2nd Armoured Cavalry Regiment has a support troop and an air troop at Feucht. The 295th Aviation Company at Coleman Barracks has CH-47Cs and UH-1Hs for assault support, while a mixture of helicopter types is operated by the 233rd Aviation Battalion at Stuttgart. The 394th Transportation Battalion at Bad Tolz was the first unit in Germany to receive the UH-60A Black Hawk, in 1982.

Canadian Armed Forces — Transport and other units. The CAF combat units in 4 ATAF are supported by No 412 Squadron at Lahr, which operates seven CC-117 Falcon 20s, two CC-132 Dash 7s and two Canadair CC-144 Challengers. No 444 Squadron, also at Lahr, operates thirteen CH-136 Kiowa helicopters in the scouting and liaison roles.

Luftwaffe — Transport and other units. Luftwaffe combat units and II and III Corps of the Bundeswehr in 4 ATAF/CENTAG are supported by one fixed-wing Lufttransportgeschwader, LTG 61 at Landsberg, south of Augsburg. LTG 61 operates 28 C-160D Transall twin-engined transports, 41 UH-1D helicopters and four Dornier Do 28D Skyservants. At Köln-Bonn there is a Flugbereitschaftstaffel (readiness squadron) which is responsible for all long-range VIP and transport flights and which operates four Boeing 707s, six Hansa Jets, three VFW-614s, six Skyservants, five UH-1D helicopters, and three VC-140 JetStars. In 1986 the latter were due for replacement by seven Canadair Challengers.

Also in the CENTAG area are two Bundeswehr helicopter regiments: Leichtes Heeresflieger Transportregiment (Light Army Aviation Transport Regiment) 30 at Niederstetten, south of Wurzburg, with forty UH-1D Iroquois, and Mittleres Heeresflieger Transportregiment (Medium Army Aviation Transport Regiment) 35 at Mendig with 36 Sikorsky CH-53G Stallion heavy assault transport helicopters.

The Lockheed C-130 Hercules is NATO's transport workhorse. The aircraft seen here is one of six belonging to the Royal Norwegian Air Force's No. 335 Squadron at Gardermoen; this particular aircraft has clearly been tasked with supporting the Norwegian contingent of a UN peacekeeping force.

Air superiority nowadays depends on adequate
warning of low-level attackers. Pictured is one of
eighteen Boeing AWACS aircraft assigned to NATO.

CHAPTER FOUR
The United States Third Air Force: NATO'S 'big stick'

The US Third Air Force, which was formed on 1 May 1951 and replaced the former Third Air Division — activated to control USAF strategic operations from Britain at the time of the Berlin Airlift in 1948 — represents a vital component of NATO's tactical air arm. Its principal mission is to prepare for and conduct tactical air operations to include ground attack, interdiction, reconnaissance, close air support and tactical airlift in the fulfilment of the US NATO commitment. It also provides NATO's theatre nuclear force.

The Third Air Force, which is under the command and control of USAFE, has its headquarters at Mildenhall, in Suffolk. Also at Mildenhall is the HQ 513th Tactical Airlift Wing of Military Air Command's 332nd Air Division, which is responsible for the administration of detachments (usually sixteen aircraft strong) of C-130E/H Hercules transports visiting the UK base on 75-day periods of temporary duty from the continental United States; the 513th TAW is also responsible for the 10th Airborne Command and Control Squadron, which operates four Boeing EC-135Hs of the European Command's airborne command post function (Silk Purse Control). Also based at Mildenhall is Detachment One, 306th Strategic Wing of Strategic Air Command, which handles deployments of up to sixteen KC-135 and KC-10 tanker aircraft assigned to the European Tanker Task Force on six-week periods of temporary duty from the US. The principal tanker base in the UK, however, is Fairford in Gloucestershire, which is the headquarters of the 11th Strategic Group, Strategic Air Command. This unit operates KC-135s and KC-10s with the 34th and 922nd Strategic Squadrons, deploying detachments overseas to Zaragoza in Spain and Hellenikon in Greece.

The largest unit in the Third Air Force is the 81st Tactical Fighter Wing, which occupies the twin airfields of Bentwaters and Woodbridge, in Suffolk. The 81st TFW comprises the 78th and 91st Tactical Fighter Squadrons at Woodbridge and the 92nd, 509th, 510th and 511th Tactical Fighter Squadrons at Bentwaters. With a total of 119 aircraft the 81st TFW is the biggest in the USAF, in keeping with the sizeable task it has to perform. It is equipped with the Fairchild A-10A Thunderbolt II, one of the most remarkable — and certainly one of the ugliest — combat aircraft ever developed.

The A-10 concept originated during the Vietnam War, when a serious lack of aircraft designed specifically for ground attack and close support was revealed. The result was a series of stop-gap measures (which in practice worked quite well) such as the use of the elderly Douglas A-1 Skyraider, which had performed well in Korea in the ground-attack role. What NATO urgently needed, however, was a modern ground-attack aircraft for use in the European environment against a massive assault by Warsaw Pact armour — an aircraft that could destroy enemy tanks in all weathers and survive in an environment dominated by enemy SAMs, fighters and the deadly ZSU 23/4 Shilka anti-aircraft artillery. Very heavy armour coupled with high manoeuvrability and enormous firepower were the keypoints of the design. Fairchild met the first requirement by seating the pilot in what was virtually a titanium 'bathtub', resistant to most firepower except a direct hit from a heavy-calibre shell, and added to this a so-called redundant structure policy whereby the pilot could retain control even if the aircraft lost large portions of its airframe, including one of the two rear-mounted engines.

The core of the A-10's built-in firepower is its massive GAU-8/A seven-barrel rotary cannon, which is mounted on the centreline under the forward fuselage. The gun fires up to 4200 rounds per minute of armour-piercing ammunition with a non-radioactive uranium core for greater impact, and is quite capable of destroying a light tank or armoured car. The aircraft also has eight underwing and three under-fuselage attachments for up to 16,000 lb of bombs, missiles, gun pods and jammer pods, and carries the Pave Penny laser system pod for target designation. It is fitted with very advanced avionics including a central air data computer, an inertial navigation system and a headup display.

From Bentwaters, the 81st TFW deploys its A-10s to Forward Operating Locations (FOLs) in Germany, usually in clutches of eight or nine aircraft. FOL 1 is at Sembach, FOL 2 at Ahlhorn, FOL 3 at Leipheim and FOL 4 at Norvenich, so the spread of A-10 deployment supports both 2 and 4 ATAF. Flying in Germany is intensive, for the A-10 pilots must become thoroughly familiar with the West German terrain. Each FOL has a computer link with Bentwaters, so that when spares are needed they can be flown out rapidly, as can ground crews to undertake major servicing. This arrangement does away with the need to maintain large stocks of spares in Germany, with the attendant need for more personnel and resulting logistics problems.

The Lockheed C-141 Starlifter is a frequent sight at RAF Mildenhall in Suffolk.

A Lockheed TR-1A of the 17th Strategic Reconnaissance Wing, RAF Alconbury. The TR-1, orbiting at up to 90,000 feet over Europe, has advanced systems that can 'see' many miles into Warsaw Pact territory and also incorporates 'Stealth' technology.

The A-10 is designed to fly a very high sortie rate, and consequently the servicing procedure is simplified to cut down turnround time. Most of the aircraft's inspection panels can be reached by a man standing on the ground, and an automatic loading system assures rapid re-arming of the 1350-round GAU-8/A ammunition drum. During exercises, the 81st TFW has flown 86 sorties with eleven aircraft between dawn and dusk, which gives a good idea of the A-10's capability; in fact the sortie rate is determined by pilot fatigue — which is high, for operational sorties require a great deal of high-g manoeuvring at low level.

In time of tension the number of A-10s deployed at the FOLs would be substantially reinforced and the aircraft dispersed in two- or four-ship flights to other locations throughout the operational area. The A-10 can operate from short, unprepared strips less than 1500 feet long; there are literally thousands of fields that fall into this category in West Germany, together with sections of road. Operating in pairs, the A-10s can cover a swathe of ground up to six miles wide, giving each other mutual support. More normally, two A-10s cover a swathe width of two to three miles, so that an attack can quickly be mounted by the second aircraft once the first pilot has made his firing pass on the target. The optimum range for engaging a target is 4000 feet, and the A-10's gunsight is calibrated for this distance. As the manoeuvrable A-10 has a turning circle of 4000 feet, this means that the pilot can engage a target without having to pass over it. A one-second burst of fire will place seventy rounds of 30 mm shells on the target, and as a complete 36-degree turn takes no more than sixteen seconds a pair of A-10s can bring almost continuous fire to bear.

Opposite: General Dynamics F-16 Fighting Falcons of the 401st TFW, Torrejon.

General Dynamics F-111E of the 20th Tactical Fighter Wing, Upper Heyford.

McDonnell Douglas F-18 Hornets.

In order to survive in a hostile environment dominated by radar-controlled AAA, A-10 pilots train to fly at 100 feet or lower, never remaining straight and level for more than four seconds. One of the aircraft's big advantages in approaching the combat zone is that its twin General Electric TF34-GE-100 turbofan engines are very quiet (this fact, together with its overall ugliness, resulting in the A-10's nickname of 'Whispering Warthog') so that it can achieve total surprise as it pops up over a contour of the land for weapons release. Attacks on targets covered by AAA involve close co-operation between the two A-10s; while one engages the target the other stands off and engages anti-aircraft installations with its TV-guided Maverick missiles, six of which are normally carried. The A-10's air-to-air combat capability has also surprised pilots of air superiority fighters engaging it during exercises: the

tactic is to turn head-on to the attacking fighter and use coarse rudder to spray it with 30 mm shells.

The A-10 has a combat radius of 250 nautical miles, enough to reach a target area on the East German border from a FOL in central Germany and then move on to another target in northern Germany. The aircraft has a $3\frac{1}{2}$ hour loiter endurance, although wartime sorties in Europe would probably last from one to two hours. The 30 mm ammunition drum carries enough rounds to make ten to fifteen firing passes.

One of USAFE's key reconnaissance elements is based in the United Kingdom under Third Air Force command. This is the 10th Tactical Reconnaisance Wing at RAF Alconbury, near Huntingdon. The 10th TRW's 1st Tactical Reconnaissance Squadron has 21 McDonnell Douglas RF-4C Phantoms and shares USAFE's tactical reconnaissance task with the 26th TRW at Zweibrucken, in Germany. (The RF-4C and its role are described in chapter three.)

Also at Alconbury are the Lockheed TR-1A tactical reconnaissance aircraft of the 95th Tactical Reconnaissance Squadron, which is a Strategic Air Command unit with the task of providing day and night all-weather surveillance of battle areas in direct support of US and allied ground and air forces during crisis and war situations. Developed from the earlier U-2, the TR-1A is equipped with a wide range of highly secret sensory systems; about half the total force of 24 aircraft, which are deployed at various locations throughout the world under the command of the 17th Strategic Reconnaissance Wing, are equipped with the Precision Location/Strike System (PLSS), enabling them to detect and locate enemy emitters and direct strike aircraft on to them. In carrying out its task the TR-1A orbits unseen at up to 90,000 feet over Europe, from which height its advanced systems can 'see' many miles into hostile territory.

Other Strategic Air Command reconnaissance detachments are deployed to Mildenhall in the form of Lockheed U-2Rs and SR-71A Blackbirds of the 9th Strategic Reconnaissance Wing (HQ Beale AFB, California). The remarkable SR-71A, which incorporates design technology that has never been equalled or surpassed since the aircraft first flew more than twenty years ago, can fly at 100,000 feet and hold a speed of Mach 3 at 78,000 feet for one and a half hours, during which time it can cover a distance of nearly 3000 miles. It carries a crew of two, the pilot and reconnaissance systems officer, the latter being responsible for operating a mass of highly classified equipment ranging from simple battlefield surveillance systems to multiple-sensor high-performance systems for strategic reconnaissance that can survey 60,000 square miles of the earth's surface in one hour from an altitude of 80,000 feet.

The secret activities of the U-2Rs and SR-71As provide vital intelligence for the operational planning connected with USAFE's medium-range strike force of General Dynamics F-111 fighter-bombers, and also the constant updating of geographical factors associated with the inertial navigation systems and terrain-following systems of ground-launched cruise missiles based in the United Kingdom.

There are two F-111 strike wings in the UK: the 20th at RAF Upper Heyford and the 48th at RAF Lakenheath. The 20th Tactical Fighter Wing comprises three squadrons — the 55th, 77th and 79th TFS — with a total of 76 F-111Es, and is supported by the 42nd Electronic Combat Squadron of the 66th Electronic Combat Wing with twelve Grumman EF-111A Raven tactical jamming aircraft. The 'Electric Fox' EF-111A is equipped with the ALQ-99 jamming system which, originally developed for the Grumman EA-6B Prowler, is automated for one-man operation.

Tactical Jamming System — Grumman EF-111A Raven.

F-15 Eagles of the 36th TFW, Bitburg.

The development history of the F-111 — one of the most potent strike aircraft in the world, and one which was years ahead of its time in terms of technology — goes back to 1962, when the General Dynamics Corporation, in association with Grumman Aircraft, was selected to develop a variable-geometry tactical fighter to meet the requirements of the USAF's TFX programme. An initial contract was placed for 23 development aircraft, including eighteen F-111As for the USAF and five F-111Bs for the US Navy. Powered by two Pratt & Whitney TF30-P-1 turbofan engines, the prototype F-111A flew for the first time on 21 December 1964, and during the second flight on 6 January 1965 the aircraft's wings were swept through the full range from 16 degrees to 72.5 degrees.

F-4E Phantoms of the 52nd Tactical Fighter Wing, Spangdahlem.

F-4E Phantom of the 86th TFW, Ramstein. The Wing is now equipped with F-16s.

One hundred and sixty production F-111As were built, the first examples entering service with the 4480th Tactical Fighter Wing at Nellis AFB, Nevada, in October 1967. On 17 March the following year six aircraft from this unit flew to Takhli AFB in Thailand for operational evaluation in Vietnam (Operation 'Combat Lancer'), making their first sorties on 25 March. The operation ended unhappily when three of the aircraft were lost as the result of metal fatigue in a control rod, but the problem was rectified and in September 1972 the F-111As of the 429th and 430th Tactical Fighter Squadrons deployed to Takhli and performed very effective service in the closing air offensive of the war, attacking targets in the Hanoi area at night and in all weathers through the heaviest anti-aircraft concentrations in the history of air warfare.

The F-111E variant, which superseded the F-111A in service, featured modified air intakes to improve performance above Mach 2.2. Re-equipment of the 20th TFW at Upper Heyford with the F-111E was completed in the summer of 1971, and in its war role the 20th is committed to 2 ATAF, under whose control the F-111s would interdict targets deep inside enemy territory. The 48th TFW at Lakenheath is assigned to 4 ATAF in its war role, and could penetrate as far as the Adriatic. The 48th TFW is equipped with the F-111F, a fighter-bomber variant combining the best features of the F-111E and the FB-111A (the strategic bomber version assigned to some units of Strategic Air Command) and fitted with more powerful TF30-F-100 engines. The 48th TFW's aircraft are equipped to carry two B43 nuclear stores internally, as well as a variety of ordnance under six wing hardpoints, and form the core of NATO's theatre nuclear strike force.

In the conventional role, on which a great deal more emphasis is now placed, the F-111F's primary precision attack weapon system is the Pave Tack self-contained pod containing a laser designator, rangefinder and forward-looking infrared equipment for use with laser-guided bombs like the 2000 lb Mk 82 Snakeye, the GBU-15 TV-guided bomb or the Maverick TV-guided missile. The Pave Tack pod is stowed inside the F-111's weapons bay in a special cradle, rotating through 180 degrees to expose the sensor head when the system is activated. The sensor head provides the platform for the FLIR seeker, the laser designator and rangefinder, so that the Weapon Systems Operator is presented with a stabilised infrared image, together with range information, on his display.

As the F-111 runs in at low level towards the target, the WSO's primary display shows a radar ground map which enables major course corrections to be made. All the information from the aircraft's systems is processed by a CP-2A digital computer, which presents it to the crew in intelligible form. The aircraft's General Electric APQ-113 multi-mode radar operates in the J-frequency band; as well as providing accurate air-to-ground navigation it also supplies ranging and weapon delivery facilities, and in the air-to-air role it can track and scan hostile targets and control the aiming and launch of Sidewinder AAMs.

The WSO activates Pave Tack at a range of about four miles from the target. This provides more accurate steering information, and at the same time the infrared image appears on the display. After selecting the correct infrared field of view the WSO centres a recticule on the target and fires the laser, which is kept in target by the F-111's inertial navigation system even when the aircraft is taking

violent evasive action to avoid enemy defences. The WSO uses a hand controller for fine tuning of the laser line of sight. With the laser illuminating the target the F-111's CP-2A computer initiates a pull-up and automatically releases the weapons at the optimum height for an accurate toss-delivery attack; as the aircraft turns away from the target Pave Tack's sensor head rotates so that it continues to illuminate the target until bomb impact. The pod is then retracted and the cleaned-up F-111, having pulled round hard and dived back to low level, accelerates to supersonic speed for its escape from the target area.

The use of Pave Tack and the F-111's associated weaponry was dramatically demonstrated under operational conditions when, in the early hours of 15 April 1986, F-111Fs of the 48th Tactical Fighter Wing struck at targets in Libya in a calculated response against a growing tide of international terrorism allegedly being supported by that nation. The operation is worth examining in some detail, because it provides a good yardstick on how the F-111 force and its associated support elements might be used in a conflict with the Warsaw Pact.

On 11 April, the USAF (Europe) was placed on alert in readiness to undertake a strike against Libyan targets in conjunction with air elements of the United States Sixth Fleet, which was on station between Sicily and the Gulf of Sirte. Within the next twelve hours the USAF's tanker task force in Britain was reinforced by the arrival of 24 McDonnell Douglas KC-10 Extenders, sixteen of which went to Mildenhall and the remainder to Fairford. Mildenhall's complement of fourteen KC-135 tankers was also increased to twenty aircraft, including a single KC-135Q; this variant, two of which were already located at Mildenhall, is used to refuel the SAC detachments of 9th Strategic Reconnaissance Wing SR-71As.

The amazing Lockheed SR-71 Blackbird, already in service for two decades, uses technology which has never been surpassed. Aircraft belonging to the 9th Strategic Reconnaissance Wing are deployed to bases in the United Kingdom and elsewhere.

Close-up of the Fairchild A-10's 30 mm seven-barrel rotary cannon installation. Note the different air-cooling configuration in the two photographs.

These tanker movements took place under the guise of preparations by the Third Air Force and associated UK air units to take part in a NATO exercise, 'Salty Nation', but as the weekend of 12/13 April progressed the level of USAF readiness made it increasingly clear that a war operation was being prepared. At Lakenheath, the engines of a proportion of the 48th TFW's F-111Fs were being ground run all through Saturday, and eight more KC-10 tankers landed at Mildenhall between 02:00 and 10:00 hours on Sunday, breaking Mildenhall's long-standing embargo on Sunday morning flying. The arrival of a large number of KC-10s was significant, because — unlike the KC-135 — they are equipped with both boom and probe-and-drogue refuelling systems and are therefore capable of refuelling US Navy as well as USAF aircraft, an indication that a combined operation was about to be mounted.

In the evening of Monday, 14 April, the tanker force left Mildenhall and Fairford to position itself at intervals along the F-111's planned approach route. The original plan had envisaged a flight of around 1600 nautical miles directly across continental Europe, but since the French, Spanish and Italian Governments had all refused permission for the strike force to overfly their territories the route had to be rescheduled so that it crossed only international waters.

A Grumman EF-111A Raven tactical jamming aircraft of the 42nd Electronic Combat Squadron, 66th ECW, RAF Upper Heyford.

Two F-5E Aggressors flank an RF-4C Phantom of the 10th Tactical Reconnaissance Wing, RAF Alconbury.

At 21:30 hours GMT on 14 April fifteen F-111Fs of the 48th TFW took off from RAF Lakenheath and were joined by three EF-111 Ravens from the 42nd Electronic Combat Squadron, RAF Upper Heyford. The total length of the flight, which now had a series of dog-legs to take it clear of France and Spain, was some 2800 nautical miles, and as the F-111's combat radius with a 6000 lb warload is about 1000 nautical miles the outbound flight required three refuelling contacts. The first of these was made off the Cherbourg Peninsula at around 50°N 03°W, the F-111s subsequently continuing on a south-westerly heading out into the Atlantic to latitude 46°N before turning south to fly parallel with the Atlantic coasts of Spain and Portugal. The second refuelling contact was made west of Lisbon and the strike force then continued south before swinging east along the 36th Parallel to pass through the Strait of Gibraltar. The flight so far had been made at high level, but the F-111s now descended to medium level for their third refuelling contact over the Mediterranean, off the Algerian coast.

With this final contact completed the F-111s now descended to low level, turning south at a point to the west of Sicily and by-passing the island of Lampedusa as they headed towards their assigned Libyan targets. There were three of these: the Libyan Air Force side of Tripoli Airport, the Al Azziziyah barracks in Tripoli, and the Sidi Bilal port facility ten miles west of Tripoli, where the Libyan Navy based its 'Nanuchka' Class missile corvettes and La Combattante missile patrol boats. The F-111 formation accordingly split into three waves.

Those aircraft tasked with the strike on the airfield and port facility were armed with Mk 20 Rockeye 500 lb laser-homing cluster bombs, while those assigned to the attack on the Tripoli barracks area and its associated command centre carried Mk 82 2000 lb laser-guided bombs for greater effect against hardened targets. At the same time, fifteen Grumman A-6 Intruders and Vought A-7 Corsairs from the Sixth Fleet carriers USS *America* and *Coral Sea,* also armed with 2000 lb and 500 lb laser-guided weapons, headed in across the Gulf of Sirte to hit two targets near Benghazi: the Al Jumahiraya Barracks, which according to US Intelligence was a back-up command centre to the one at Tripoli, and the military airfield at Benina.

Throughout the operation, which was carried out through moderate and disorganised AAA and SAM fire (the heaviest of which was apparently put up after the strike aircraft had long gone), top cover was provided by Sixth Fleet F-14 Tomcats and F-18 Hornets, directed by Grumman E-2C Hawkeye command and early warning aircraft. Effective countermeasures were provided by the EF-111 Ravens, and also by US Navy Grumman EA-6 Prowlers.

The F-111s flight-refuelled on the way back to the United Kingdom. One F-111F diverted to Rota, in Spain, with engine trouble and another was missing as a result of the operation. Post-strike reconnaissance was carried out by two Lockheed SR-71A Blackbirds from Mildenhall, which photographed both target areas after dawn on 15 April from very high altitude; it revealed that all the assigned targets had been hit, albeit with a certain amount of collateral damage to civilian property in Tripoli, and a number of aircraft destroyed. These included MiG-23 Floggers, Mi-8 helicopters, Il-76 transports and Mi-24 Hind helicopter gunships.

The attacks on Libya, although the subject of much controversy, showed that the F-111 was still quite capable of carrying out the low-level interdiction task for which it had been designed. The Libyan operation was characterised by surprise, coupled with effective ECM and the cover of darkness, all of which are essential ingredients of the F-111's success. On this occasion the F-111s made single passes through the target areas at around 630 mph, but under other circumstances the aircraft is capable of an over-the-target speed of Mach 1.2 while still retaining weapons delivery accuracy.

Carrying a payload of the size used in the Libyan attacks, the combat radius of UK-based F-111s is sufficient to put them in reach of many key eastern European targets without flight refuelling. For example, an F-111F with a 6000 lb warload could fly at high level across the 'neck' of Denmark, descend to low level at a turning point over the Baltic, and penetrate Russian territory as far as Minsk. Alternatively, flying directly across central Europe, the F-111 could cover the whole of Poland and Czechoslovakia — and from advanced NATO bases, say in Turkey, its combat radius would enable it to strike at targets in Russia's vital Caucasian oilfields. In the ground support role, the F-111 can lift a maximum warload of 24,000 lb over a combat radius of 350 nautical miles, so UK-based aircraft — assuming that their bases survived — could deliver a very heavy weight of ordnance on enemy forces that succeeded in breaking through into West Germany.

In a NATO/Warsaw Pact war scenario, while Tornados and Buccaneers of RAF Strike Command carried out anti-shipping attacks and strikes on enemy ports, airfields, radar complexes and missile sites in the Soviet Arctic — at Murmansk and Archangelsk, for example — the F-111 force would penetrate Warsaw Pact territory from a variety of directions to hit command and communications centres, supply bases, road and rail links, fuel depots and possibly oilfield installations. In summary, the primary roles of the UK-based F-111 force are theatre nuclear strike, conventional interdiction and counter-air attack; secondary roles are close air support, air defence suppression and maritime air support.

Each squadron of the two F-111 wings in the UK carries an identification colour coding on the radar warning antenna on top of the fin. In the case of the 20th TFW the colours are grey (42nd ECS), blue (55th TFS), red (77th TFS) and yellow (79th TFS),

while the 48th TFW's colours are blue (492nd TFS), yellow (493rd TFS), red (494th TFS) and green (495th TFS). All F-111 units train intensively for their war roles over the UK low-level military routes and, on occasions, venture much farther afield. A typical sortie over the UK might involve an hour of high-level cruise, half an hour of low-level practice with fifteen minutes or so spent in dropping practice bombs or illuminating targets by radar, and high-level cruise back to base. However, airframe, systems and engine checks, together with briefings and debriefings and half an hour spent in the circuit at the end of the sortie, will extend the F-111 crew's time spent on all phases of the sortie to about six hours.

Fairchild A-10A Thunderbolt II of the 81st TFW, Bentwaters.

During training, the F-111 force, RAF and other NATO low-level strike aircraft are subjected to simulated attacks over the UK low-level routes by RAF Phantoms, Lightnings and Tornado F 2s, and also by the Northrop F-5E Tiger IIs of the 527th Aggressor Squadron. Assigned to the 10th Tactical Reconnaissance Wing at RAF Alconbury, the 527th AS is unique in the European theatre. Its role is to provide Dissimilar Air Combat Tactics (DACT) training for USAF and NATO air units.

The Tiger II was selected for this specialised role because of its small profile, which approximated that of Warsaw Pact fighter aircraft in the MiG-21 class. It has a wingspan of only 26 feet 8 inches and a length of 48 feet 3 3/4 inches. It weighs 9425 lb

Lockheed C-5A Galaxy, used to ferry heavy materials — including cruise missile and components - across the Atlantic to locations in the UK.

empty, increasing to an all-up weight of 25,488 lb with fuel and armament. The Tiger II, which is basically a day and night fighter with limited all-weather capability, is powered by two General Electric J85-GE-21 turbojets, each producing 5000 lb thrust with reheat. Maximum level speed at 36,000 feet is about Mach 1.4, and its service ceiling is 50,000 feet. The 527th AS aircraft, which are painted in Warsaw Pact colour schemes, have a fighter/attack role in wartime. Ordnance includes two AIM-9L Sidewinder AAMs on wingtip launchers, two 20 mm cannon in the nose with 280 rounds per gun, and up to 7000 lb of mixed ordnance on four underwing attachments and one under-fuselage station.

In providing Dissimilar Air Combat Tactics Training, the 527th AS places emphasis on two areas: combat training and air-to-air exercises, and academic instruction on the ground and air components of the Warsaw Pact air defence system. In-theatre training of USAFE and NATO fighter crews is in three stages. In the first, the host-unit pilots fly against the Tigers in basic size and performance exercises; these one-v-one missions expose the fighter crews to the advantages and disadvantages of NATO types, which tend to have high wing loadings, versus Warsaw Pact types, which have low wing loadings.

The second stage consists of offensive and defensive exercises involving multiple aircraft. The offensive two-v-one missions review the basics of fluid tactics, with the emphasis on teamwork, radio procedures and flight discipline. Disengagement techniques are practised during this type of mission because they stress the team effort necessary for offensive aircraft to get in, complete their mission and get out as a unit. In defensive exercises, the host-unit aircraft practice initial move reactions from a position of disadvantage. The objectives during these missions are to react to a defensive situation as a fighting unit and continue to an offensive position, or disengage as a fighting unit, depending on the tactical situation.

The third and last stage of progression is multi-aircraft exercises, involving building on the combat lessons learned on previous missions to practice more dynamic and tactically flexible scenarios. In carrying out its mission, the 527th Aggressor Squadron deploys its aircraft to locations all over the European NATO area.

Il-86 Candid transports seen during the F-111 strike on Tripoli, April 1986.

Since 1983, the US Third Air Force has been responsible for the administration and tactical control of the 501st Tactical Missile Wing, which deploys the General Dynamics BGM-109G Tomahawk Ground Launched Cruise Missile (GLCM) at RAF Greenham Common, in Berkshire. A second GLCM Wing will be deployed at Molesworth, Suffolk, by 1987. The BGM-109G has a range of 1500 miles and carries a 200-kiloton nuclear warhead, but warheads ranging in yield from ten to fifteen kilotons — and also conventional warheads, for that matter — maybe fitted depending onoperational requirements. The BGM-109G is subsonic, with a speed of Mach 0.7 (530 mph) at sea level.

In peacetime, GLCM flights are housed in concrete shelters hardened to withstand a direct hit from precision-guided weapons with conventional warheads. Each shelter is divided into three cells, each containing two launch vehicles. When a GLCM flight is deployed to its war station it travels as two separate elements, each comprising two launchers and a control centre, and the vehicles themselves are armoured against small-arms fire. This is a necessary precaution, for in time of war cruise missile sites and launch vehicles en route would come under attack by subversive groups and Spetsnaz, the Soviet Special Forces.

The GLCM is transported, erected and launched from a 78,000 lb cross-country vehicle comprising a semi-trailer with an elevating armoured launcher containing four GLCM rounds, and a MAN tractor. The launch control centre is a similar cross-country vehicle with a semi-trailer mounting an armoured shelter and generators. Each GLCM flight has a primary and backup control centre linked by fibre-optic, electromagnetic pulse resistant cable.

The 501st TMW's GLCMs can be deployed to pre-surveyed sites almost anywhere in southern England, as far west as the Welsh border, and once on site it takes about an hour of planning to prepare the mission. This is done with the aid of the Theatre Mission Planning System, which enables the operator to select appropriate waypoints and terrain contour matching maps for the best route to the target. En-route navigation at low level is achieved by INS, the TERCOM information being stored in the GLCM's on-board computer. A continuous stream of height data supplied by the missile's radar altimeter is used to produce a profile of the ground over which the GLCM is flying; this is compared with stored data and the INS updated accordingly. The missile's memory contains up to twenty TERCOM maps; between the TERCOM fields — surveyed and constantly updated by satellite and other reconnaissance methods — the GLCM navigates by a series of pre-programmed waypoints, its route taking advantage of local terrain for concealment and to avoid known defences. As the flight progresses the TERCOM maps become smaller and more detailed until the terminal matrix is reached just before the target. The missile is then programmed to pop up and dive on the target in a manoeuvre designed to clear any defensive barriers such as cables or earthworks.

The GLCM has sufficient range to attack targets along an arc stretching from Murmansk in the north to Odessa in the south from its launching sites in Britain. It will remain a viable weapon system for a long time to come, despite the growing sophistication of Warsaw Pact air defences, and will continue to be the mainstay of NATO's theatre nuclear force.

CHAPTER FIVE
The Southern Flank: From the Atlantic to the Black Sea

Although NATO describes its southern flank in terms of the three member nations of Italy, Greece and Turkey, in practical terms the actual southern flank extends much farther westward to encompass Spain and Portugal. Although these last two countries have an important role to play in NATO's Iberian Atlantic Command, they would also, in time of war, play an equally important part in establishing NATO control of the approaches to Gibraltar and the Mediterranean, without which the southern flank would be indefensible. In this chapter, therefore, we shall look at the air strengths of the NATO member nations that run west to east from the Atlantic to the Black Sea, along the line of the 40th Parallel of Latitude.

Portugal

The Portuguese Air Force — Força Aérea Portuguêsa — has been constantly plagued by economic problems, and much of its equipment is in need of updating. Two squadrons, Nos 301 at Montijo and 303 at Lajes, are at present equipped with a total of 42 Fiat G 91R-3/R-4 fighter-bombers in the interceptor and attack roles, and also with eight G 91Ts for training. These aircraft are ex-Luftwaffe machines and are scheduled for replacement by more modern aircraft, the Northrop F-20A Tigershark being one of the possibilities under consideration. Portugal's G 91s have been updated in the meantime with modern mission avionics and AIM-9 Sidewinders. Built-in armament comprises four 0.5-inch Colt-Browning machine-guns or two 30 mm cannon, fuselage-mounted on either side of the cockpit; underwing pylons can also accommodate 500 lb bombs, three-inch air-to-ground rocket clusters, folding-fin rockets or 250 lb bombs. The G 91R has a maximum level speed of 650mph at 5000 feet and a service ceiling of 40,000 feet.

Two attack squadrons, Nos 302 and 304 at Monte Real, are equipped with a total of 44 Vought A-7P Corsair IIs and six two-seat TA-7C trainers. The Corsair II also equips units of the Greek Air Force and the US Navy/Marine Corps. Powered by an Allison/RR TF41-A2 turbofan engine (a licence-built Rolls-Royce Spey), the Corsair II has a maximum speed of 660 mph with a 3000 lb bomb load and a combat radius of 580 nautical miles hi-lo-hi, carrying an 8000 lb bomb load. It carries one 20 mm M61 cannon and its eight underwing and underfuselage hardpoints can accommodate a warload of up to 20,000 lb.

The Portuguese Air Force maintains a small force of five Lockheed C-130H Hercules with No 501 Squadron at Montijo; these aircraft are used for various tasks, including transport, reconnaissance and maritime patrol. An additional four Hercules were on order for delivery in 1986, as were six Lockheed P-3B Orions for the ASW/Maritime Patrol tasks. Other Portuguese AF units include No 103 Squadron with Lockheed T-33As and RT-33As for training and reconnaissance and No 201 Squadron with Northrop T-38A Talons, both at Monte Real; Nos 551 and 751 Squadrons with Alouettes and Pumas at Montijo for utility and transport; Nos 503 and 752 Squadrons with C 212 Aviocars and Pumas at Lajes for SAR and transport; and Nos 502 (Aviocar), 552 and 111 Squadrons (Pumas) at Tancos for transport, liaison and utility duties.

Spain

The Spanish Air Force — Ejército del Aire — has four operational commands, the foremost of which is the Mando Aéreo de Combate (Air Combat Command). This consists of three combat wings, each with two squadrons. No 11 Wing (Nos 111 and 112 Squadrons) at Manises operates nineteen Mirage IIIEE and six Mirage IIIED aircraft; No 12 Wing (Nos 121 and 122 Squadrons) at Torrejon operates 35 F-4C and four RF-4C Phantoms; and No 14 Wing (Nos 141 and 142 Squadrons) at Los Llanos flies 44 Mirage F 1CEs and four F 1BEs.

Also part of Air Combat Command is No 901 Squadron, with Dornier Do 27s for liaison, and each combat wing has a Do 27 flight.

The Dassault Mirage IIIEE (the second 'E' denotes 'Espagne') began to come on to the Spanish Air Force's inventory in April 1970. The long-range fighter-bomber/intruder version of the celebrated Mirage III line, it is powered by a SNECMA Atar 09C turbojet fitted with an overspeed system which is engaged automatically from Mach 1.4 and permits a thrust increase of about eight per cent in the high supersonic speed range. It gives the Mirage IIIE a maximum level speed at sea level of 870 mph, and 1460 mph (Mach 2.2) at 40,000 feet. Built-in armament of the Mirage IIIE consists of two 30 mm DEFA cannon, and external stores include Sidewinder or MATRA AAMs, 1000 lb bombs or a variety of air-to-ground rockets and missiles.

Fiat G.91 of No. 310 Squadron, Portuguese Air Force, pictured at RAF Bruggen in 1982 in company with a Jaguar of No. 14 Squadron, RAF.

The Mirage F 1, originally conceived by Dassault as a single-seat strike fighter as a private venture, is roughly the same size as the Mirage III and has a swept wing fitted with high-lift devices that enable the aircraft to take off in 1600-2600 feet at normal operating weight. The type's primary role is all-weather interception at any altitude for which it is produced in the F 1C version, while the F 1A is a ground-attack fighter with an extra fuel tank in place of some of the interceptor's avionics. The F 1C is powered by a SNECMA Atar 9K-50 turbojet rated at 15,785 lb thrust with reheat; maximum speeds are 1450 mph at 40,000 feet and 915 mph at sea level, and service ceiling is 65,700 feet. The F 1C carries two 30 mm DEFA cannon, two MATRA 530/550s and two Sidewinder AAMs.

The second operational command is the Mando Aéreo Táctico (Tactical Air Command), which has a close-support element comprising forty Northrop SF-5A/B Freedom Fighters in Nos 211 and 214 Squadrons, No 21 Wing, at Moron. No 22 Wing comprises the six P-3A Orions of No 221 (Maritime Reconnaissance) Squadron at La Parra, with six P-3Cs on order, and No 407 Squadron at Tablada with Dornier 27s and 28s and Cessna 0-1Es for liaison.

Cessna T-37 trainers of the Portuguese Air Force.

The Mando Aéreo de Transporte (Transport Command) has three wings: No 31 comprises No 311 Squadron with seven C-130H Hercules and No 312 Squadron with four KC-130H tankers, both units at Zaragoza; No 35 Wing's 351 and 352 Squadrons at Getafe use C 212 Aviocars and C 207 Azors, while No 37 Wing's sole squadron, No 372, uses DHC-4 Caribous at Villanubla.

The fourth operational command is the Mando Aéreo de Canarias (Canaries Air Command) which has a single wing — No 46 — of four squadrons: No 461 with C 212s, No 462 with Mirage F 1CEs, No 464 with twenty SF-5As/RF-5Bs and No 802 with three F 27s and three Pumas for SAR. All these units are based at Gando. The Mirage IIIs and F-4Cs in the combat commands are being replaced by the F-18 Hornet, 72 of which are on order, and the SF-5As will probably be replaced in the 1990s by the European Fighter Aircraft, for which Spain has expressed a 100-strong requirement.

In addition to the four combat commands, the Spanish Air Force has a Training Command of sixteen squadrons, operating a wide variety of aircraft such as the C 101 Aviojet, T-34A, T-33, T-35, Bell UH-1H and Hughes 300. Eight more squadrons are assigned to Air Force Headquarters for VIP transport (DC-8, Falcon 20, Navajo, Puma), fire-fighting and SAR.

The Spanish Naval Air Arm (Arma Aérea de la Armada) has recently received an important boost with the introduction into service of the new Carrier *Principe de Asturias*, which replaced the elderly 1943-vintage ex-US Navy *Dedalo*. The new vessel's 575-foot flight deck is equipped with a ski jump, and there is hangarage space for twenty aircraft. From the end of 1986, the nine AV-8A Matadors (Harriers) equipping No 008 Squadron will be replaced by twelve new AV-8Bs. The *Principe de Asturias* will also accommodate No 005 Squadron, which currently operates fourteen SH-3D/G Sea King helicopters; in 1987 three of these aircraft will be fitted with Searchwater radars to provide airborne early warning coverage for the fleet, and in 1988 some of them are scheduled to be replaced by six SH-60B Seahawk helicopters.

The Spanish Army Aviation (Fuerza Aeromoviles del Ejército de Tierra) is a relatively new organisation, having been formed in 1965, but it now operates some 165 helicopters in five battalions and a number of support units. Attack battalions, consisting of two aviation companies, are equipped with the Bölkow Bö105 helicopter, one company having 28 aircraft equipped with HOT anti-tank missiles and the other with eighteen aircraft armed with cannon. The sole transport battalion operates twelve CH-47C Chinook heavy-lift helicopters, with a further six on order, and UH-1H Iroquois. Reconnaissance and battalion support is undertaken by OH-58 Kiowas and Bö105s.

Spain is the headquarters of the USAFE's 16th Air Force, which is located at Torrejon. Also at Torrejon is the 401st Tactical Fighter Wing with the 612th, 613th and 614th Tactical Fighter Squadrons, operating F-16A/B Fighting Falcons. It is a large unit, with 96 F-16As and six F-16Bs, and would rapidly deploy to other European locations — Italy, for example — if hostilities threatened. The United States Navy maintains a sizeable intelligence-gathering force at Rota, where Navy squadron VQ-2 operates the McDonnell Douglas EA-3B Skywarrior, Lockheed P-3A and EP-3E Orion; VR-22 operates Lockheed C-130F Hercules from the same base. Rota also acts as host base for frequent USAF and USN deployments from the continental USA, while a detachment of the 11th Strategic Wing's KC-135 tankers is rotated to Zaragoza from RAF Fairford in the United Kingdom.

Vought A-7P Corsair II of the Portuguese Air Force. The Corsair II equips two Portuguese AF attack squadrons Nos. 302 and 304.

Italy

Italy makes a sizeable contribution in terms of both air and naval power to the NATO alliance. The Italian Air Force — Aeronautica Militare Italiano — forms the core of the 5th Allied Tactical Air Force, with nineteen squadrons NATO-assigned. Total Air Force strength is currently some 900 aircraft, and the principal combat types are the Tornado and the F-104S Starfighter. The F-104S was developed from the F-104G, which it replaced in Italian Air Force service, to carry out interception as its primary role; it is powered by a

The Mirage IIIs and F-4Cs in the Spanish Air Force's Combat Commands are being replaced by the F-18 Hornet, 72 of which are on order.

General Electric J79-GE-19 turbojet with a redesigned afterburner, giving 17,900 lb st. There are nine external stores attachments for Sidewinder AAMs, rockets and bombs and the normal primary armament of Raytheon Sparrow AAMs. Aeritalia produced a total of 205 F-104S Starfighters, about a quarter of which have been subsequently lost in accidents.

Two ASW squadrons, 86° Gruppo of 30° Stormo at Cagliari and 88° Gruppo of 41° Stormo at Catania, are equipped with Dassault-Breguet Atlantics.

The Italian Air Force is organised on a Stormo (Wing), Gruppo (Squadron) and Squadriglia (Flight) basis with the exception of the Gruppi of the tactical transport force, which come under the control of an Aerobrigata (Air Brigade). Many of the first-line squadrons are concentrated on the major airfield complexes in the plain of the River Po and around Foggia on the southern Adriatic coast.

The Tornado IDS equips three squadrons: 154° Gruppo of 6° Stormo at Ghedi, 156° Gruppo of 36° Stormo at Giola del Colle, and 155° Gruppo of 51° Stormo at Piacenza (the latter unit equipping in 1986). Each Gruppo has sixteen aircraft, some equipped for reconnaissance and others, like those of the Federal German Navy, with MBB Kormoran missiles for the anti-shipping role. A fourth Tornado squadron is scheduled to form in 1987-8.

Of the other NATO-dedicated first-line units, 3° Stormo (28° and 132° Gruppi) still operates the F-104G Starfighter at Villafranca; its total strength is 32 aircraft. The 4° Stormo (9° Gruppo) at Grosseto, 5° Stormo (23° and 102° Gruppi) at Rimini, 9° Stormo (10° Gruppo) at Grazzanise, 36° Stormo (12° Gruppo) at Giola del Colle, 37° Stormo (18° Gruppo) at Trapani, 51° Stormo (22° Gruppo) at Istrana and 53° Stormo (21° Gruppo) at Cameri all operate the F-104S, while 20° Gruppo at Grosseto flies the F-104G and TF-104G. This unit is in fact the Starfighter OCU, and like other OCUs has a war role. There are also twelve RF-104Gs for tactical reconnaissance, mostly assigned to 3° Stormo.

The Italian Air Force still has a substantial number of Fiat G 91s (sixty G 91Ys, 57 G 91Rs and 71 G 91Ts). The G 91Y is a twin-engined development of the basic G 91 design, giving up to sixty per cent more take-off thrust at the cost of a relatively small weight increase and a substantial boost in payload. The aircraft can cruise on the power of one engine for greater endurance. It is faster than the basic G 91, with a maximum speed at sea level of 690 mph, and has a service ceiling of 41,000 feet. Armament comprises two 30 mm DEFA cannon in the nose, together with cameras, and there are four underwing attachments for 1000 lb bombs, 750 lb napalm tanks, seven two-inch rocket packs, 28 two-inch rocket packs or four five-inch rocket containers. The G 91Y also has a more advanced nav/attack system than earlier models, including the Computing Devices of Canada 5 C-15 position and homing indicator, Sperry SYP twin-axis gyro platform, Bendix RDA-12 Doppler radar and AiResearch air data computer. The G 91Y is operated by 101° Gruppo of 8° Stormo at Cierva-San Giorgio and 13° Gruppo of 32° Stormo at Brindisi, while the G 91R-1 is used by 14° and 103° Gruppi of 2° Stormo at Treviso-San Angelo in the strike and PR roles. The G 91T trainers are operated by 201°, 204° and 205° Gruppi at Foggia-Amendola. The G 91 units are not assigned to NATO, but in the event of a war threat they would come under the command of 5 ATAF.

From 1989, the Fiat G 91 force will begin to be replaced by the first of 187 examples of the Aeritalia/Aermacchi/Embraer AMX light ground-attack fighter, developed under an Italian and Brazilian partnership. The first of six prototypes flew on 2 May 1984. The AMX design emphasizes low cost, combined with small size, STOL operation from semi-prepared strips and the maximum degree of survivability. The single-seat aircraft is designed for daylight low-level attack and for tactical reconnaissance with a centreline reconnaissance pod in addition to a forward-

In 1986, the Italian Army was evaluating the Agusta
A.129 Mangusta anti-tank helicopter, which can carry
eight TOW missiles.

The Fiat G.91Y is operated by 101° Gruppo of 8° Stormo at Cierva-San Giorgio and 13° Gruppo of 32° Stormo at Brindisi.

fuselage pallet with three sensor options. Power is provided by a single Rolls-Royce Spey turbofan, which gives the AMX a maximum speed low down of Mach 0.8. The aircraft has a hi-lo-hi combat radius of 325 nautical miles; built-in armament comprises one 20 mm cannon, with provision for two Sidewinder AAMs on wingtip stations. There are four underwing hardpoints for ordnance and two for fuel tanks. There are also plans for a single-seat anti-ship version, fitted with new radar and carrying either Kormoran or Exocet ASMs, and for a two-seat version for all-weather and night attack and operational training, with electronic warfare another possible role.

At Pratica di Mare, the 14° Stormo — comprising 8° and 71° Gruppi — uses twenty aircraft for electronic warfare and calibration; types in service with the Stormo are the Piaggio PD-808, the Aeritalia G 222RM, the Macchi MB 326RM and MB 339. The transport force is provided by 46 Aerobrigata, whose 2° and 98° Gruppi operate G 222s and 50° Gruppo the Lockheed C-130H Hercules. Total strength is 32 G 222s and twelve C-130s, all located at Pratica di Mare. Rome-Ciampino is the Italian Air Force's VIP base, from which 31° Stormo's 306° Gruppo operates ten PD-808s and two DC-9s.

The transport force is provided by 46 Aerobrigata, whose strength includes thirty-two Aeritalia G.222 transports.

Two ASW squadrons, 86° Gruppo of 30° Stormo at Cagliari and 88° Gruppo of 41° Stormo at Catania, are equipped with Dassault-Breguet Atlantics. Although these eighteen maritime patrol aircraft, known as the 'Aviazione per la Marina' — Naval Aviation — are under naval control, the Italian Navy is forbidden by law to operate fixed-wing aircraft, and so the Atlantics actually belong to the Air Force. The latter also controls the search and rescue helicopter force, which consists of 15° Stormo's 84° and 85° Gruppi, respectively operating twenty Sikorsky HH-3s and a mix of thirty or so Agusta-Bell AB 204s and '212s (the latter gradually replacing the '204s). There are SAR flights at Brindisi, Rimini, Trapani, Cameri, Ciampino, Amendola and Decimomannu.

The Helicopter Component of the Italian Navy (Reparti elicotteri della Marina) is primarily equipped with the Agusta-built Sikorsky SH-3D, in service with 1° Gruppo at Luni Sarzana and 3° Gruppo at Catania. Armed with Sea Killer anti-ship missiles, these helicopters deploy from their home bases to fleet warships, mainly the new helicopter carrier Giuseppe Garibaldi, commissioned in 1985. If the Italian Navy succeeds in pushing through a reform of the law governing its use of fixed-wing aircraft, it may acquire some British Aerospace Sea Harriers to form a strike component. Sixteen SH-3Ds are assigned to the Garibaldi; other vessels, such as destroyers and frigates, operate smaller helicopters like the AB 212, which is deployed by 2° Gruppo at Catania-Fontanarossa, 4° Gruppo at Grottaglie and 5° Gruppo at Luni Sarzana. In this case too the AB 212 has replaced the earlier AB 204 in the ASW role, although some '204s still remain in service.

The AB 204, however, is still widely used by the Italian Army Aviation (Aviazione Leggera dell'Esercito). Thirty-four are used for liaison, but the main helicopter type for this role is the AB 206B JetRanger, 136 of which are in service, and the Army also uses 94 AB 205As for transport work. Between them, these three types equip twenty Army Aviation squadrons and flights. Two Gruppi, 11° and 12° at Viterbo, use 26 CH-47C Chinooks and provide a capable heavy-lift force. In 1986, the Italian Army was evaluating the Agusta A 129 Mangusta anti-tank helicopter, which can carry eight TOW missiles.

Greece

Greece's commitment to the NATO alliance is important for two principal reasons. Firstly there are major port facilities at Suda Bay, where the anchorage is big enough to accommodate the whole of the US Sixth Fleet; and secondly, Greece's membership is critical in denying the Warsaw Pact access to the Aegean shore of the Mediterranean in Thrace, which borders on Bulgaria. The Greek Army, although deficient in modern equipment, would be capable of defending Thrace for some time in the event of hostilities. The problem is that Greece's confrontation in this area is not so much with the Warsaw Pact but with her traditional enemy and fellow NATO member, Turkey.

The Hellenic Air Force (Elliniki Aeroporia) forms part of NATO's 6th Allied Tactical Air Force and is organised into three main elements: Tactical Air Force, Air Training Command and Air Material Command. The commands are sub-organised on a wing (Pterix, plural Pterighe) and squadron (Moira, plural Moire) basis. The Tactical Air Force has seven wings, each of two squadrons. At Larissa, the 110 Pterix's 337 Moira operates the F-4E Phantom in the fighter-bomber role, while the 347 Moira uses the A-7H Corsair II in the strike role. Also under the control of 110 Pterix is 348 Moira, which is a photo-reconnaissance unit equipped with RF-4E Phantoms and RF-5A Tigers. Greece was the last NATO country to operate the Republic RF-84F Thunderflash, a few of which were still serving in 1985.

The 111 Pterix (341 and 349 Moire) at Nea Ankhialos and 113 Pterix (343 Moira) at Thessalonika-Mikra all operate Northrop F-5A/B Tigers, some of them purchased from Jordan, in the fighter-bomber role. An interceptor force is

Carrying out periodic depot maintenance on an A-7H Corsair II of the Hellenic Air Force.

provided by 33 Dassault-Breguet Mirage F 1CG (G for Greece) fighters with 334 and 342 Moire of 114 Pterix at Tanagra, while the 115 Pterix (340 and 345 Moire) at Suda Bay operates A-7H Corsairs in the strike role, concentrating mainly on anti-shipping work. The 116 Pterix (335 and 336 Moire) at Araxos is equipped with F-104G Starfighters, most of which are assigned to attack duties. Finally, the 117 Pterix (338 and 339 Moire) at Andravida operates F-4E Phantoms in the fighter-bomber role. Each Pterix has a station flight with six Lockheed T-33A Shooting Stars and one AB 205 helicopter for liaison.

Hellenic F-4E Phantom of 337 Moira undergoing servicing in the low bay hangar at Larissa which can accommodate fifty fighters and twelve helicopters simultaneously.

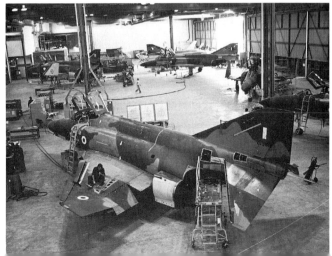

The Hellenic Air Force's 347 Moira uses the A-7H Corsair II in the strike role.

Two wings of the Hellenic Air Force operate Northrop F-5A/B Tigers, some of them purchased from Jordan, in the fighter-bomber role.

At Larissa, the 110 Pterix's 337 Moira operates the F-4E Phantom in the fighter-bomber role.

Numbers of Tactical Air Force types in service in 1986 included 48 Corsair IIs and five two-seat TA-7Hs, sixty F-104Gs, twelve TF-104Gs and two RF-104s, 54 F-5As and eight F-5Bs, ten RF-5As, 47 F-4E and seven RF-4E Phantoms, 33 Mirage F 1CGs, ten RF-84F Thunderflashes and 59 T-33A Shooting Stars. The Hellenic Air Force has ordered forty Dassault-Breguet Mirage 2000s and forty General Dynamics F-16s to replace the Phantoms and F-5s.

The Air Material Command has four squadrons, all based at Elefsis. The 353 Moira has eight Grumman HU-16B Albatross for ASW and SAR under naval control; 354 Moira has twenty ex-Israeli and German Noratlas transports; 355 Moira operates six ex-Olympic Airlines YS-11A Nihons and ten CL-215s; and 356 Moira has twelve Lockheed C-130H Hercules. Nine C-47 Dakotas are also in service with the various transport squadrons, and the command has a requirement to replace both these and the Noratlas in the near future.

The Air Training Command's 359 Moira mainly operates AB 205, AB 206 and Bell 212 helicopters; 360 Moira, which constitutes the Air Academy at Dekelia, uses Cessna T-41As/Ds; 361 Moira has Cessna T-37Bs/Cs; while 362 and 363 Moire use the North American T-2E Buckeye. The last three squadrons are based at Kalamata.

The Hellenic Navy has a squadron of sixteen AB 212 helicopters for ASW and a few Alouette IIIs for liaison. There is a small Army Aviation force based at Megara, with twenty Bell AH-1 TOW-armed anti-tank helicopters either in service or on order, five CH-47C Chinooks and a mixture of Bell 47G, UH-1D and AB 204/205 helicopters for utility work.

Turkey

There can be no doubting Turkey's strategic importance as a member nation of NATO. She controls the passage from the Black Sea to the Mediterranean; moreover, she has the military power to close the passage and to keep it closed. It is for this reason that the Soviet Union's naval presence in the Mediterranean is composed mainly of units on rotation from the Baltic and Northern Fleets, even though the USSR has the right, under the terms of the 1936 Montreux Convention, to pass warships of specified types through the Dardanelles.

Yet Turkey's adherence to NATO has suffered its traumas, not least from 1974 to 1977, when the United States imposed an arms embargo as a consequence of the Turkish invasion of Cyprus. In those years Greece withdrew from NATO, and the stability of the southern flank was seriously compromised. Today, matters have improved; Greece is back, and the Turkish armed forces are undergoing a modernisation programme. However, Turkey is by no means a wealthy nation, and she is still forced to depend to some extent on equipment handed down by other NATO countries.

The mainstay of the Turkish Air Force (Turk Hava Kuvvetleri) is the F-104G/S Starfighter. In 1986 190 F-104Gs and 36 F-104Ss were in service in the interception and strike roles. Many of these aircraft have served with other NATO air forces; the Netherlands, for example, has supplied 51 F-104Gs to Turkey, while Belgium has transferred eighteen and Denmark twelve. The next most numerous type is the ageing F-100 Super Sabre, of which 123 are in service; 25 of these also came from

Ex-German Noratlas transports are operated by 354 Moira at Elefsis.

The Hellenic Air Force's 356 Moira has twelve Lockheed C-130H Hercules transports.

The Hellenic Navy has a squadron of sixteen AB.212 helicopters for ASW.

Mirage F.1C fighters of No 114 Pterix, Hellenic Air Force.

The Hellenic Air Force's 353 Moira has eight Grumman HU-16B Albatross for ASW and SAR under naval control.

The Dornier Do.28 Skyservant is widely used for liaison duties by the Hellenic Air Force.

Denmark. More modern equipment comprises 97 F-4E Phantoms; fifteen of these were purchased from Egypt, with negotiations in progress at the time of writing for the purchase of 22 more from that source. Spain has also offered to provide thirty Phantoms as she re-equips with F-18s. Eighty-two F-5As and twelve F-5Bs are used in the ground-attack role. Many of the above types will eventually be replaced by the F-16 Fighting Falcon, 160 of which are on order, and Turkey has also expressed interest in buying up to forty Tornado IDS, although this has been frustrated — at least for the time being — by financial problems.

The Turkish Air Force is subordinate to the Turkish General Staff and has four main Commands: the 1st and 2nd Tactical Air Forces, Air Support Command and Air Training Command. The commands are organised on a squadron (Filo) basis rather than on wing-and-squadron lines.

The 1st Tactical Air Force, Eskisehir Air Division, is the largest command, with eleven Filos. Three of the squadrons, 111 Filo at Eskisehir and 131 and 132 Filos at Konya, operate the F-

The Hellenic Air Force's 362 and 363 Moire use the North American T-2 Buckeye for advance training at Kalamata.

100C/D/F Super Sabre; 141 Filo at Murted and 191 Filo at Balikesir use the F-104G Starfighter in the fighter-bomber role, while 142 Filo at Bandirma operates the F-104S interceptor. The 1st TAF has two F-4E units, 113 Filo at Eskisehir and 162 Filo at Bandirma, the former with four RF-4Es for tactical reconnaissance. Finally, 112 Filo at Eskisehir, 161 Filo at Bandirma and 192 Filo at Balekesir operate the F-5A/B Freedom Fighter.

The F-5A/B also equips three Filos of the 2nd Tactical Air Force, Diyarbakir Air Division; these are 151 and 152 Filos at Merzifon and 181 Filo at Diyarbakir. There is also a tactical reconnaissance unit at Diyarbakir, 183 Filo, which is equipped with RF-5As. The third squadron at Diyarbakir, 182 Filo, is an interceptor unit and is equipped with F-104S Starfighters. Lastly there are two F-4E Phantom strike squadrons, 171 and 172 Filos at Erhac-Malataya.

The Air Support Command, as its name implies, is a transport force, with its HQ at Kayseri. Two squadrons are based here: 221 Filo with twenty ex-Luftwaffe C 160D Transalls, and 222 Filo with seven C-130E Hercules brought up to C-130H standard. A VIP flight at Etimesgut operates three

Lockheed F-104S Starfighters of the Turkish Air Force.

The Turkish Air Force uses ninety-seven F-4E Phantoms in the strike role; fifteen of these were purchased from Egypt with negotiations in progress for the purchase of twenty-two more from that source.

Viscounts, while forty C-47 Dakotas and three C-54 Skymasters are deployed to various locations for Army support. There are also some UH-1D/H helicopters for utility work.

Air Training Command, Izmir Air Division, has three squadrons, all based at Cigli. Lockheed T-33As and Northrop T-38A Talons are used by 121 Filo, while 122 Filo operates Cessna T-37s. Primary training is the responsibility of 123 Filo, with T-34s, T-41s and T-42s.

The Turkish Army has a considerable mixed force of fixed- and rotary-wing types for utility work, and now has an anti-tank capability in the form of 26 AH-1S Cobra helicopters armed with TOW missiles. The Navy has a small number of AB 205 and AB 212 helicopters for liaison, and a squadron of twenty Grumman S-2 Trackers based at Topel in the ASW role. These aircraft are operated by the Air Force, although they come under naval control.

The US Navy' strike squadrons are now progressively re-equipping with the McDonnell Douglas Hornet which comes in two versions: the F-18A single-seat fighter-interdictor to replace the F-4 Phantom, and the A18-A single-seat attack aircraft to replace the A-4 Skyhawk and the A-7 Corsair II.

F-18A Hornet prepares for launch from a US Navy attack carrier.

A-7E Corsair IIs of Navy Attack Squadron VA-27 in formation. Markings carried aft of the cockpit on the nearest aircraft show that it flew nine bombing missions over Vietnam.

The United States Sixth Fleet

In time of war, the Mediterranean-based US Sixth Fleet would make an important, and probably decisive, contribution to the security of NATO's southern flank. The fleet has eight task forces, covering the whole spectrum of warfare from air strike through amphibious assault to submarine attack. At the heart of the whole organisation is the Battle Force; in the case of the Sixth Fleet this is Task Force 60, which comprises two carriers — a nuclear-powered attack carrier, usually a 95,000-ton vessel of the USS *Nimitz* Class, and a smaller attack carrier of the USS *Forrestal* or *Midway* Class. The larger carriers have an air wing of 90-95 aircraft, the smaller vessels about 75 aircraft.

The interceptor element of a USN Carrier Air Wing is provided by two squadrons of Grumman F-14 Tomcats. The variable-geometry Tomcat is powered by two 20,900 lb st Pratt & Whitney TF30-P-414A turbofans which give it a maximum low-level speed of 911 mph (Mach 1.2) and a high-altitude speed of 1544 mph, or Mach 2.34. It is equipped with the Hughes AN/AWG-9 weapons control system, enabling the two-man crew to detect airborne targets at ranges of up to 170 nautical miles, depending on their size, and small targets such as cruise missiles at 65 nm. The system can track 24 targets and initiate attacks on six of them at the same time, at a variety of altitudes and ranges.

The Tomcat's built-in armament consists of one General Electric M61A1 20 mm Vulcan gun mounted in the port side of the forward fuselage, with 675 rounds. Main missile armament comprises four Sparrow AAMs partially recessed under the fuselage, or four Phoenix AAMs mounted below the fuselage. In addition, four Sidewinder AAMs, or two Sidewinders plus two Phoenix or two Sparrow, can be carried on underwing pylons. The Tomcat can also carry a mixture of ordnance — missiles or bombs — up to a maximum of 14,500 lb, and is fitted with an array of ECM equipment.

A Task Force's Tomcats are normally tasked to fly three kinds of mission: Barrier Combat Air Patrol, Task Force CAP and Target CAP. Barrier CAP involves putting up a defensive screen at a considerable distance from the Task Force under the direction of a Grumman E-2C Hawkeye command and control aircraft, which carries the General Electric APS-120/125 search and surveillance radar. In conjunction with the Tomcats, the E-2Cs police the sky at a radius of 200 nm or more from the fleet, their radar searching for hostile targets at all levels from the sea up to 100,000 feet. Standing off from the Task Force at a range of between 50 and 100 nm on the threat side, the E-2 can track up to 200 targets simultaneously and provide automatic directions to a Tomcat via data link, assigning targets in order of threat priority. In war or a real threat situation, one Hawkeye would be airborne over the fleet 24 hours a day. The E-2C also has a valuable secondary role in directing returning aircraft to their carrier in bad weather.

Since fighters flying Barrier CAP are likely to encounter the greatest number of incoming enemy aircraft, Tomcats usually carry their full armament of six Phoenix AAMs. These weapons, which carry a 132 lb HE warhead, reach a speed of more than Mach 5 and have a range of over 125 miles, which

From the end of 1986, the nine AV-8A Matadors equipping the Spanish Navy's No. 008 Squadron will be replaced by twelve new AV-8Bs.

Lockheed F-104S Starfighter of the 23° Gruppo, 5° Stormo, Rimini. Three Italian Air Force Wings still operate the F-104.

makes them highly suitable for long-range interception of aircraft flying at all levels and also sea-skimming missiles. Hostile aircraft that survive the attentions of the Tomcats on Barrier CAP are engaged by fighters of the Task Force CAP, which operate within sight of their ships and which are armed with a mixture of Phoenix, Sparrow and Sidewinder AAMs. If targets still show signs of breaking through and all defensive AAMs are expended, the Tomcats can continue the engagement with their Vulcan cannon at close range.

Macchi MB 339A advanced jet trainer of the Italian Air Force with rocket pods.

On Target CAP, when the Tomcats escort the Carrier Air Wing's strike aircraft, the F-14s carry the medium- and close-range Sparrow and Sidewinder, backed up by the M61 cannon. The US Navy's strike squadrons are now progressively re-equipping with the McDonnell Douglas Hornet, which comes in two versions: the F-18A single-seat fighter-interdictor to replace the F-4 Phantom, and the A-18A single-seat attack aircraft to replace the A-4 Skyhawk and the A-7 Corsair II. Each Carrier Air Wing has two squadrons of attack aircraft, and a further important strike element is provided by a squadron of Grumman A-6E Intruders. Together with the A-7 Corsair, the Intruder provided the US Sixth Fleet's contribution to the American air strikes on Libya in April 1986.

From 1989, the Fiat G.91 force will begin to be replaced by the first of 187 examples of the Aeritalia/Aermacchi/Embraer AMX light ground-attack fighter.

Designed specifically as a carrier-based low-level attack bomber with the ability to deliver both nuclear and conventional warloads with high accuracy and in all weathers, the Grumman A-6A Intruder prototype first flew on 19 April 1960 and the first operational aircraft entered service with VA-42 in February 1963. The A-6A saw extensive action over Vietnam, providing the US Seventh Fleet with a formidable strike force. Each aircraft could carry up to 15,000 lb of bombs and employed a Digital Integrated Attack Navigation System, enabling the crew to pre-select an attack pattern for the aircraft, which left the target area under automatic control after weapons release. The next variant was the EA-6A, which — although retaining a reduced strike capability — had the primary task of supporting air and ground forces by detecting, locating, classifying, recording and jamming enemy transmissions, for which purpose it was fitted with over thirty different kinds of antenna. The EA-6B Prowler was a development of the EA-6A with advanced electronics and a longer nose to accommodate two extra ECM specialists; each Carrier Air Wing currently has a squadron of Prowlers, usually with four aircraft.

The A-6E Intruder was developed from the basic A-6A mainly as a result of the latter's poor serviceability record. The A-6E is fitted with a Norden APQ-148 multi-mode radar assisted by a Hughes target recognition and attack multisensor, comprising a FLIR sensor, laser spot tracker, rangefinder and designator housed in an under-nose turret. Powered by two Pratt & Whitney J52-P-8A turbojets, the Intruder has a maximum speed of 640 mph at sea level and a range of 2700 miles in combat configuration with maximum fuel. Plans are currently in hand to produce an uprated version, the A-6F, with a new radar that will detect ground targets at twice the range of the current A-6E equipment and track them at all target speeds.

Mirage F1-CE fighters of No. 14 Wing, Spanish Air Force, Los Llanos.

The A-6F weapons systems officer will be able to recognise and select targets at extended range and launch stand-off weapons while still out of range of the sophisticated defences the aircraft is likely to encounter in the 1990s.

Completing the Carrier Air Wing's inventory is a squadron of Lockheed SA-3 Viking ASW aircraft, described in Chapter One, which operate in conjunction with SH-3H Sea King helicopters and also with hunter-killer submarines of the Sixth Fleet's Task Force 69.

The primary task of the Sixth Fleet in time of war, when it would come entirely under NATO control, would be first of all to secure the Mediterranean area and deny it to the Soviet Navy's battle groups by destroying those already on station. With this achieved, the Sixth Fleet could then turn its attention to supporting NATO land operations on the southern flank.

The Soviet Union maintains three air armies on the southern front, which includes the Odessa, Trans-Caucasus and Turkestan Military Districts. The total air strength is between 800 and 900 aircraft, most of them tactical and many suffering from the fact that the best equipment goes to the units facing NATO's central front. To these must be added the air forces of Bulgaria and Romania, both of which are organised on Soviet lines.

The Greek Air Force's interceptor force is provided by thirty-three Dassault-Breguet Mirage F.1CG fighters with 334 and 342 Moire of 114 Pterix at Tanagra.

103

Vought A-7E Corsair II of Navy Attack Squadron VA-12, USS *Dwight D. Eisenhower*, one of the big nuclear-powered carriers that deploys periodically to the Mediterranean for Sixth Fleet duty.

The Bulgarian Air Force has a tactical element composed of five air regiments, three with four squadrons each and two with three. The biggest regiment has eighty MiG-21PFMs, which have an air defence role as well as a tactical one; two more regiments have 32 MiG-23s and 36 MiG-19s. The three-squadron regiments operate a total of sixty MiG-17s, and there is also a regiment of two squadrons assigned to the tactical reconnaissance role. There is a forty-strong fixed-wing transport force of An-2s, An-14s, An-24s, An-30s and Il-14s,

Grumman F-14A Tomcat, the mainstay of a US carrier task force's air defence element.

with an equal number of Mi-4 and Mi-8 transport helicopters and a single squadron of about twenty Mi-24 gunships.

The Romanian Air Force (Fortele Aeriene ale Republicii Socialiste Romania) has two air divisions, each with two air regiments. One air division is tasked with air defence and each of its two air regiments has six squadrons, operating about 150 MiG-21s and fifty MiG-23s in total. The other air division is tactical and each of its regiments has three squadrons, operating a total of some seventy MiG-17s and an equal number of Su-7s. Plans for the replacement of all the MiG-17/Su-7 ground-attack force with the IAR-93 Orao (Eagle), developed jointly by Soko of Yugoslavia and CNIAR of Romania, have not reached fruition because of the type's slow introduction into service, and it is possible that Romania may re-equip some of her ground-attack squadrons with the Su-17/20 Fitter.

The Orao, which made its first flight in both Yugoslavia and Romania in October 1974, was conceived as a joint requirement for a single-seat close-support, ground-attack and tactical reconnaissance aircraft. It is powered by two licence-built Rolls-Royce Viper Mk 663 turbojets and has a maximum speed of 665 mph at sea level. Built-in armament is two 23 mm GSh-23L 23-mm twin-barrel cannon in the lower fuselage, and there are five external stores stations to accommodate ordnance up to a maximum of 3307 lb. The Orao also has a secondary low-level interception role. Romania has a requirement for 200 aircraft, but only a few of these have yet been delivered.

CHAPTER SIX
The French Connection

Although she has not been a member of NATO's integrated military structure since 1966, France remains a member of the Atlantic Alliance and has several times affirmed her loyalty and adherence to it; her armed forces frequently train and co-operate with those of NATO members in defensive scenarios. What France has said over the past twenty years, quite simply, is that loyalty to her Alliance commitments must not be allowed to interfere or restrict her national sovereignty; in the event of an outright crisis, France intends to remain mistress, entirely and under all circumstances, of the form and timing of her commitment. That is the keystone of France's defence policy, and one that has to be thoroughly understood as a prelude to any examination of her considerable military power.

The French Air Force (Armée de l'Air) has three operating commands — Air Defence, Tactical and Air Transport — and the territory of metropolitan France is divided into four Air Regions (Régions Aériennes) with their respective headquarters at Metz (1re RA), Paris (2e RA), Bordeaux (3e RA) and Aix-en-Provence (4e RA). The 1re RA covers the whole of north-eastern France, and because of the likelihood that much of France's tactical air power would be used in this area in the event of hostilities, its commander is also the General Officer Commanding the Tactical Air Force.

France's deterrent capability is concentrated in the Strategic Air Forces (Forces Aériennes Stratégiques) which, although now predominantly reliant on surface-to-surface missiles, still retain an airborne nuclear delivery system in the shape of the Dassault Mirage IV. Thirty-five of these aircraft equip two bomber squadrons, Escadres de Bombardement 91 and 94, flights of which are deployed at Mont de Marsan, Cazaux, Orange, Avord, St Dizier and Luxeuil; twelve more Mirage IVs are used in the strategic reconnaissance and ECM roles, and the whole Mirage IV force is supported by eleven Boeing KC-135F tankers of Escadre de Bombardement 93.

The Mirage IV, which was selected to be the carrier of France's first atomic bomb, made its first flight in June 1959 and entered service with EB91 in 1964. Sixty aircraft were subsequently delivered and at one time equipped three squadrons. Powered by two SNECMA Atar 09K turbojets, the Mirage IV is extremely fast at high level, with a speed of over 1500 mph at 40,000 feet. Service ceiling is 65,000 feet and its unrefuelled combat radius around 800 nautical miles. The aircraft carries a single seventy-kiloton free-falling nuclear bomb recessed in the underside of the fuselage. The Mirage IVs currently in service have all been stressed for the low-level role, and the force is now being modified to carry the Aérospatiale ASMP (Air-Sol Moyenne Portée) ramjet-powered supersonic air-to-surface missile, which has a range of about sixty nautical miles and carries a nuclear warhead. The missile entered service with EB1/91 'Gascoigne' in May 1986, followed by EB2/91 'Bretagne' in December.

The Air Defence Command (Commandement de la Défense Aérienne, or CAFDA) controls two air defence zones covering northern and southern France. The north-eastern zone, corresponding with the area covered by the 1re RA, is a separate entity and comes under the control of the Tactical Air Force. The system relies on a sophisticated network of radar stations for early warning and control, the principal ones being situated at Romilly, Doullens and Tours in the north and at Lyon, Nice, Narbonne and Mont-de-Marsan in the south. The Tactical Air Force controls two more, at Drachenbronn and Contrexeville.

CAFDA has nine interceptor squadrons, all equipped with the Mirage F 1C and organised in four fighter wings (Escadres de Chasse). Each squadron should have an establishment of eighteen aircraft, although most are slightly under strength with sixteen or seventeen. EC5, at Orange, has two squadrons totalling 33 aircraft; it shares the airfield with the Mirage F 1 OCU, Escadre de Transformation (ECT) 3/5, which has nineteen two-seat F 1Bs and three F 1Cs, and is a fully operational combat unit in addition to its training role. EC10 at Creil has one F 1C squadron and was in fact the last CAFDA unit to convert from the Mirage IIIC; in 1986 it was due to move to Reims. EC12 at Cambrai has three F 1C squadrons, while EC30 at Reims, with two squadrons, is an all-weather fighter unit.

Mirage F 1C of Escadre de Chasse EC12, Cambrai.
The aircraft is carrying Matra Super 530 AAMs.

The Mirage III continues to serve in the tactical role,
and can carry the AN52 25-kiloton free-falling nuclear
weapon.

A Mirage F 1 in formation with its direct ancestor,
the Mirage III.

The latest edition to the Tactical Air Force (Force Aérienne Tactique, or FATAC) is the Dassault-Breguet Mirage 2000, which in December 1975 was selected to be the French Air Force's principal combat aircraft from the mid-1980s. It was initially developed as an interceptor and air superiority fighter, but is equally suitable for reconnaissance, close support and low-altitude attack missions in areas to the rear of a battlefield. Powered by a SNECMA M53-P2 turbofan engine producing 21,385 lb st with afterburning, the single-seat Mirage 2000C has a maximum level speed of Mach 2.2 and a service ceiling of 59,000 feet. In the interceptor role, carrying two Matra Super 530 AAMs inboard and two Matra 550 Magic AAMs under the wings, it can intercept a Mach 3 target flying at 80,000 feet in less than five minutes from brake release. Built-in armament comprises two 30 mm DEFA 554 cannon with 125 rounds per gun, and there are nine attachments for external stores, five under the fuselage and two under each wing.

In the air-to-ground role the Mirage 2000 can carry up to 13,890 lb of external stores, including a whole range of cluster bombs, air-to-surface, anti-radar and anti-ship missiles, reconnaissance pods, ECM pods and underwing tanks. The Mirage 2000N version, which made its first flight in February 1983, will be armed with the ASMP nuclear missile and will replace the Armée de l'Air's Jaguar and Mirage IIIE nuclear attack aircraft. The Mirage 2000N is stressed for missions at 690 mph and 150 feet and is specifically designed for the penetration role.

The first Mirage 2000Cs for FATAC were delivered in the summer of 1984, equipping EC1/2 — the famous 'Cigognes' squadron — of Escadre de Chasse EC2 at Dijon. The squadron became operational on the Mirage 2000 in July and was followed, in 1985, by EC3/2 'Alsace'. The Tactical Weapons Unit, Escadre de Chasse Tactique (ECT) 2/2 'Côte d'Or' was due to re-equip with the type in 1987. Most of the aircraft assigned to the latter unit will be the two-seat Mirage 2000B variant, numbers of which have already been allocated to the two squadrons so far equipped with the Mirage 2000C.

At Nancy, Escadre de Chasse EC3 has three squadrons, two equipped with Mirage IIIEs and the other with Jaguars. French Air Force Jaguars are fitted with a stand-off bomb release system consisting of two parts, the first of which is the ATLIS (Automatic Tracking Laser Illumination System) fire control equipment, contained in a pod mounted on the aircraft's centreline. The pod contains a laser designator and a wide-angle TV camera whose field of view is centred down the line of the laser beam. The assembly is stabilised and held steady regardless of aircraft movement. The second part of the system consists of a modular laser guidance unit called ARIEL, which is implanted in the nose cone of rockets, missiles or bombs.

In operation, when the pilot recognises the target, he takes a rough line-of-sight through his headup display, switches his gaze to the TV monitor and makes an accurate fix with the hand controller. He then initiates laser emission to determine the distance to the target, and commences automatic target tracking. Immediately he is within missile range, he launches his weapon and banks away from the danger area. Regardless of how violent his evasive manoeuvre, the laser beam will remain locked on to the target until impact.

The latest addition to the Tactical Air Force is the Dassault-Breguet Mirage 2000, which in December 1975 was selected to be the French Air Force's principal combat aircraft from the mid-1980s.

A French Mirage IIIE at RAF Wildenrath during an exchange visit.

Even after leaving the area, the pilot can continue to make fine adjustments on his monitor or even to switch to another target, provided it is in close proximity and visible on his screen. As a safety device, a pitch-and-roll indicator and dangerous height warning marker are displayed on the screen to advise the pilot of his aircraft's attitude while carrying out head-down, follow-through procedures. In bad weather conditions, when visibility is poor, the pilot relies on his navigational computer to bring the pod to bear in the vicinity of the target. The camera operates near infrared in the electromagnetic spectrum and the enlarged picture on the monitor will display a target that remains unseen by the naked eye. The system is very flexible, and it is possible for one aircraft to illuminate the target with its ATLIS pod while another aircraft releases its own laser-guided weapons. In the case of a mass air attack, when several neighbouring targets such as a squadron of tanks are illuminated simultaneously, confusion can be avoided by using a code that governs the laser pulse rate to which the associated missile detector is tuned. The weapon will thus only recognise the target designated by its parent launch aircraft.

The air-to-surface laser missile used by FATAC's Jaguars in conjunction with the ATLIS fire control system is the AS 30. Developed by Aérospatiale, it is supersonic and powered by a two-stage solid fuel motor. It is controlled by a two-phase guidance system, the first phase being a gyroscopic pre-guidance fit which initially keeps the missile parallel to the launch axis; the second is the terminal guidance system, which activates as soon as the laser energy reflected back from the target is sufficiently strong to lock on to the spot illuminated by ATLIS. The flight path to the target during this second phase is maintained by a series of guidance jets, located at the outlet of the sustainer motor, which respond to commands from the computer that steers the missile by proportional navigation, from error detector signals issued by the auto-director. On impact, which occurs at around 1500 feet per second, a 500 lb charge — either general-purpose or SAP — is detonated and is especially effective against hardened targets. The AS 30 missile is stored in two sealed containers and requires only periodic inspection; it can be quickly fitted under the aircraft's wing with a minimum of final safety checks. The missile has a range of about seven miles.

Mirage IIIR of Escadre de Reconnaissance (ECR) 33 which is based at Strasbourg.

In the nuclear role, the Jaguars and the Mirage IIIEs of the Tactical Air Force carry the 25-kiloton Arme Nucléaire AN52, a free-fall weapon that will eventually be replaced by the ASMP when the Mirage 2000N comes into service. The first unit to receive the Mirage 2000N, in 1988, will be Escadre de Chasse EC4 at Luxeuil, which currently operates two squadrons of Mirage IIIEs; this will be followed shortly afterwards by EC7 at St Dizier, which has four squadrons of Jaguars (one of which is based at Istres).

FATAC's tactical weapons training unit is Escadre de Transformation 8, which has two squadrons of Alpha Jets, totalling 42 aircraft, at Cazaux. EC11 at Toul is another Jaguar unit with four squadrons, one of which is located at Bordeaux, while EC13 operates one squadron of Mirage IIIEs and two squadrons of Mirage 5Fs from Colmar. Completing FATAC's line-up is Escadre de Reconnaissance (ECR) 33, which is based at Strasbourg and has one squadron of Mirage F 1CRs, one of Mirage IIIRs and one of Mirage IIIRDs. The last two units operate in support of the three French Army divisions stationed in Baden-Württemberg, which are supported by four more divisions in Alsace-Lorraine.

The Mirage IIIR/RD equips two squadrons of ECR33 at Strasbourg in support of three French Army Divisions based on West German soil.

The Mirage 5 serves with one squadron of EC13 at Colmar. The example pictured here is carrying two Sidewinder AAMs and an AS 30 air-to-surface missile.

Mirage IIIR of ECR33.

The Armée de l'Air's third operating command is the Commandement de Transport Aérien Militaire (CoTAM), the nucleus of which comprises two wings of C 160 Transall transports. These are Escadre de Transport (ET) 61 at Orleans, and ET64 at Evreux. ET61 is the larger of the two units, with two squadrons totalling 46 aircraft; ET64 has a single squadron of 22 aircraft. ET63 at Toulouse still operates ten Noratlas; other units, such as ET60 at Villacoublay, operate a mixture of types including the Falcon 20, Caravelle and DC-8 in the VIP role.

High on the list of France's military priorities is her ability to defend the maritime approaches to western Europe in conjunction with the other partners of the Atlantic Alliance, and in this respect the Naval Air Arm (Aéronautique Navale, or more popularly Aéronavale) plays a key role. The Aéronavale has two 27,300-tonne aircraft carriers, *Clemenceau* and *Foch;* these will be withdrawn on the commissioning of two new 39,680-tonne nuclear-powered carriers, the *Richelieu* and *Charles de Gaulle*, construction of which will begin in 1988. The new carriers will each have a 644-foot angled deck, two steam catapults, two fifty-tonne lifts each capable of carrying two aircraft at a time, and a hangar surface that is one and a half times bigger than the present carriers' hangar space.

Mirage IIIE of EC13 at Colmar.

In the meantime, the *Clemenceau* and *Foch* are undergoing modifications to extend their operational lives. Both carriers have been refitted with Telecom 1A satellite communications terminals (Système Radio Communications Utilisant un Satellite — SYRACUSE) and are to be fitted with more powerful catapults to accommodate the fifty Dassault-Breguet Super Etendards which are being modified to carry the ASMP nuclear missile. The Super Etendard began life as an updated version of the Etendard IVM, which had been the Aéronavale's principal carrier-borne strike fighter since 1962, but the installation of a more powerful SNECMA Atar 8K-50 turbojet engine, together with an advanced and very accurate Sagen-Kearfott ETNA inertial nav/attack system, made the aircraft ninety per cent new.

The Super Etendard carries a built-in armament of two DEFA 30 mm cannon with 125 rounds per gun. There are under-fuselage attachments for two 500 lb bombs and four underwing attachments for 900 lb bombs, Magic AAMs or rocket pods. An AM39 Exocet ASM may be carried under the starboard wing, offset by a fuel tank under the port wing. The Super Etendard has a maximum speed of 733 mph at sea level, and its radius of action with one Exocet and two external tanks, hi-lo-hi, is 460 nautical miles.

The first Super Etendards were delivered to the Aéronavale in June 1978 and the Service eventually received a total of 71 aircraft, of which sixty remain. These equip Flottilles 11F and 14F at Landivisiau and Flottille 17F at Hyeres. Also at Landivisiau is Flottille 16F, a photo-reconnaissance unit with Etendard IVPs and IVMPs, and Flottille 12F, which provides the Aéronavale's interceptor force with 29 Vought F-8E (FN) Crusaders. These aircraft, which have been in French Navy service since 1965, have been constantly updated with new avionics and are now armed with the MATRA R550 AAM; they will remain in service until 1991-95, when they will be replaced by a new aircraft — the future Avion de Combat Marine, or ACM. The ACM is based on the Avion de Combat Expérimental (ACX), built by Dassault as a technology demonstrator; the prototype was due to fly in the summer of 1986.

The Aéronavale type that is perhaps the most remarkable in terms of longevity is the Breguet Alizé carrier-based ASW aircraft, which first entered service in 1959. The Alizé is powered by a Rolls-Royce Dart Mk 21 turboprop and carries a crew of three; it has a maximum speed over the target of 280 mph and an endurance of seven hours at economical cruise. Its armament comprises torpedoes, either in the weapons bay or under the wings, rockets, depth charges and anti-ship missiles. Thirty-four Alizés are still in Aéronavale service and 28 of these have undergone a modernisation programme designed to extend their useful life into the 1990s. Work includes the installation of a new Thomson-CSF Iguane retractable ASW radar, a Cruozet Omega Equinox navigation system and ECM equipment. The Alizé currently equips Flottilles 4F at Lann-Bihoue and 6F at Nimes-Garons.

The Aéronavale has a considerable fixed-wing shore-based ASW force in the shape of 24 Breguet Atlantic maritime patrol aircraft. These equip Flottilles 21F and 22F at Nimes-Garons and Flottilles 23F and 24F at Lann-Bihoue. The aircraft at present in service will be replaced, from 1987, by the Atlantic Generation 2 (ATL2) for which the Aéronavale has an initial requirement of 42 aircraft. The ATL2 incorporates a number of important structural changes, including better anti-corrosion protection and design improvements offering longer fatigue life and more economical maintenance. This will all add up to a big increase in serviceability, with 75 per cent of squadron aircraft permanently available for operations and capable of taking off within thirty minutes of an order to go being received. The modifications will also give the ATL2 a life of about twenty years, or at least 12,000 flying hours per aircraft. The basic mission requirements are more or less the same as those of

The elderly Breguet Alizé continues to render excellent service in the carrier-borne ASW role, and a modernisation programme will extend their useful life into the 1990s.

the Atlantics now in service: a high cruising speed to the operational area, a quick descent from cruising altitude to patrol height, a lengthy patrol endurance at low altitude and a high degree of manoeuvrability at sea level. Like the original Atlantic, the ATL2, in addition to its primary ASW role, can perform minelaying, logistic support and transport operations.

The Aéronavale has a considerable fixed-wing shore-based ASW force in the shape of twenty-four Breguet Atlantic maritime patrol aircraft.

Dassault-Breguet Atlantic on patrol.

The Aéronavale also has a number of rotary-wing ASW units. Flottilles 31F (Saint-Mandrier), 34F and 35F (Lanveoc) operate the Lynx in this role, while Flottilles 32F (Lanveoc) and 33F (Saint-Mandrier) use the Super Frelon. Light transport and liaison duties are carried out by nine Support (Servitude) squadrons: 2S, 3S, 11S, 20S, 52S, 55S, 56S, 57S and 59s. These are based at various naval airfields and use a variety of types such as the Nord N 262 and the Piper Navajo.

France maintains a large Army Aviation (Aviation Légère de l'Armée de Terre, or ALAT) with six regiments of combat helicopters, each comprising seven squadrons. Two of these are scouting units, with SA 41L Gazelles, three are anti-tank units with HOT-armed SA 342M Gazelles or SS-12 armed Alouette IIs, and the other two are transport squadrons equipped with Pumas. Two regiments are attached to each of the Army's I and II Corps in Federal Germany, a fifth to III Corps, and the sixth to the Force d'Action Rapide (Rapid Deployment Force) which became operational in the summer of 1985. Total helicopter strength available to the ALAT includes 130 Pumas, 190 Alouette IIs, 70 Alouette IIIs, 170 SA 341 Gazelles and 90 SA 342 Gazelles (128 having been ordered). Other duties are performed by small numbers of fixed-wing Cessna 0-1 Bird Dogs and MH 1521 Broussards. No 1 Combat Helicopter Regiment is based at Phalsbourg, No 2 at Friedrichshafen, No 3 at Etain, No 4 at Trier and No 5 at Pau.

Exactly how the French would act in the event of an outbreak of hostilities between NATO and the Warsaw Pact is open to conjecture. France's defence concepts are based on a resolute wish for national independence; she has no wish to be drawn, against her wishes, into conflicts which are irrelevant to her and which she condemns. However, this position of principle in no way precludes France's being a loyal and faithful ally within the Atlantic Alliance. The presence of French troops in the Federal Republic of Germany is proof of this, as is the creation of the Rapid Deployment Force; the latter has the capability to intervene immediately in the European Theatre, which was the precise reason for its formation. Should a serious crisis develop in Europe, there can be little doubt that France will be at the side of her allies. Nor can there be any doubting the power and efficiency of the contribution she would make.

CHAPTER SEVEN
NATO air exercises

In air warfare, although — as history has shown — victory might not always go to the strongest, it will certainly go to the better-trained. Constant training under realistic war scenarios, with equally realistic simulated threats, is consequently of paramount importance to NATO's air arms, confronted as they are by a potential enemy who, at least in the early stages of a conflict, would enjoy a considerable numerical superiority.

The Royal Air Force's Tornado strike squadrons have provided a number of good examples of what can be achieved by highly-trained aircrews flying some of the world's finest combat aircraft. By October 1984 the RAF was operating seven

Symbolic of the Hawk's versatility, this aircraft of No. 1 Tactical Weapons Unit, RAF Brawdy, carries two Sidewinder AAMs and a Sea Eagle anti-ship missile as it turns in towards a 'County'-Class guided missile destroyer.

Tornado squadrons: No 9 at RAF Honington, Nos 27 and 617 at RAF Marham — all dedicated to SACEUR — and Nos 15, 16, 20 and 31 in Germany. In the following month, 617 Squadron's Tornado GR 1s were entered in the prestigious Strategic Air Command Bombing Competition (Prairie Vortex) in the USA, supported by Victor K 2 tankers from No 55 Squadron, also based at Marham.

The Tornados showed their capabilities by winning two trophies in the face of strong competition from SAC B-52s and FB-111s, and F-111Cs of the RAAF. In all, 42 crews took part. The Curtis E. LeMay bombing trophy, which is awarded to the crew compiling the most points in high- and low-level bombing and time control, was won by Squadron Leader Peter Dunlop (pilot) and Flight Lieutenant Dick Middleton, who scored 2616 points out of a possible 2650. Second place was won by Flight Lieutenant Steve Legg and Squadron Leader Vic Bussereau, with 2612 points.

The John C. Meyer memorial trophy, awarded to the F-111 or Tornado team compiling the highest damage expectance from their bombing, was won by a team comprising two Tornados. Their scores were assessed in both low-level bombing and evasive tactics using ECM. The award went to Squadron Leader Dunlop and Flight Lieutenant Middleton in one aircraft, and Flight Lieutenant Ian Hunter and Flight Lieutenant Dermot Dolan in the second aircraft. They achieved a score of 90.43 per cent while the second team, an American pair, achieved 86.5 per cent. Third place also went to a Tornado team. It was the first time that teams from outside the United States had won the LeMay or John C. Meyer trophies.

Apart from low-level (500 foot) sorties, the competition also included legs at 15,000-20,000 feet, with flights lasting several hours and covering 1500-2000 miles. This meant that the Tornados proved their lethal bombing accuracy in missions for which they were not specifically designed, while operating under the disadvantage of being the only aircraft in the contest needing air-to-air refuelling. The competition was spread over eight weeks and involved attacks on targets and intercept evasion at low level over ranges in Nevada, Wyoming, Montana and South Dakota, sometimes 900 miles from the aircraft's operating base.

The contest was in two phases. The first involved dropping a 6.6 lb bomb on each of two targets, neither of which was visible to the crews, who had to use offset blind bombing techniques. They also had to evade a simulated ground-to-air attack by SA-2 and SA-4 missiles, as well as a fighter attack. The Tornados used the Sky Shadow pod to provide the necessary countermeasures. In the second phase, night and day sorties utilised simulated electronic bombing, with scoring tracked from the ground. These sorties took an average of five hours and involved several mid-air refuelling rendezvous which required split-second accuracy to avoid losing penalty points. Normally, Tornado sorties would average less than two hours, so the increased flying time was an unfamiliar experience for the crews. Again during these sorties, the aircraft had to evade SA-2, SA-4 and fighter attacks.

In November 1985 the Tornados did it again. This time the aircraft involved came from No 27 Squadron; they came first and second in both the Curtis E. LeMay and John C. Meyer trophy competitions, and second in the Mathis Trophy competition. The Mathis Trophy is awarded to the bomber unit with the highest points for both high- and low-level bombing; No 617 Squadron had achieved second and sixth places in this contest the year before.

Expertise of this kind could not be achieved without frequent participation in gruelling exercises which simulate war conditions as realistically as possible and tax men, machines and equipment to the utmost. One of the better-known, and certainly the most arduous, of such exercises is 'Red Flag', which provides combat training under simulated war conditions for USAF, RAF, NATO and other allied air forces. 'Red Flag' is centred on Nellis Air Force Base, which lies eight miles to the north-east of Las Vegas. Together with its associated bombing and gunnery ranges it extends across more than three million acres, which makes it the biggest USAF base complex of any. In fact, it is bigger than the home countries of some of the foreign pilots who come here for combat training. Nellis AFB is part of USAF Tactical Air Command; its principal unit is the Tactical Fighter Weapons Center, which conducts advanced tactical fighter training for the visiting aircrews.

Opposite: Aircraft Directors prepare to move an A-7 Corsair aboard the *USS Saratoga* during flight operations in the Mediterranean Sea.

General Dynamics F-16 Fighting Falcons of the 401st Tactical Fighter Wing, Torrejon, Spain.

B.Ae Hawk armed with Sidewinder AAMs for the air defence role.

The US Navy has its own air combat school in which aircrews from other NATO naval air arms (ie, the Fleet Air Arm and Kriegsmarine) also participate. Known as 'Top Gun', and more properly the Fighter Weapons School, it is located at Miramar Naval Air Station near San Diego, California. A 'Top Gun' course lasts five weeks and includes ninety hours of classroom work and thirty training sorties. The US Navy also has an aggressor squadron at NAS Oceana, Virginia, equipped with twelve Israeli Aircraft Industries F-21A Kfirs on lease; the Kfir is a fair approximation in profile and performance to the MiG-23/27 Flogger. At the time of writing, negotiations were under way to lease a second Kfir squadron, to be based at the US Marine Corps Air Station Umah, Florida.

In the European NATO area, one of the most important air exercises is 'Mallet Blow', which is organised four times a year by the Royal Air Force to allow aircrew to practise attacks against ground targets, and to provide realistic training for attacking aircrew, defending fighter squadrons, communications and jamming personnel, and surface-to-air missile units. Apart from the RAF, strike squadrons from the Luftwaffe and Kriegsmarine, the USAF and the Royal Danish Air Force usually participate in the week-long exercise, which is focused on the Otterburn military training area in Northumberland. Two ranges are used, designated Bravo and Charlie, and are alternated daily throughout the exercise period. Bravo is the interdiction range, and pilots have to aim at a bridge or at one of more than seventy derelict vehicles scattered across the firing area, simulating a deployed motor rifle regiment. Charlie, the counter-air range, is provided with a simulated runway and SAM site.

Participating aircraft are allocated TOT (Time on Target) slots by RAF Strike Command and enter the ranges either singly or in formations of up to eight aircraft. No live firings can take place because of the nature of the range area, which is in the middle of a national park, so ordnance consists of small practice bombs that produce a flash and/or smoke for visual reference and scoring. The Harriers fire inert rockets, other RAF aircraft drop 1000 lb retarded bombs and USAF F-111s drop 500 lb retarded bombs.

A formation of Hawks from No. 2 Tactical Weapons Unit, RAF Chivenor, breaking to join the circuit. All aircraft bear the markings of No. 151 'shadow' Squadron, and the code letters on their fins spell out the name of their home airfield.

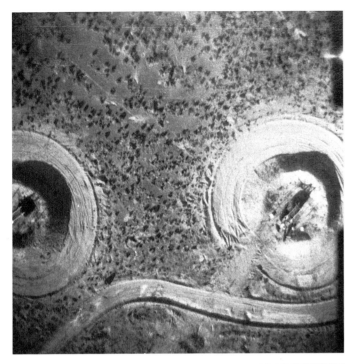

Simulated SAM sites and 'enemy' airfields provide realistic training for NATO strike crews in 'Red Flag' exercises.

The latter is situated at Indian Springs Air Force Auxiliary Field, 45 miles north-west of Las Vegas; this is the home of the 554th Support Squadron of the 554th Range Group, and the 350 personnel based there provide bombing and gunnery range support for the tactical air operations out of Nellis.

The Filter Center relays its information to Red Force Brigade commanders who initiate defensive operations. More than fourteen different types of radar unit simulate those used by Warsaw Pact countries, operating at the same frequencies, pulse widths, pulse repetition roles, scan patterns and power levels. TV cameras are fitted to many of these units to cover the same area as the radar; other instruments report factors such as threat switch positions and transmit to Range Control.

All data collected on the range is processed by computers which can generate not only plots of an engagement or of a single aircraft's entire mission, but also several different kinds of two- or three-dimensional graphic displays from different perspectives. When pilots return from a sortie, the Range Control Center provides computer plots of a mission; pilots can view video tapes of their aircraft as seen in the sights of enemy surface-to-air missile controllers, anti-aircraft guns or camera-gun film shot by aggressor aircraft. The latter are mainly Northrop F-5Es and T-38s of the 57th Tactical Training Wing, whose two squadrons, the 64th and 65th, fly aircraft camouflaged in patterns typical of Warsaw Pact colour schemes. Also at Nellis is the 474th Tactical Fighter Wing, with F-16 Fighting Falcons.

The second major war-simulation exercise in North America — which is run by 'Red Flag' personnel — is 'Maple Flag'. This is centred on Canadian Forces Base Cold Lake, Alberta, adjacent to some 3500 square miles of muskeg and silver birch forest, with many hundreds of lakes set amid low, rolling hills. Located at about 54° 30'N — the same latitude as the boundary between North Yorkshire and South Durham — and set 1770 feet above sea level, the area offers the same weather conditions as those prevailing in north-west Europe, and from this point of view is perhaps more realistic than the conditions of the arid Nevada Desert. Even so, the weather at Cold Lake is generally clearer than that of northern Europe; the airfield can usually be seen from the air at a range of fifty miles.

The 'Maple Flag' range measures 100 miles by forty and is virtually flat, which presents a considerable challenge to pilots trained to use the contours of the terrain as their primary aid to survival in a hostile environment. The task of aggressor pilots is also made easier by the fact that camouflage is of little use when a target aircraft is flying over a frozen lake. For the strike pilots, camouflaged sites among the trees and dummy tanks in clearings present difficult targets for an aircraft flying at 150 feet and over 500 mph.

The exercise pattern for 'Maple Flag' broadly follows that established for 'Red Flag', and begins with large numbers of aircraft carrying out attack, reconnaissance, combat air patrol, escort and defence suppression roles. At a later stage, participating aircraft are switched from Blue Force (attack and CAP) to Red Force (defensive) to give crews experience on both sides of the fence. 'Maple Flag' also includes search and rescue missions; pilots designated as shot down are flown out to the range area to be picked up by fighter-escorted bombers.

The 'Red Flag' 'playpen' encompasses a ten-million-acre block of airspace reserved exclusively for military flying. Within it lie the three million acres that constitute the actual range area. The range includes fifty different types of target, including airfields and industrial complex outlines, two vehicle convoys — one of which is more than seventeen miles long, correctly spaced and protected by tracked anti-aircraft guns — ten miles of railway with a ten-car train, and armoured replicas of Soviet T-62 tanks deployed for battle.

These targets are defended by 35 threat simulators which are similar visually, and in most cases electronically, to Soviet-built equipment. Organised into two brigades, early warning radars detect aircraft at 300 miles and pass data to the Red Force Filter Center at the Range Control Center.

The daily sortie rate averages 170, and each attack on the ranges is recorded on video tape which is despatched to the relevant units after the exercise so that each crew can assess their own attacks and compare them with the way other crews tackle the problem of approaching the target. 'Mallet Blow' is not a competitive exercise, so no comparison is made — officially, at any rate — between squadrons and air forces as far as scoring is concerned. The exercise is purely tactical, with the emphasis on creating a realistic wartime environment — something that the planners take great pains over, although it is not always possible to update and improve the facilities as they would like because of the conditions and restrictions imposed by the environment.

Attacking aircraft have to evade defending fighter aircraft, which have their own test of efficiency in air defence exercises such as 'Elder Forest', when the United Kingdom Air Defence Region is subjected to multiple simulated attacks over a period of several days by aircraft drawn from several NATO air forces. The United Kingdom forms one of four NATO air defence regions and as such is part of the area under SACEUR; the responsibility for its integrity falls on No 11 Group, RAF Strike Command, which has the broad task of providing an air defence force and its associated control system wherever the need arises, including air defence for ships of the Royal Navy, and of exercising control over the United Kingdom airspace in peace and war.

It is a NATO requirement that commanders with responsibilities other than air defence shall appoint a deputy for air defence only, and so, while the AOC-in-C Strike Command is the Air Defence Commander and Commander of the NATO UK Air Defence Region, he delegates his responsibilities for the direct day-to-day operational control to the AOC No 11 Group, while retaining overall responsibility for the policy, planning, supervision and support of the air defence forces.

The UK air defence responsibility is considerable; the ADR extends for 1600 nautical miles from north to south, with radar coverage stretching from just to the south of Iceland to encompass the whole of the British Isles, the west coast of Norway, the Low Countries and northern France. The nerve-centre of the whole system is the Air Defence Operations Centre, which is housed in a hardened underground HQ at High Wycombe and has a completely centralised command picture of the UK ADR. Tactical air defence control is exercised by three Sector Operations Centres, which are at RAF Neatishead in Norfolk, RAF Boulmer in Northumberland and RAF Buchan in the north of Scotland. The SOCs are fed from various quarters with information regarding attack threats; sources include the NATO Air Defence Ground Environment, with which the UK SOCs are integrated, the Ballistic Missile Early Warning System at Fylingdales, which can be used to track aircraft as well as missiles, and early warning aircraft. In 1986 the elderly Shackleton AEW 2 was still being used in this role, six aircraft being operated by No 8 Squadron at RAF Lossiemouth and long overdue for replacement.

Each SOC has its own Command and Reporting Centres (CRCs), which are responsible for tracking and interceptor control, and Command and Reporting Posts (CRPs) which provide limited backup tracking and fighter control, while a network of radar sites or Reporting Posts (RPs) essentially form the front line. The SOC/CRC at Buchan, for example, receives data from CRPs and RPs at Benbecula in the Hebrides, Saxa Vord in the Shetlands and a station in the Faeroes, the latter under Danish control, while Boulmer is fed by Bishop's Court in Northern Ireland and Staxton Wold in Yorkshire. Farther south, Neatishead receives information from Hartland Point in Devon and Portreath in Cornwall.

Jaguar of No 41 Squadron, RAF Coltishall. Jaguars are among the most numerous participants in Exercise 'Mallet Blow'.

RAF Jaguars have the ability to defend themselves in a hostile fighter environment; this example is carrying two Sidewinder AAMs.

The acquired data is processed through ADOC at High Wycombe, where military plots are sifted from civil aircraft movements, and passed back via HQ 11 Group to the SOCs for action; if the threat is real, fighters held on Quick Reaction Alert are scrambled. Recently, the whole United Kingdom Air Defence Ground Environment (UKADGE) system has been substantially updated to cope with the changing threat, which now comes from all-weather aircraft armed with stand-off missiles and protected by advanced ECM. Fixed radars, with their powerful electromagnetic emissions, have become vulnerable to anti-radiation missiles, so No 11 Group is now equipped with the S723 Martello transportable three-dimensional air defence radar, which is used in conjunction with the fixed-site arrays. The new system enables radar sensors to be remotely deployed at will almost anywhere in the UK, and new telecommunications technology provides a nationwide network of lines and exchanges that routes both voice and data along any path as long as some physical connection remains, even if the main systems are seriously disrupted by enemy action.

The capability of European NATO's air defence squadrons has been greatly enhanced in recent years by the use of the Air Combat Manoeuvring Instrumentation (ACMI) range at Decimomannu in Sardinia. The ACMI became operational here in 1979 for the training of NATO fast jet pilots and its funding is shared by the USA, Federal Germany, Britain and Italy, which are the facility's main users. 'Deci' is one of twelve such ranges throughout the world and currently the only one in Europe. Together with its counterparts, the facility provides fighter pilots with the opportunity for aggressive fighter combat in a realistic scenario without requiring special targets, live weapons or, more importantly, involving the possible loss of an aircraft and pilot.

The range itself is a circle thirty nautical miles in diameter over the sea, about fifty nm off the west coast of Sardinia, with a base height of 5000 feet and a ceiling of 50,000 feet. Any aircraft straying from the circle, unless in transit to or from the range, can be recalled to base by the local coastal radar at Mirto. This applies particularly to the adjacent north-west area outside the range, where there is a civilian air route.

The ACMI (which is designated Tactical Aircrew Combat Training System, or TACTS, by the US Navy) was built by the Cubic Corporation of San Diego, the principal contractor, and is operated by a twenty-man team. It consists of four principal interfaced elements, the first of which is an Airborne Instrumentation Subsystem (AIS), a pylon-attached transponder pod with locking and connection points identical to those of the AIM-9 Sidewinder and linked to the aircraft's electrical, avionic and weapon systems. The AIS pod communicates directly with equipment in four 35-ton buoys — the Tracking and Communication Subsystem (TCS) — which are moored at sea beneath the range, one in the centre and the others around the circumference at 045 degrees, 180 degrees and 315 degrees. Two additional land-based monitoring units located on mountains to the north and south of Deci complete the remote part of the TCS.

The information is passed to the land-based TCS master station situated some 4000 feet up a mountain north of Deci and from there fed by microwave to the Computer and Computation Subsystem (CCS) at Deci. This processes the data received from each aircraft: altitude, speed, bearing, angle of attack, what types of missiles are programmed into it, and range and simulated track of the missile in relation to the dynamic track of its selected target. From the CCS computers, the data is passed to two six-foot square graphical VDU screen displays above the Range Training Officer's (RTO) console, where it can be viewed by an audience of up to twenty people. It is the responsibility of the RTOs to monitor the exercise, vector their pilots to the opposition (saving range time and simulating ground radar control) and have radio contact with their own pilots.

Hawk T.1 of No.1 Tactical Weapons Unit landing at RAF Brawdy. Note the practice bomb dispenser under the outboard wing pylon.

Not only can the audience see the aircraft in plan view, but the image can be rotated through ninety degrees to give an elevation. Moreover, a second screen which is normally used for an alpha-numeric display of the aircraft data can be used to show a graphical cockpit view of any selected combatant. When an aircraft is 'killed' a coffin shape appears around it and the pilot is vectored out of the fight by his RTO for 45 seconds, at which point he is free to return and the coffin is removed. During this period the computer will not recognise, nor therefore record, any missile launch or gun firing from the killed aircraft.

The length of combat time over the range is strictly controlled to twenty-minute slots for the aircraft using the facility. At the end of their slot the pilots return and debrief using a video recording of the combat at the Display and Debrief Subsystem (DDS). They can view this recording, freezing a frame or using play-back to identify mistakes, lost opportunities and incidents during the range slot and get a clear and complete overall picture of the recently concluded combat. The training at Decimomannu, apart from improving a fighter pilot's skills, is important because it helps to standardise the tactics employed by the various NATO air forces. Luftwaffe F-4 crews, for example, can learn a lot from Royal Navy Sea Harrier pilots, who in turn learn how to cope with Mach 2-plus aircraft like the F-15.

In all NATO training activities and exercises the level of international co-operation is high. Nowhere is this more evident than in the Tactical Air Meets that are held periodically at a major base in AAFCE's operating area; such events involve participating aircraft and crews from Belgium, Canada, Federal Germany, the Netherlands, United Kingdom and the United States, with the French often taking part as guests. A typical Air Meet consists of two major parts: Tactics, involving twelve missions, and the Competition, involving two missions. The tactics phase encompasses interdiction, offensive air support, offensive counter-air strikes and ground defence suppression, all carried out in a simulated high-threat environment. Attack forces are supported by ECM and defence suppression aircraft (F-4G Wild Weasels), and targets are heavily defended by combat air patrols, SAMs and AAA. Simulated targets are airfields, armoured vehicle parks, radar and SAM sites, and live weapons are dropped on designated ranges.

The competition phase revolves around two major events: weapons delivery/navigation, and tactical air reconnaissance. In the first event, weapons delivery teams comprising a team leader and two aircrews from each attack unit are selected to fly two daily missions appropriate to their NATO role, which covers strafing, rocket firing, low-angle and low-level bombing, visual laydown and visual low-level retarded delivery and toss bombing. In the reconnaissance phase, selected crews fly two missions a day and overfly three targets on each sortie.

AAFCE's operational abilities are tested under more realistic conditions in large-scale exercises such as 'Lionheart', which was held in the Harz Mountains area of Germany in September 1984. During the second week of the exercise, the friendly 'Blue Forces', mainly comprising the British 4th Armoured Division, advanced north of Hildesheim to retake ground captured the week before by the enemy 'Orange Forces' — the 1st US Tiger Battalion with their new Abrams M-1 battle tanks — which had thrust westwards from a simulated eastern state border.

Although there was a considerable amount of confusion on the ground (mainly because some of the 'enemy' forces ignored the decisions of umpires) the air operations proceeded fairly smoothly. Blue Forces were supported by the Harriers of Nos 3 and 4 Squadrons, and Orange by the A-10 Thunderbolts of the 81st TFW. Blue Force's anti-tank operations were also carried out by Army Air Corps Lynx I helicopters, armed with TOW missiles, at all times flying 'nap-of-the-earth' under power lines and using all available tree cover. The helicopter squadrons were reported to have completed a highly successful exercise, without 'losing' a single Lynx to enemy action. Gazelles were used for scouting, and Harriers were called in to knock out tanks which had escaped the Lynx units.

The Harriers of Nos 3 and 4 Squadrons operated from five field sites during the first week of the exercise, and in one day of clear weather the two squadrons flew 120 sorties in four hours. More than 100 sorties were flown by Tornados and Jaguars of Nos 15, 16 and 20 Squadrons from Laarbruch, and Nos 14, 17 and 31 Squadrons from Bruggen. Chinook and Puma helicopters played a vital role in support of battlefield operations, using Exercise 'Lionheart' as the first major chance to test operations with the 6th Air Mobile Brigade. The two types lifted nearly 4½ million pounds of freight, guns, ammunition and supplies, and more than 10,300 troops. In an air support exercise called 'Full Flow', the RAF's transport squadrons also airlifted 25,000 troops to Germany in the course of 249 flights, some in very bad weather. Very few of the flights were subject to delay, and only one had to be diverted.

Since the essential task of the NATO forces in place on the European continent is to hold the line until the arrival of massive reinforcements from the United States, much emphasis is placed in training on refining the techniques necessary for the rapid deployment of such forces. For example, the USAF's Exercise 'Blue Flag' is designed to train command-control and communications (C^3) personnel to operate under wartime conditions, and training is tailored to simulate theatres in which the C crews might have to operate, such as Europe, Korea or the Arabian Gulf; 'Checkered Flag' is an exercise whereby Tactical Air Command units based in the continental United States deploy to overseas bases, usually of other tactical Commands, from which they would have to operate in time of crisis. Crews learn the peculiarities of the emergency base to which they are assigned, such as runway layout, facilities available and local weather — the latter a very important factor in the European context, where weather conditions can come as a nasty surprise to pilots used to operating in much clearer skies.

The USAF's main annual readiness exercise aimed at the rapid reinforcement of Europe is code-named 'Reforger', and its broad aim is to fly military formations at short notice from the USA and marry them up with equipment already stockpiled in the German Federal Republic. 'Reforger' is a major test for the USAF Military Airlift Command and its three main heavy-lift transport types: the Lockheed C-130 Hercules, C-141 Starlifter and C-5 Galaxy. Military Airlift Command in fact comprises three Air Forces, the 21st, 22nd and 23rd. It is the 21st AF, operating out of McGuire AFB in New Jersey, that controls airlift operations eastward through Canada, Greenland, Iceland, NATO Europe, Africa and the Middle East and southward into the Caribbean and South America; the 22nd AF covers the Pacific area, Antarctica and the Indian Ocean westward to the Arabian Peninsula, where it meets the 21st AF's sphere of operations. The 23rd AF has no geographic boundary, but controls the USAF's Special Operations and the Aerospace Rescue and Recovery Service.

In NATO air exercises, much emphasis is placed on the rapid reinforcement of the European theatre by combat groups based in the continental United States. The photograph shows an F-15 Eagle refuelling from a McDonnell Douglas KC-10 tanker.

Military Airlift Command's massive C-5 Galaxy has a payload in excess of 100 tons, and its flight refuelling capability enables it to move any item of equipment in the US Army's arsenal anywhere in the world in a matter of hours. Its four General Electric TF39-GE-1C turbofans give it a maximum speed of 570 mph and a service ceiling of 34,000 feet; it carries a crew of five, with a rest area for fifteen personnel (relief crews, etc). As a typical payload it can carry 73 fully equipped troops, plus 36 standard 463L transport pallets or assorted vehicles, including two main battle tanks or three Chinook helicopters; alternatively, it can lift 343 fully equipped troops. MAC has 77 C-5A Galaxies, a fleet that is gradually being augmented with the delivery of fifty C-5Bs. Under 21st Air Force Command, the Galaxy equips the 436th Military Airlift Wing at Dover AFB, Delaware. The only other operational C-5 unit is the 60th MAW at Travis AFB, California, under 22nd AF command; the 443rd MAW at Altus AFB, Oklahoma, also flies C-5s, but in the crew training role.

The 21st Air Force has four wings of Lockheed C-141 Starlifters: the 437th MAW and the 315th MAW (Air Force Reserve) at Charleston AFB, South Carolina, and the 438th MAW plus the 514th MAW (Air Force Reserve) at McGuire AFB. Under 22nd Air Force command, C-141s operate with the 62nd MAW and the 446th MAW (AFRES)

at McChord AFB, Washington, the 63rd MAW and the 445th MAW (AFRES) at Norton AFB, California, and the 349th MAW (AFRES) at Travis AFB, California. C-141s are also assigned to the 443rd MAW at Altus AFB for crew training. The C-141B Starlifter, 234 of which are in Military Air Command service, is powered by four Pratt & Whitney TF33-P-7 turbofans; it has a maximum speed of 466 mph, a service ceiling of 41,600 feet and a range of 4080 miles. It can carry thirteen standard cargo pallets, up to a maximum payload of 90,200 lb.

The 21st Air Force has two C-130 Hercules wings, the 317th Tactical Airlift Wing at Pope AFB, North Carolina, and the 459th Tactical Airlift Wing (AFRES) at Andrews AFB, Maryland. The latter unit was scheduled to re-equip with C-141s in 1986.

Air Force Reserve and Air National Guard units play an important part in European reinforcement exercises. AFRES is an integral part of the United States Air Force; its funding comes from the active-duty budget and it constitutes about thirty per cent of the active force strength. It operates 56 flying units with more than 430 aircraft, including the F-16, F-4, A-10, C-130 and C-141. AFRES personnel, who as their reserve status implies are part-time, are recruited and trained alongside active Servicemen and are then committed to one weekend a month of active duty plus fifteen days of summer camp, which usually takes the form of a tour. Reservists are divided into three categories: Ready, Standby or Retired. Ready Reservists can be called to active duty by the President with a declaration of emergency; Standby and Retired Reservists can be called to active duty only by a special Act of Congress. However, the President can mobilise up to 100,000 selected reservists from AFRES and the ANG for up to ninety days without declaring a national emergency.

While AFRES is an agency of the USAF, the Air National Guard operates independently, although its aircraft are owned and allocated by the USAF. There are 54 Guards in all — one for each of the fifty States, plus those in Puerto Rico, the Virgin Islands, Guam and the District of Columbia. Each Guard is under the command of the State Governor, but in time of war the President may 'nationalise' the National Guard, at which time units join the regular US Army and Air Force overseas. Units across the USA fly KC-135 Stratotankers, C-130 Hercules, A-7 Corsairs, A-10 Thunderbolts, F-16 Fighting Falcons — and now the F-15 Eagle, which was first assigned to the 159th Tactical Fighter Group, Louisiana ANG, in 1985.

Because of its front-line role, the Air National Guard regularly takes part in military exercises in the USA and abroad, and also enters combat efficiency competitions with the USAF. In 1983, in the 'Gunsmoke' contest for fighter units, the Guard beat the regulars by a handsome margin. Every three years the ANG holds Operation 'Readiness Express', which evaluates how quickly units can be moved to where they are needed — either to augment the regular USAF or to supply additional squadrons and aircraft to reinforce NATO. In 1983, for example, the 113th Tactical Fighter Wing of the District of Columbia ANG deployed its entire force of F-4D Phantoms to RAF Finningley, Yorkshire, to work alongside the Royal Air Force and other NATO air forces. There can be no doubt that, if there is ever a hot war in Europe, the ANG will be among the first to arrive in support of NATO's battle; nor can there be any doubting the vital contribution the Guard would make.

Britain's air defences are periodically put to the test by aircraft such as No 360 Squadron's electronic countermeasures Canberra T 17s, which are based at RAF Wyton.

CHAPTER EIGHT
NATO and Warsaw Pact missile forces

Any major conflict between NATO and the Warsaw Pact would involve the use of missiles of all types in overwhelming numbers; the great majority would be air-launched, so no survey of the relative capabilities of the NATO and Warsaw Pact air forces would be complete without an assessment of the missiles at their disposal. The survey does not include strategic ballistic missiles, which are not part of the NATO armoury, nor cruise missiles, which are described elsewhere and which, as part of NATO's Theatre Nuclear Force, would only be used as a last option.

NATO: Tactical missiles
The oldest of the tactical missiles still in service with NATO is the Honest John unguided spin-stabilized rocket, which in fact was the first post-war American missile to become operational and which was designed by the Douglas Aircraft Corporation. Designated MGR-1A/B, the 24 foot 10 inch Honest John is launched from a six-wheeled truck and has a range of between $4\frac{1}{2}$ and 23 miles. Its usual warhead is a thirty-inch HE round, but it can also be fitted with chemical or nuclear warheads (the latter only applied to weapons which served with the US Army). Honest John has now been phased out of service with most NATO forces, but Greece still operates two battalions with eight launchers and Turkey has eighteen missiles deployed with four battalions. Operationally, the problem with Honest John is that it is no more accurate than artillery shells and is more susceptible to wind effect. In flight, the missile reaches a speed of about Mach 1.5.

The Honest John has been replaced in most NATO armies by the Vought Corporation's MGM-52A/B/C/D Lance, which has a simplified inertial guidance system and is just over twenty feet long. Powered by a Rocketdyne P8E-9 liquid rocket motor, the Lance weapon system is deployed on two M113 amphibious tracked vehicles, the M752 erector/launcher and the M688 resupply unit with two Lances and a hoist. Alternatively, the weapon can be used from a lightweight launcher developed by Hawker Siddeley Canada, which can be transported by helicopter and air-dropped. The missile, which has a range of up to 75 miles when fitted with a ten-kiloton, 474 lb M234 nuclear warhead or 45 miles with a Honeywell 1000 lb XM251 cluster warhead, is deployed with the Belgian Army (one battalion with four systems), the Bundeswehr (four battalions with 26 systems), the

Italian Army (one brigade), the Netherlands Army (one battalion with six systems), the United Kingdom (one regiment of four batteries, each with three launchers) and the United States Army (72 launchers). The British Army is the only one still retaining the combination of Lance and the M234 nuclear warhead.

An important guided weapon system in service with AFCENT is the Martin Marietta MGM-31 Pershing. The Pershing 1A is widely used by the US Army and the Bundeswehr; it is 34 feet 9 inches long, has a range of 100-460 miles, depending on its warhead — which can be between sixty and 400 kilotons nuclear, to fit varying operational requirements — and is mounted on a set of wheeled vehicles based on the M656 five-ton truck. It is also air-transportable in a C-130 Hercules. The Pershing 1A is powered by a Thiokol XM105 solid fuel rocket motor and has a Bendix inertial navigation and control system. The Federal German Luftwaffe operates two missile wings with a total of 72 Pershing 1As, their nuclear warheads being under US control, and the US Army has 108 rounds. The Pershing 1A will remain in Luftwaffe service, but in the US Army it is being replaced by the Pershing II; this carries a new terminally-guided re-entry vehicle with Goodyear RADAG (Radar Area Guidance) which compares live radar returns from the target with stored images of the area. Control signals are then initiated to manoeuvre the warhead. The resulting increase in accuracy allows low-yield nuclear warheads to be used, increasing the number of target types that can be attacked with the weapon. Pershing II uses an earth-penetration warhead that can be effective against underground command centres at depths of up to 100 feet.

The French Army's principal tactical missile is the Aérospatiale Pluton, which equips five regiments, each with six launchers. Pluton is 25 feet long and is powered by an SEP Styx dual-thrust motor with SNPE solid propellant. The missile is mounted in a box container on top of an AMX-30 tracked AFV chassis; alternative warheads are the 25-kiloton AN-51 (which is also fitted to free-falling nuclear bombs used by the Armée de l'Air) for use against rear areas, and a fifteen-kiloton device for use against targets close to the front line. Pluton, which has a minimum range of $6\frac{1}{4}$ miles and a maximum of 75, incorporates stringent safety systems which are active before, during and after launch to safeguard friendly troops. A more advanced tactical missile, Hades, is under development as a longer-range successor.

NATO's rocket forces are being greatly enhanced with the introduction of new systems such as the Vought Multiple Launch Rocket System (MLRS), which is a battlefield artillery system mounted on a tracked self-propelled launcher that can fire twelve rockets either singly or in ripples up to a range of nineteen miles. Each rocket warhead carries more than 600 M77 submunitions, which have about the same destructive power as a hand grenade and contain a shaped charge enabling them to penetrate light armour. MLRS is already in service with the US Army, and a phase 3 version with a payload of six homing submunitions is under development. Federal Germany has ordered 198 MLRS, which will be fitted with the AT-2 anti-tank mine, and the system is on trial with the UK, Italian and French forces.

Warsaw Pact: Tactical missiles

Although the Soviet Union is currently deploying a new generation of tactical missiles, the bulk of the Warsaw Pact armies are still equipped with weapons that have been in service for many years. The most widely-used tactical missile is the Scud-B, which equips the armies of Bulgaria (three brigades with 27 launchers), Czechoslovakia (three brigades with 27 launchers), East German (two brigades with eighteen launchers), Hungary (one brigade with nine launchers), Poland (four brigades with 36 launchers), Romania (two brigades with fifteen launchers) and the Soviet Union (number unspecified). Scud-B is launched vertically from a MAZ-543 eight-wheel articulated vehicle and has a simple inertial guidance system. It can be fitted with either a conventional or nuclear warhead and has a range of 100-175 miles. The Scud-B, or SS-1C to give it its more correct designation, was used in small numbers by Egypt during the Yom Kippur War of 1973 and was notable mainly for its inaccuracy.

The excellent MAZ-543 vehicle is also used to launch and transport the SS-12 Scaleboard tactical missile, which is 37 feet 9 inches long and is thought to have a warhead in the megaton range. The missile has an estimated range of up to 500 miles, which would give it the ability to hit targets in East Anglia from forward sites in East Germany. About 120 rounds are deployed with the Soviet Army. The SS-12 is progressively being replaced by the SS-22, a development with an estimated range of 1000 miles.

The Soviet Army has also deployed two new-generation battlefield missiles, intended as replacements for the ageing Scud and Frog. The first is the SS-21, which is similar in configuration to the US Lance and which is mounted on a similar vehicle to that used to transport the SA-8 Gecko SAM system. The SS-21 is thought to have a range of about sixty miles and, like the Lance, can carry either conventional or tactical nuclear warheads. The SS-23, which was developed as a Scud-B replacement, has a range of about 300 miles and offers increased accuracy and payload. It has a short reaction time and the launcher can quickly be reloaded with fresh rounds. According to US Intelligence estimates, some 600 SS-23 rounds will be deployed with the Soviet Army when the Scud is eventually withdrawn from use.

NATO: Air-to-surface missiles

One of the oldest and most successful air-to-surface missiles still in service with the USAF and US Navy is the AGM-62 Walleye unpowered TV-guided glide bomb, which is carried by the F-4 Phantom and A-7 Corsair II. The pilot or WSO of the carrier aircraft identifies the target, aims the missile camera at it, focuses it and locks it on the target using a monitor screen in the cockpit. The missile is then released and the aircraft turns away. Walleye steers itself to the target automatically, but can be guided manually if necessary. Walleye II is a larger development with bigger wings to improve the glide ratio, and can be launched at a greater distance from the target. Walleye is an extremely accurate weapon and was used very successfully by the US Navy against bridge targets in Vietnam.

NATO's most widely-deployed ASM is the Hughes AGM-65 Maverick, of which some 30,000 rounds have been produced in several versions. The original AGM-65A Maverick has automatic TV homing; it is fitted with a TV seeker with a five-degree field of view and a target tracker that relies on contrast to steer the missile to the centre of its target. The AGM-86B 'scene-magnification' Maverick is a variant with a 2.5-degree field of view TV, which increases the range at which a typical target can be acquired. With TV Maverick the target is located visually, and the aircraft is then turned towards it while the missile's TV seeker is slewed until the target appears in the centre of the cockpit CRT. The missile can be fired as soon as lock is achieved, allowing the aircraft to turn away or to fire a second Maverick.

To obtain line-of-sight contact with the target, the launch aircraft pops up to 500-800 feet and remains exposed for up to fifteen seconds. Lock-on requires from four to eight seconds, and the missile can be fired at dive angles of up to sixty degrees. The maximum range of the missile is twelve nautical miles, although in practice TV lock-on is usually achieved at two or three nautical miles. Minimum range is about half a nautical mile. Three Mavericks can be fired in rapid succession, thanks to a modification that slaves the seeker of the second missile to that of the first.

Maverick, which is powered by a Thiokol TX-481 dual-thrust solid-fuel rocket motor, can be fitted with either a 132 lb hollow charge or a 300 lb fragmentation warhead. It is carried by the F-4, A-7, A-10, F-111 and F-16. The AGM-65D IIR Maverick is an imaging infrared version for use at night, the AGM-65E Laser Maverick has been developed for use as a close support weapon by the US Marine Corps, and the AGM-65F Navy Maverick is a specialised variant for use against ships and coastal targets. Apart from the US forces, Maverick is also in service with the air forces of Greece and Turkey.

One of the most important — and most accurate — tactical weapons in NATO's armoury is the Texas Instruments Paveway laser-guided 'smart bomb' family, which is in service with the US forces and the Royal Air Force. The name Paveway actually applies to the guidance units that can be fitted to a very wide variety of bombs, including the 2000 lb Mk 84 GP bomb, the 3000 lb M118 demolition bomb, the 500 lb Mk 82 Snakeye GP bomb, the 500 lb Rockeye Mk 20 cluster munition, and the 2000 lb SUU-54B cluster munition. Targets can be marked by airborne lasers carried by the parent aircraft in designator pods such as Pave Tack and Pave Knife, or by ground troops. The usual tactic is for the carrier aircraft to release the laser-guided bomb in the climb, so that the weapon follows a ballistic trajectory. Its sensor unit picks up the source of reflected laser light, and the bomb is steered to the impact point by its control fins.

The Rockwell International GBU-15, deliveries of which to the USAF began in 1982, also comes into the smart bomb category. The designation

GBU-15 applies to a whole family of winged stand-off missiles for use against targets such as mobile radar and missile sites. The cruciform-winged Rockwell GBU-15 can be released from altitudes down to 200 feet and, if desired, can be launched at extended ranges and guided by command from the parent aircraft until the bomb's electro-optical (or infrared) seeker can lock on to its target. The GBU-15 can be fitted with a number of bomb payloads, including the SUU-54B cluster munition for use against soft, dispersed targets, or the 2000 lb Mk 84 bomb. Carriers include the F-4E (two GBU-15s plus datalink pod), and the F-111F (four GBU-15s plus pod and the Pave Tack FLIR/laser pod).

Anti-radiation missiles form a vital component of NATO's tactical air-to-ground weaponry; without their support, ground-attack aircraft would be subjected to unacceptable losses from enemy SAM and AAA. The US Air Force and the US Navy are now standardising on the Texas Instruments AGM-88 HARM High-Speed Anti-Radiation Missile, the first of which was delivered to the USN in December 1982 and for which there is a requirement of about 20,000 rounds. HARM is intended as a replacement for the AGM-45A Shrike, which has been in service with the US forces for many years but which is far from ideal as an air-launched ARM and which is not effective against the latest Soviet SAM and other radars. HARM is faster than Shrike, with a maximum speed in excess of Mach 2; it also has a longer range, improved sensitivity, flexible logic and broadband coverage with a single seeker head.

Prototype for a supersonic V/STOL fighter? A Harrier fitted with a Rolls-Royce Pegasus engine equipped for plenum chamber burning being tested on a special rig at Shoeburyness in 1984.

HARM equips A-7E, F/A-18 and A-6E aircraft of the US Navy, and also F-4G Wild Weasel defence suppression aircraft of the USAF. In May 1986 the Federal German Government also placed an order for more than 350 HARMs to equip the Navy's Tornados. In US Navy service, hostile radars to be attacked with HARM are first of all detected by an Itek ALR-45 radar warning receiver or by the missile's own seeker operating in the search mode. Threat priorities are then computed by a Magnavox ALR-50 missile launch warning receiver with its associated digital interface, allowing HARMs to be fired against radars which are actively engaged in the guidance of surface-to-air missiles. In the USAF's Wild Weasel Phantoms, HARM is interfaced with the McDonnell Douglas APR-38 radar homing and warning system. The missile has three operating modes. In Self-Protect, it locks on to targets designated by the RWR; in Seeker-Search it conducts its own search for hostile radars; and in Pre-Brief it is launched and then climbs to altitude to conduct a search for hostile emitters whose signatures are stored in the computer's memory. Operationally, HARM is similar to the British Aerospace ALARM anti-radar missile, which will be carried by the RAF's Tornado GR 1s and which is described in Chapter Two.

France's standard air-launched tactical missile is still the well-tried Aérospatiale AS 30, which has a 500 lb warhead and a range of about seven miles. The operator watches tracking flares on the missile and keeps them aligned with the target by means of a radio link which sends signals to a pair of spoilers mounted in the rocket exhaust. The missile autopilot interprets the guidance command to interrupt the appropriate nozzle efflux and steer the AS 30 left or right, up or down.

A laser-guided version of the basic AS 30, the AS 30L is also in service with the Armée de l'Air's Jaguar and Mirage 2000 aircraft. The missile closely resembles its predecessor, but carries a Thomson-CSF Aeriel laser in the nose, replacing the radio-command guidance in the original version. The AS 30L homes on to radiation generated by a Cilas ITAY-71 illuminator and reflected by the target. The illuminator is installed in a Thomson-CSF/Martin Marietta Atlis 2 pod; this incorporates an automatic TV tracker which allows single-seat aircraft to locate and attack hardened targets accurately. The AS 30L carries a 500 lb X12 GP warhead or an X35 semi-armour-piercing charge; impact with the target occurs at a velocity of around 1600 feet per second.

French Air Force Jaguars also carry the AS 37 Martel TV-guided anti-radar missile, developed jointly in the 1960s by Engins Matra of France and Hawker Siddeley Dynamics. The missile is steered by the operator's control stick via a streamlined underwing pod, which also receives the TV signals from the weapon. Martel also has a passive radiation seeker, which searches a pre-set frequency band; when a hostile emission is detected the seeker sweeps through ninety degrees in azimuth to pinpoint the source and lock on to it. The missile will continue to home after launch as long as the frequency remains within the preset band. Martel has a range of eighteen miles when launched from

The cockpit of the Hawk 200 represents the latest state of the art equipment: pilot workload is eased with the introduction of advanced avionics including HUD, INAS, HOTAS, Digital Databus and colour multi-purpose electronic display.

low level, and 37 miles when launched from altitude. The weapon carries a 330 lb warhead and has a speed of Mach 0.9. In 1986, an anti-radiation variant known as Armat, for use against long-range surveillance radars, was under development to arm the Mirage 2000. The new design uses a basic AS 37 airframe mated to an ESD (Electronique Serge Dassault) homing head.

Matra also produces a laser-guided bomb for use with all types of French tactical aircraft. The weapon is similar in configuration to the US Paveway, with tail-mounted steering fins and a Thomson-CSF Elbis seeker. The bomb is available with either a 900 lb or a 2240 lb warhead and can be released at low level at up to five miles from the target.

Warsaw Pact: Air-to-surface missiles
Although the Soviet air forces have had a considerable array of long-range stand-off missiles at their disposal for many years, these properly fall into the strategic systems category. The Soviet Union has been slow to develop short-range air-launched tactical missiles, or at least to get them into service, which is a curious omission for a nation that used all kinds of tactical airborne ordnance to such effect during the Second World War. Soviet Frontovaya Aviatsiya aircraft are equipped with a wide variety of free-falling bombs and unguided rockets, but it is only comparatively recently that they have received operational tactical guided weapons.

The first such missile reported to be in service was the AS-7 Kerry, a radio-command missile which is carried by the Su-20/22 and the Su-24. The weapon, which has a conventional warhead, a range of about six miles and a speed of Mach 0.6, can reportedly be launched at heights of between 1000 and 10,000 feet. Another missile in service with the FA is the AS-10 which is a semi-active laser-guided weapon; it also has a range of around six miles and is powered by a solid-fuel rocket motor that gives it a speed of Mach 0.8. Other tactical guided weapons are known to be under development, but their status is uncertain. Soviet tactical air units have also been issued with laser-guided bombs similar in concept to Paveway.

NATO: Anti-ship missiles
One of the most important anti-ship missiles in the NATO inventory is the McDonnell Douglas Harpoon, which comes in two categories: the RGM-84A ship- and submarine-launched version and the air-launched AGM-84A. In United States service the AGM-84A is carried by the P-3C Orion and the A-6E Intruder and the RGM-84A is widely deployed throughout the US Navy's surface fleet, where it is installed in a variety of launchers; Canada has 36 RGM-84A systems on order for use in six planned ASW frigates; Denmark deploys the surface-to-surface variant on two 'Peder Skram' Class and three 'Niels Juel' Class frigates, as well as on ten 'Willemoes' Class fast attack craft; Federal Germany operates it on six 'Bremen' Class frigates; Greece on two 'Kortenaer' Class frigates; the Royal Netherlands Navy has 96 rounds deployed on two 'Tromp' Class destroyers and nine 'Kortenaer' Class frigates; Spain operates the missile on five 'Baleares' Class frigates and six 'Descubierta' Class frigates; Turkey deploys the system on one MEKO 2000 frigate and five 'Dogan' Class fast attack craft; the Royal Navy uses the RGM-84A on thirteen nuclear attack submarines, and the Royal Air Force employs the air-launched version on No 18 Group's Nimrod maritime patrol aircraft.

US Navy guided missile frigates (USS *Preble* nearest the camera) engaged in practice launch of Terrier SAMs).

The AGM-84A air-launched version of Harpoon is virtually identical to the surface vessel and submarine-launched RGM-84A. Because of the deletion of the tandem booster motor it is slightly shorter, with a length of twelve feet seven inches, and there are necessary modifications to enable the missile to interface with its various carrier aircraft.

The AGM-84A has a maximum range of seventy miles, a speed of Mach 0.85, and it carries a Naval Weapons Centre 500 lb penetration blast warhead with proximity fuzing. An Aerojet rocket motor boosts the weapon to its cruising speed of Mach 0.75, after which a Teledyne CAE J402-CA-400 turbojet takes over. The powerplant has an endurance of fifteen minutes. Guidance systems comprise a Lear-Siegler or Northrop strapdown platform, IBM 4PiSP computer and a Honeywell AN/APN-194 radar altimeter for cruise, with a Texas Instruments PR-53/DSQ-28 two-axis active radar seeker governing the attack phase of the flight.

The main purpose behind the development and deployment of anti-ship missiles is to eliminate enemy naval weapons systems before they become threats. It was for this purpose that British Aerospace developed the Sea Skua, the only missile in the western world specifically designed to take the offensive against small, fast and highly manoeuvrable attack craft. To keep an enemy fast attack craft out of missile range of a capital ship, the Sea Skua has to be deployed well out beyond the ship itself; for this purpose it is mounted on helicopters such as the Royal Navy's Lynx, with four missiles per aircraft. When a target is located, the helicopter pilot sets a radar altimeter to allow the missile to skim just above the waves, then launches it while still well outside the enemy's defences. Sea Skua is only nine and a half feet long; it cruises at high subsonic speed under the power of its solid-fuel rocket motor and has a range of about

ten miles. Target illumination is by Ferranti Seaspray radar, and the missile has a semi-active radar homing seeker.

The outer layer of the Royal Navy's anti-ship defence is provided by one of the newest and most advanced weapons in the arsenal of naval missiles, the British Aerospace Sea Eagle air-to-surface, long-range, fire-and-forget sea-skimming cruise missile. Sea Eagle is being produced to arm Sea Harriers of the Royal Navy as well as land-based Buccaneers and Tornados of the Royal Air Force, and is described in Chapter One.

Federal Germany, Italy and Norway have all developed anti-ship missiles, either indigenously or as part of an international programme. Federal Germany's principal air-launched anti-ship weapon is the MBB Kormoran, the Mk I version of which is in service with the Navy's Tornado and F-104G maritime attack squadrons. Kormoran was, in fact, the first major post-war missile programme in West Germany, and was based on a Nord-Aviation missile project, the AS 34. The basic Kormoran closely follows the French design, but has a more advanced guidance system. After launch, twin SNPE Prades booster motors burn for one second and boost the missile to a speed of Mach 0.9, whereupon an SNPE Eole IV sustainer motor takes over 100 seconds. Guidance systems comprise a Stena/Bodenseewerk inertial platform plus a modified TRT AHV-7 radio altimeter, while a modified Thomson-CSF RE576 two-axis active radar seeker is used in the attack phase. The warhead comprises 369 lb of explosive in sixteen radial charges which project fragments with sufficient velocity to penetrate up to seven bulkheads, together with a central 125 lb explosive charge fitted with a delayed-action fuze. A Mk II version of Kormoran with an improved guidance seeker, better ECM resistance, longer range (forty miles) and a larger warhead is under development.

Italy's Oto Melara Otomat, developed in conjunction with Engins Matra of France, is a ship-launched sea-skimming missile, but the Mk II version incorporates a TG-2 radio link which allows mid-course guidance updates to be transmitted from helicopters such as the Agusta-Bell A 109 or the ASW version of the AB 212. The Otomat Mk II, which is just under sixteen feet long, reaches a speed of Mach 0.9 and has a range of 62 miles. Power is provided by two Hotchkiss-Brandt/SNPE solid fuel boosters which burn for four seconds and are then jettisoned, a Turbomeca TR281 Arbizon sustainer turbojet then taking over for cruise flight. The latter is controlled by an autopilot and radio altimeter, while the attack phase is controlled by an SMA single-axis active radar seeker. The warhead comprises 145 lb of HE, plus incendiary material; this, together with residual fuel, gives a total of 560 lb. The warhead can penetrate 40 mm of armour plate.

Norway's Penguin anti-ship missile, developed by the Kongsberg Vapenfabrikk, comes in two variants: the Mk II ship-launched passive homing missile, which is in service with the Royal Norwegian and Greek Navies, and the Penguin Mk III air-launched version, which is on order to equip the Royal Norwegian Air Force's F-16s. The Mk III has a maximum range of 38 miles, and a solid fuel rocket sustainer motor gives it a speed of Mach 0.9. Cruise flight is commanded by inertial midcourse guidance, pre-programmed via waypoints, and attack is governed by infrared search and homing. The missile is fitted with a 268 lb SAP warhead with a delayed impact fuze.

The most widely-used French anti-ship weapon is the Aérospatiale Exocet, which in its ship-launched version is also in service with the Royal Navy, the Greek Navy and the Federal German Kriegsmarine, as well as with a considerable number of non-NATO navies. France deploys the surface-launched MM 38 Exocet on the helicopter carrier *Jeanne d'Arc* and on its fleet of destroyers and frigates, and also employs the AM 39 air-launched Exocet on the Aéronavale's Super Etendard strike force. The AM 39 Exocet can be launched at any altitude from 150 feet up to the carrier aircraft's normal operating ceiling and has a normal range of between thirty and 43 miles, depending on the launch altitude and conditions. The missile is boosted by an SNPE Dondor rocket with a two-second burn and sustained by an SNPE Helios rocket motor that burns for a maximum of 150 seconds, producing a cruising speed of Mach 0.9. Cruising flight is controlled by an inertial guidance system plus a TRT AHV-7 radio altimeter, and for the attack phase the weapon has an EMD Adec X-band single-axis monopulse radar seeker that begins searching about nine miles from the target. The missile has a 370 lb GP1 blast/fragmentation warhead, fitted with delay and proximity fuzes.

Warsaw Pact: Anti-ship missiles
The Soviet Union has always concentrated on the development of ship- and submarine-launched anti-ship missiles, to the detriment of air-launched types. Those of the latter which are in service are mainly large and of aircraft configuration; they carry nuclear warheads which could be used against concentrations of warships as well as against area targets on land. The AS-4 Kitchen and AS-6 Kingfish are typical examples. The former, which is powered by a liquid rocket motor, has a range of about 250 miles and a speed in excess of Mach 2, is carried by the Soviet Naval Aviation's Tupolev Tu-22 Blinder bombers; the AS-6 equips the Backfire and has a range of about 140 miles at Mach 3. Cruise flight is inertially-guided, and the missile, which is thought to have a 200-kiloton warhead, has either an active radar or passive radiation seeker for the attack phase. The AS-5 Kelt is another aircraft-configured missile and is carried by the Tu-16 Badger; this weapon, unlike the others, is fitted with a large HE warhead, has a range of around 200 miles and a high subsonic speed. Powered by a liquid rocket motor, it is fitted with either an active radar seeker or passive radiation seeker and may be primarily intended to attack large surface units such as nuclear attack carriers. Another air-launched missile, the AS-9, is equipped with a passive radiation seeker, presumably for anti-ship operations, and has a range of around fifty miles, while a new Mach 3.5 missile with a range of around 500 miles is being developed to replace the AS-6 with the Backfire force.

In 1982, Soviet Backfire bombers carried out their first simulated attacks on US Navy aircraft carriers when eight aircraft flew to within 120 miles of the carriers USS *Enterprise* and *Midway* in the North Pacific and locked on to the task force with their AS-6 missiles before returning to new Far East bases which now permit the Backfires to patrol the Sea of Japan. Manoeuvres of this kind have since been repeated, both in the Pacific and North Atlantic.

NATO: Surface-to-air missiles
The armed forces of NATO employ no fewer than twenty different surface-to-air missile types, on land and at sea. For many years, European NATO's standard long-range interceptor SAM has been the Nike Hercules, a missile that stands 41 feet high with its booster and has a range of more than 87 miles. Nike Hercules is capable of carrying out interceptions at up to 150,000 feet and reaches a speed of Mach 3.65. It is operated by eight NATO countries: Belgium has 36 rounds grouped into four missile squadrons, Federal Germany has 24 batteries, Greece deploys 36 rounds, Italy has eight batteries with a mixture of Nike Hercules and Spada SAMs (see below), the Netherlands has 23 missiles in two squadrons, Norway has four batteries, each with 32 missiles, Spain has ten rounds, Turkey has eight squadrons, and the United States Army retains four batteries for training purposes in Florida and Alaska.

The problem with the Nike Hercules system is that it is cumbersome and obsolescent, but for the time being it is the only long-range, high-altitude SAM system NATO has got. It should have been replaced from 1975 by the Raytheon MIM-104 Patriot, but this system has been subjected to serious delays and cost escalation and is only now being deployed with the US Army. Patriot is designed to intercept air-breathing targets at all altitudes and in the face of heavy countermeasures; its phased-array radar and launcher are operated remotely from the engagement control station, which contains display and control systems, a high-speed digital computer and communications. Patriot is powered by a Thiokol TX-486 single-stage rocket motor, which boosts the eighteen-foot missile to a speed of Mach 3. Maximum range is 37 miles, and upper altitude limit in the region of 80,000 feet. The system has also been ordered by the Netherlands and Federal Germany.

The Bloodhound Mk 2 SAM still provides the RAF's primary area defence system. Modifications have given Bloodhound enhanced capability, such as relatively low-level interception.

Patriot is also intended to replace, at least in part, another long-serving NATO SAM system: the Raytheon MIM-23B Improved Hawk. This system, whose name stands for Homing All-the-Way Killer, was conceived in 1954 to fill a requirement for a mobile SAM that was capable of engaging low-flying aircraft. The earlier MIM-23A system has now been superseded by the MIM-23B in NATO service. Belgium, Denmark, West Germany, Greece and the Netherlands each deploys 36 Improved Hawk systems, each with a total of 216 rounds; France deploys eleven batteries with 66 Hawks; Italy has three battalions with sixty rounds; Spain has 24 systems, and Norway has 36 on order. In US service, the missile is being gradually replaced by Patriot.

Improved Hawk is boosted to a speed of Mach 2.5 by an Aerojet/Hercules Mk 56 dual thrust rocket motor; minimum and maximum effective altitudes are 100 feet and 60,000 feet, and maximum range is 25 miles. The weapon has semi-active radar guidance, and the 120 lb warhead is fitted with impact and proximity fuzes.

Britain's long-serving area defence SAM is the BAe Bloodhound, originally developed by the Bristol Aeroplane Co and Ferranti under the code-name Red Duster. The current Bloodhound Mk 2 version, once deployed at British bases overseas, is now operated by No 25 Squadron RAF, with launch sites at Barkston Heath, Wyton and Wattisham, and by No 85 Squadron with sites at Bawdsey, West Raynham and North Coates. Both squadrons are under the control of No 11 Group. The Bloodhound Mk 2 system uses either a portable or fixed-base form; the portable system uses a Ferranti Firelight target illuminating radar, while the fixed-base set employs the more powerful AEI Scorpion. The TIR is directed towards the target by surveillance radar and the reflected radar energy is used by the Bloodhound's guidance system to direct the missile to its target. The weapon is launched with the aid of data from a high capacity computer, which monitors missile readiness as well as acting as fire control computer. Bloodhound is boosted by four solid fuel rockets which are then jettisoned, two Rolls-Royce Bristol Thor ramjets taking over. Maximum speed is Mach 2+ and range fifty miles. Bloodhound has a high explosive warhead, is ECM-resistant and can engage targets flying between 200 and 65,000 feet.

Arguably the most effective land-based short-range SAM system currently deployed by NATO is the British Aerospace Rapier, which is fully described in Chapter Two. An indication of its efficiency is that it was selected to protect the USAF's strike bases in the United Kingdom. The US Army's primary short-range SAM system is the MIM-72C/F Improved Chaparral, 400 units of which are in service. Chaparral, which was developed by Ford Aerospace, also serves with the Greek Army (37 units) and Spain has 96 units on order. Chaparral is basically a land-mobile version of the Sidewinder AAM, four rounds being mounted on an M730 tracked vehicle. The launcher is retracted for travelling and is equipped with eight reload rounds. The missile is fitted with a Mk 50 rocket motor and has infrared homing; the warhead is an M-250 blast fragmentation type with an M817 proximity fuze. Maximum range is in the order of $3\frac{1}{2}$ miles.

Federal Germany, France, Spain and the United States all operate the short-range Roland SAM system, developed by Aérospatiale and MBB under the guise of a company called Euromissile. There is no doubt that Roland is a successful weapon, but production has not reached the anticipated levels. For example, the US Army, which was originally to have purchased 184 Roland fire units, eventually took only 31 to equip a National Guard unit assigned to the Rapid Deployment Force. The Bundeswehr has 143 Roland systems, France twenty batteries of Roland I and II, and Spain has eighteen systems on order. Roland I is mounted on an AMX-30 tracked carrier which is fitted with a Siemens/Thomson CSF pulse-Doppler search and surveillance radar; when a target is acquired the threat azimuth is scanned through the missile operator's optical sight, and when a hostile aircraft is sighted a missile is launched by foot button. The missile is automatically gathered by an IR system which transmits steering commands by centimetric radio link, the operator continuing to track the target until warhead detonation. Roland II is an all-weather variant, mounted on a Marder chassis and tracked by radar throughout the engagement. Roland has an SNPE booster motor and an SNPE Lampyre sustainer which burns for 13.2 seconds, giving the missile a speed of Mach 1.6. Roland's upper altitude limit is 10,000 feet, maximum range just under four miles and its warhead, weighing $14\frac{1}{2}$ lb, contains 65 projectile charges which are lethal up to twenty feet. An IR proximity fuze is fitted.

To protect its strategic nuclear force bases against low-level attack, the Armée de l'Air deploys 24 batteries of Thomson-CSF/Matra R 440 Crotale SAMs, each with one radar vehicle and two fire units. Crotale was originally developed for the South African armed forces; each fire unit has four rounds, together with a Thomson J-band pulse-Doppler radar. An E/F band surveillance radar is mounted on the Hotchkiss-Brandt electrically-driven target acquisition unit. The missile is powered by a single-stage SNPE Lens rocket motor which accelerates it to Mach 2.3 in a fraction over two seconds. The weapon then coasts and is gathered by an IR system, subsequently guiding to the target via a monopulse Ku-band radar with a 1.1 degree beam. The system has a standby X-band command and optical (TV) backup for low level. Crotale has a maximum altitude of 12,000 feet and a range of $5\frac{1}{4}$ miles; the warhead, which is fitted with an IR proximity fuze, is a 31 lb focalised fragmentation type which emits fragments at 7590 feet per second. Fourteen units of a navalised version of Crotale are also in service with the Aéronavale.

The latest SAM system to enter service with the French armed forces is the Matra SATCP (Sol-Air très Courte Portée) Mistral, a very short range lightweight weapon which, in its basic configuration, is mounted in its launch container on a short vertical pedestal. Mistral was due to be deployed in 1986 with the French Army and the Armée de l'Air, and was also on order for the Belgian Army. The missile itself is six feet long and is powered by an SEP solid-propellant booster and sustainer. Speed is Mach 2.6, maximum range $3\frac{3}{4}$ miles, guidance is passive IR homing and the warhead is a 7 lb HE charge, proximity fuzed.

The second component of the Italian Air Force's SAM system, shared with Nike Hercules, is the Selenia Spada, which is based on the Aspide AAM. The basic Spada system consists of three six-round launchers controlled by a G/H band radar tracker incorporating an I-band illuminator; four systems can be controlled by one E/F band search radar. The missile is powered by a single-stage SNIA-Viscosa solid-fuel rocket motor giving a speed of Mach 4 at burnout, and reportedly has a range of up to sixty miles. Spada is fitted with a 77 lb fragmentation warhead.

NATO ground forces are equipped with three types of man-portable SAM: Blowpipe, Redeye and Stinger. Developed by Short's Guided Weapons Division, Blowpipe can engage oncoming targets and has a very fast reaction time. The operator sights the target visually, interrogates it by IFF, and fires the missile if no correct response is received. The round is popped from its tube by a booster charge that burns for 0.2 seconds, and a Crake sustainer rocket then takes over to accelerate it to Mach 1.5. Initial guidance is by IR autogathering, followed by command line of sight to the target. The missile, which has a range in excess of two miles, is fitted with a 4.85 lb blast/shaped charge warhead with a proximity fuze. Blowpipe is in service with the British Army, the Royal Marines and the Canadian Army. An improved version of Blowpipe called Javelin is just entering service.

The FIM-43A Redeye was developed in the late 1950s by the Pomona Division of Convair (later General Dynamics), but because of a protracted development history it did not become operational until 1968. Redeye is supplied in a sealed container which also acts as a launch tube. On sighting a hostile aircraft the operator tracks it in an open sight, at the same time energising the gas-cooled infrared seeker. A buzzer sounds when the weapon is ready to fire. A boost motor propels the missile from its tube, the sustainer igniting some twenty feet from the operator to protect him from exhaust blast. The missile has a maximum speed of Mach 1.4, a range of two miles and an altitude limit of 8250 feet. Guidance is IR homing, and the missile has a fragmentation warhead. Redeye is in service with the armed forces of the United States, Denmark, Federal Germany and Greece.

Redeye is progressively being replaced in US and German service by the General Dynamics Pomona FIM-92A Stinger man-portable SAM system, which entered service with the US Army in 1981.

Stinger is fitted with a Passive Optical Scanning Technique (POST) seeker system, in which two detectors — one operating in the infrared region of the spectrum and the other in the ultraviolet — pass data to two micro-processors. The system is designed to cope with current and anticipated countermeasures. Stinger has a range of just over three miles, an altitude limit of 16,000 feet and a speed in excess of Mach 2. The missile is powered by an Atlantic Research dual-thrust rocket motor. Guidance is by IR homing and proportional navigation, and the missile is fitted with a 6.72 lb Arsenal fragmentation warhead.

NATO's most widely-used naval SAM system is the Raytheon RIM-7H Sea Sparrow, which is in service with the Canadian, Danish, West German, Greek, Italian, Netherlands, Norwegian, Spanish and US Navies. This point defence system is the shipboard equivalent of the air-launched AIM-7M and is mounted in an eight-cell lightweight launcher. The missile is powered by a single-stage Aerojet Mk 53 Mod 2 rocket motor with a 2.9-second burn; maximum speed is Mach 3.5, range up to 11.25 miles and altitude limit 16,500 feet. The missile has a continuous-wave semi-active radar guidance system and 67 lb warhead.

One of the older naval SAM systems is the General Dynamics Terrier, which dates back in prototype form to 1949. The version that still equips some surface units of the US and Italian Navies is the RIM-2 Advanced Terrier, a two-stage solid-fuel missile which has a range of 21 miles and can engage low-flying aircraft. Terrier is currently being phased out in favour of the General Dynamics Pomona RIM-66C/67B Standard 2 Missile, which was developed to be compatible with existing Terrier launch equipment and also to form an integral part of the US Navy's Aegis area-defence system. The Aegis Weapon System Mk 7 includes the Raytheon SPY-14 search/track radar, which can detect targets at a range of more than 200 miles.

The Standard 2 Missile is powered by a Naval Propellant Plant Mk 12 Mod 1 booster motor and an Atlantic Research Mk 30 Mod 2 sustainer; maximum speed is in excess of Mach 2.5, altitude limit is 65,000 feet and range fifty miles. Guidance is

Midships view of a Soviet 'Kresta II' Class guided missile cruiser, showing quadruple SS-N-3 surface-to-surface missile launchers. The launchers for the warship's SA-N-3 SAMs may be seen fore and aft; note the two Headlight fire control radars.

semi-active radar homing plus on-board mid-course guidance, which means that the missile does not require continuous target illumination.

Standard 2 is developed from the RIM-66B/C Standard 1, which has the same airframe but a reduced performance; maximum range of the SM1 is thirteen miles, altitude limit 65,000 feet and maximum speed Mach 2 under the power of an Aerojet/Hercules Mk 56 Mod 0 dual-thrust rocket. Standard Missiles are in service with the Italian, Netherlands, Spanish and US Navies.

The Standard 1 Missile was developed to replace the General Dynamics RIM-24 Tartar, itself a development of the Terrier with the ability to engage targets flying between 1000 and 40,000 feet. Tartar still equips two French Navy T-47 destroyers, three 'Lutjens' Class destroyers of the Federal German Navy, and some older surface units of the US Navy.

The outer layer of the Royal Navy's SAM defence is formed by the British Aerospace GWS30 Sea Dart, an area-defence, medium-range missile designed to engage aircraft and relatively large, slow-moving missiles at medium and high level. When the area protected by a vessel carrying Sea Dart is threatened, the missile director dedicates one of two Marconi radars on board the ship to the next missile to be launched. An onboard computer aims the radar at the target's approximate position, and once the radar is locked on the information is fed to the computer, which in turn points the Sea Dart launcher at the predicted interception point. Once fired, the fourteen-foot, 1200 lb weapon is boosted by an IMI rocket motor to Mach 2; a Rolls-Royce Odin ramjet then takes over and accelerates the missile to its Mach 3.5 cruise. Homing is semi-active radar. Sea Dart has a range of over fifty miles and an upper altitude limit of 82,500 feet; it is fitted with a powerful fragmentation warhead. The system is currently deployed on the three 'Invincible' Class aircraft carriers, one Type 82 destroyer and twelve Type 42 destroyers.

The Shorts Seacat, originally developed in the late 1950s as a close-range SAM system to replace rapid-fire guns, is still widely used by the Royal Navy, which deploys it in quadruple launchers on the assault ships *Fearless* and *Intrepid,* two 'County' Class destroyers, six Type 21 frigates, seventeen 'Leander' Class frigates and seven Type 12 frigates. The Royal Netherlands Navy also deploys the system on six frigates. Seacat has simple radio command guidance and is steered optically to the target by its operator, who keeps two tracking flares on the missile's fins lined up with the objective. However, Seacat can be integrated with almost any sighting and fire control system, which makes it a very versatile weapon. The missile is powered by an IMI dual-thrust rocket motor and has a blast type warhead with an EMI proximity fuze. Speed is in the order of Mach 0.9 and range is four miles.

Probably the most effective close-range naval SAM system in the world is the British Aerospace Seawolf, development of which began in 1969 under the designation Guided Weapons System (GWS) 25. In parallel, associated surveillance and tracking radars were developed by Marconi Radar Systems, and the missile launcher by Vickers Engineering. Seawolf was designed from the outset to intercept and destroy high, medium and sea-skimming aircraft or missiles travelling in excess of Mach 2 and which presented a direct threat to the vessel carrying the Seawolf system, and was to be capable of effective operation in severe weather and high sea states. The system can operate independently of human control, with the exception of being loaded. Each missile is considered a round of ammunition, like an artillery round, and is hand-loaded into the launcher, which has six missile cells.

When a threat enters the area of a vessel protected by Seawolf, a Ferranti digital computer allocates a threat priority and assigns the target to the radar. The computer instructs the radar tracker and launcher to turn towards the target, the radar locks on, and the launcher is positioned to the correct elevation. After launch, the Bristol Aerojet solid-propellant rocket motor burns for two or

The British Aerospace EAP — an experimental aircraft programme demonstrator — is a single-seat air superiority aircraft with all-moving foreplanes, an advanced compound sweep wing and powered by two Turbo-Union RB 199 Mk. 104 engines. These features, together with new light-weight materials, active control technology, result in an outstandingly agile aircraft. New developments in stealth technology are also incorporated. EAP flew for the first time on 8 August 1986 and is designed to prove systems for the European Fighter Aircraft.

three seconds and accelerates the 180 lb missile to a speed in excess of Mach 2. Once the missile is launched, the radar tracks it and the target simultaneously. Continuous steering commands are transmitted to the missile to keep it on course towards the target. If the radar has difficulty in tracing a target at extremely low level, the task can be taken over manually by a bore-sighted TV camera on the radar antenna. A controller below deck steers the camera by means of a joystick. This manual TV tracking is the only aspect of Seawolf operation, outside loading, which needs the human element. In a typical Seawolf engagement, the total elapsed time from target sighting to target destruction is approximately ten seconds.

Seawolf has successfully intercepted missiles, targets as small as 4.5-inch shells and aircraft. The missile has a range of three miles and is fitted with a proximity-fuzed 30 lb impact warhead. A vertical-launch version of the Seawolf system is currently under development; groups of its launch canisters can easily be fitted to ships without the need for a large below-deck magazine, and the system can be installed in vessels as small as fast attack craft. The VL Seawolf system will be operationally ready for the Royal Navy's new Type 23 frigates.

Warsaw Pact: Surface-to-air missiles
The Soviet Air Force, in addition to maintaining a large interceptor force, the IA-PVO, has large numbers of surface-to-air missiles and associated radar equipment. The SA-2 Guideline medium range SAM is still in widespread use within the Warsaw Pact; this radio-controlled missile has a two-stage rocket propulsion system, a slant range of 25-30 miles, a speed of Mach 3.5, a maximum altitude of around 60,000 feet and is used in conjunction with a Fan Song radar. It is fitted with a 290 lb fragmentation warhead, but is also nuclear-capable.

The SA-3 Goa is used by both the PVO, and, in its SA-N-1 version, by the Soviet Navy. It is designed for short-range defence against low-flying aircraft, is very mobile and is used in conjunction with the Low Blow radar. A radio command-guided missile, it has a speed of Mach 2, a range of fifteen to eighteen miles and is fitted with a 135 lb HE warhead.

The SA-4 Ganef, first identified in 1964, can be launched from a tracked vehicle which carries two missiles. It has solid propellant boosters and a ramjet sustainer, is used in conjunction with a Pat Hand radar, and has a range of 40-45 miles. It is widely deployed in the USSR and Warsaw Pact. Maximum speed of the SA-4 is Mach 2.5, and the missile carries a HE warhead.

The SA-5 Gammon is a long-range high-altitude SAM of which about 1100 are operational at more than 100 Soviet sites. The missile, which operates in conjunction with a Square Pair radar, has a slant range of up to 150 miles and a maximum altitude of 100,000 feet. Both booster and sustainer motors are solid fuel, giving the missile a maximum speed in excess of Mach 3.5; guidance is by radio command and the SA-5 carries a 135 lb HE warhead. The system may have a limited anti-ballistic-missile capability.

One of the most important SAM systems in the Warsaw Pact inventory is the SA-6 Gainful. It has both command and homing guidance, is fully mobile — being carried in threes on a PT-76 chassis — and is accompanied by a separate vehicle which carries its acquisition and fire control radar equipment. The SA-6 has an effective minimum capability as low as 150 feet with optical tracking, and Israeli combat aircraft such as the F-4 suffered heavy losses from it during the Yom Kippur war of 1973. Rocket power accelerates the missile at about 20g to a speed of Mach 1.5; the tail cone, which contains the rocket motor nozzle, is jettisoned at burnout and a ramjet sustainer takes the missile up to about Mach 2.8. The SA-6 has a 180 lb HE warhead.

The Warsaw Pact's standard man-portable SAM is the SA-7 Grail, which is broadly similar to early variants of the US Army's Redeye. The SA-7 has a 5.5 lb fragmentation warhead and reaches a speed of Mach 1.5. Range is about 2½ miles, and upper altitude limit approximately 11,500 feet. The weapon is powered by a dual-thrust solid motor and has infrared guidance, now fitted with a filter to screen out decoy flares. The weapon is effective against targets flying at less than 500 knots, but a Mk 2 version with enhanced performance is now in service. The SA-9 Gaskin is a vehicle-mounted derivative of the SA-7, the mounting consisting of twin quadruple canister launchers on a modified BRDM. The missile itself is larger than the SA-7 and has a far better performance; range is five miles, altitude limits 150-15,000 feet, and speed Mach 1.8. The SA-9 has a warhead of unknown weight and may be used in conjunction with the Gun Dish radar also used with the ZSU-23/4 Shilka AAA.

The Royal Air Force's long-range AAM is a British Aerospace Sky Flash which forms the primary missile armament of the Tornado F.2. Sky Flash is a derivative of the AIM-7E2 Sparrow.

The SA-8 Gecko, first identified in 1975, appears to have been designed to fill the gap between very short-range systems such as the SA-7, SA-9 and ZSU-23/4 on the one hand and the SA-6 on the other. In size and weight the SA-8 resembles the US Sparrow. The system comprises a six-wheeled amphibious vehicle carrying a rotating launcher which is surmounted by a folding surveillance-radar aerial, with a forward-mounted target tracking radar flanked by two command dishes. Two missiles can be launched at the same target and controlled by the twin-antenna I-band command link. A low-light TV camera mounted on top of the tracking command assembly is used for optical target tracking and probably for autogathering. The latest version of the SA-8 carries six rounds in storage/launch boxes. Range of the SA-8 is about 7.5 miles, speed Mach 2, and altitude limits 150-19,500 feet. The missile has a dual-thrust solid propellant motor and is fitted with a 112 lb HE warhead.

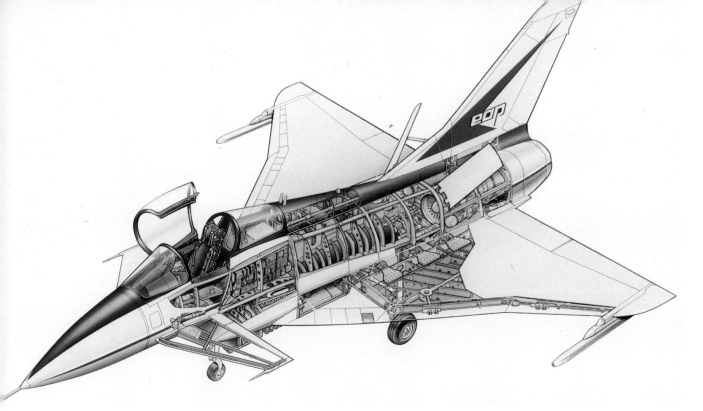

Approximately 800 Eurofighter aircraft are being developed and produced for the Air Forces of Great Britain, Germany, Italy and Spain by Eurofighter/Jagdflugzeug GmbH with its Partner Companies Aeritalia, British Aerospace, CASA and Messerschmitt-Bolkow-Blöhm (with Dornier as national co-contractor). Introduction of Eurofighter to the Services will start in 1995. The picture shows the Eurofighter configuration as agreed by the industrial partners.

The SA-10 is a rapid-acceleration SAM system now deployed in defence of key targets in the Soviet Union. The system uses a tower-mounted surveillance radar for better detection of low-flying targets such as cruise missiles. SA-10 has also been tested against Soviet re-entry vehicles, indicating that it may have a limited ABM capability. Little is known about the SA-10 other than that it is powered by a single-stage solid propellant rocket motor; its maximum speed is in the region of Mach 5.6, range thirty miles and upper altitude limit about 15,000 feet. The missile is thought to use active radar terminal homing.

Other land-based Soviet SAMs are the SA-12, which is apparently intended as SA-2/SA-5 replacement and which uses a phased array radar capable of handling several targets simultaneously at altitudes of between 100 and 100,000 feet and a range of up to sixty miles, and the SA-13, which was developed to replace the current SA-9 in the point defence of Warsaw Pact ground forces.

Apart from the SA-N-1 Goa, mentioned earlier, the Soviet Navy deploys a formidable array of SAM systems. The twenty-foot SA-N-3 Goblet, deployed on 'Kiev' Class aircraft carriers, 'Moskva' Class helicopter carriers, 'Kara' Class cruisers and 'Krivak II' Class cruisers in twin launchers, is used in conjunction with Headlight G, H and I-band radars and is an area defence weapon; the SA-N-4 is a short-range system using the same missile as the SA-8, fired from a twin launcher and associated with the Pop Group radar; SA-N-5 is the navalised version of the SA-7, using a simple pivoted mount and deployed on fast attack craft; SA-N-6 is a vertically-launched weapon, used in conjunction with the Top Dome radar, deployed on 'Kirov' Class battlecruisers and thought to be a derivative of the SA-10; and the SA-N-7, which may be a

derivative of the land-based SA-11, is deployed on 'Sovremennyy' Class destroyers in association with six Top Dome fire control and target illumination radars, the latter being assigned to individual engagements and taking command of rounds from the rapid-fire launchers.

NATO: Air-to-air missiles

NATO's standard short-range AAM is the Ford Aerospace/Raytheon AIM-9 Sidewinder. Current operational variants are the AIM-9L and AIM-9P, while an AIM-9M version, featuring improved infrared ECCM capability and a fifty per cent improvement in its ability to acquire a target against a strong infrared background such as a desert, is being developed for the US Navy. All Sidewinder variants have a range of 6.25 to 11.25 miles, depending on launch factors, and a speed of Mach 2.5. Guidance is infrared, and warhead is the blast-fragmentation type with Ir or active-optical fuze.

The Raytheon/General Dynamics AIM-7 Sparrow is a long-range dogfight-capable weapon with a speed of Mach 4. Variants in NATO service are the AIM-7E, AIM-7F and AIM-7M, the latter having enhanced resistance to countermeasures and better performance in ground clutter. Depending on the variant, Sparrow has a maximum range of 28-62 miles. Sparrow will eventually be replaced by the Hughes AIM-120A AMRAAM (Advanced Medium-Range Air-to-Air Missile), which has fire-and-forget capability and is similar in size to Sidewinder but with a Sparrow-type performance. Up to six rounds can be fired in rapid succession at a series of targets.

The US Navy's long-range AAM is the Hughes AIM-54 Phoenix, which equips the F-14 Tomcat. This formidable missile has a speed in excess of Mach 5, a range of 125 miles and is fitted with a 134 lb warhead with proximity and impact fuzing. The missile is powered by a Rocketdyne Mk 47 Mod 0 long-burning rocket motor and has an AN/DSQ-26 on-board computer; cruise is governed by pulse-Doppler semi-active radar homing, switching to pulse-Doppler active radar homing for the attack phase during the last twelve miles of the mission.

The Royal Air Force's long-range AAM is the British Aerospace Sky Flash which forms the primary missile armament of the Tornado F2. Sky

Flash is a derivative of the AIM-7E2 Sparrow, with British semi-active homing avionics and a 67 lb continuous-rod warhead with an EMI proximity fuze. Designed for use with Tornado's AI-24 Foxhunter AI radar, Sky Flash has a range of up to thirty miles and a speed of Mach 4.

Warsaw Pact: Air-to-air missiles

The most widely-used Warsaw Pact AAM is still the AA-2 (K-13A) Atoll, which is the Soviet equivalent of Sidewinder. However, it is by no means as efficient as the American missile and its performance is poor by comparison. Atoll has a range of 3.5 miles and a speed of Mach 2.5; it has infrared homing. The larger AA-3 Anab can have either IR or I/J-band SAR homing; its range is around ten miles. The AA-5 Ash is larger still, with a range of about twenty miles; like the AA-3, it too can be fitted with IR or SAR homing. Ash forms the primary armament of the Tupolev Tu-28P Fiddler long-range interceptor and is used in conjunction with Big Nose AI radar. The AA-6 Acrid, which is similar in configuration to the AA-3 but larger, was developed as the primary armament of the MiG-25 Foxbat, which carries four missiles — two using infrared and the other pair SAR homing — on underwing pylons. The missiles are ripple-fired in pairs, the IR round preceding the SAR round by one second. The AA-6 is used in conjunction with the Fox Fire fire control radar, which was developed from Big Nose. Missile range is about thirty miles in the SAR variant (fifteen miles IR), speed Mach 4.5 and the warhead is between 134 and 224 lb, probably HE.

The AA-7 Apex is the standard missile armament of the MiG-23S Flogger, and is used in conjunction with the High Lark fire control radar. One IR-guided missile and one SAR-guided weapon are carried on underwing pylons. The AA-7 is effective at low and medium altitudes; ranges are twenty miles (SAR) and nine miles (IR), the missile reaching a speed of Mach 3.5. The warhead is a 90 lb HE type, and the system has a limited look-down/shoot-down capability.

The Eurofighter is a canard delta, single-seat, twin-engined aircraft optimised for air-to-air combat with a basic mass empty of 9.75 tonnes, a thrust of 90 kN per engine and a gross wing area of 50 sgm.

The AA-8 Aphid is a dogfight missile thought to be derived from the AA-2 and roughly equivalent to the AIM-9L Sidewinder. Carriers are the MiG-21 (two on underwing pylons) and the MiG-23 (two or four under the fuselage). This weapon also forms the secondary armament of the MiG-31 Foxhound, the primary being the AA-9 active-radar homing missiles which are used in conjunction with the interceptor's long-range pulse-Doppler radar to counter low-flying aircraft and cruise missiles. The latest active-radar homing AAM to enter Warsaw Pact service is the AA-10, up to six of which are carried by the MiG-29 Fulcrum air superiority fighter and four by the Su-27 Flanker.

NATO: Anti-tank missiles

The principal types of anti-tank missile in service with NATO forces are HOT, Milan, Swingfire, TOW and the M-47 Dragon.

Shape of the future: B.Ae's EAP demonstrator on its impressive roll-out.

The Euromissile-developed HOT (which is a somewhat contrived abbreviation for Haut-subsonique Optiquement Téléguidé Tiré d'un Tube) is a heavy missile with a range of between 250 and 13,200 feet; it carries a 13.4 lb hollow-charge warhead that can penetrate 80 cm of solid armour struck at zero degrees incidence and 20 cm at 65 degrees. HOT is deployed by the French Army on VAB vehicles and Gazelle helicopters, by West Germany on RJPz AFVs, and in small numbers by Spain. Milan, also by Euromissile, has a minimum/maximum range of 80/6,600 feet; like HOT it has a semi-automatic command line-of-sight guidance system and carries a 6.6 lb hollow-charge warhead which can penetrate just over 35 cm of armour at an incidence of 65 degrees. An infantry weapon, Milan is deployed with the armies of Belgium, France, Greece, Italy, Spain and the United Kingdom.

The British Aerospace Swingfire has a minimum/maximum range of 500/13,200 feet; guidance is by command line of sight, plus velocity control and autogathering, and the missile carries a 15.6 lb hollow-charge warhead. The missile is deployed by the British Army on FV438 and Striker AFVs, each with a four-round launcher, and the Belgian Army, where the weapon is mounted on forty Striker AFVs.

The most important NATO anti-tank missile is the Hughes BGM-71 TOW, which has a minimum/maximum range of 214/12,400 feet. Guidance is by semi-automatic command line of sight, and the missile carries an 8 lb hollow-charge warhead. Improved TOW has an extendable nose spike to trigger the warhead's shaped charge at a stand-off distance of 38 cm, giving a better performance against the latest types of armour, and

TOW 2 has a 13.5 lb warhead and more powerful rocket motor. TOW is deployed by Canada (149 systems), Denmark (84 systems), West Germany (on 211 Bo 105 helicopters as well as with ground forces), Greece (on twenty AH-1S Cobra helicopters as well as with ground forces), Italy, Luxembourg, the Netherlands, Norway, Spain, the United Kingdom (on AAC Lynx helicopters, each with eight rounds) and the United States.

The McDonnell Douglas/Raytheon FGM-77A (M-47) Dragon was developed to replace the 90 mm recoilless rifle as the US Army's infantry-portable anti-tank weapon. Its minimum/maximum range is 200/3600 feet, guidance is by semi-automatic command line of sight and the missile carries a 5.4 lb M225 linear hollow charge warhead capable of penetrating 60 cm of armour. The system's reusable tracker contains a 6x optical sight, infrared sensor, electronics package and trigger. After use the tracker is removed and attached to a fresh round.

Warsaw Pact: Anti-tank missiles

The Warsaw Pact deploys five types of anti-tank missile. The AT-2 Swatter is mounted on triple launchers on BRDM-1 vehicles and also arms the Mi-24 attack helicopter; it has a range of up to 8250 feet and its warhead can penetrate 50 cm of armour. Guidance is command line of sight plus IR homing. The AT-3 Sagger is operated by a two-man infantry team and has a range of up to 10,000 feet; guidance is by command line of sight and the missile's 6 lb warhead can penetrate up to 40 cm of armour. The AT-4 Spigot SACLOS-guided missile is gradually replacing the AT-3 in the Soviet Army and is broadly similar to HOT, while the AT-5 Spandrel system, deployed on BRDM tracked vehicles, possibly uses the same round as the AT-4. Spandrel is progressively replacing the AT-2. Finally, the AT-6 Spiral is deployed on the Mi-24 Hind D attack helicopter.

CHAPTER NINE
Combat aircraft of tomorrow

Although many of the aircraft types described in this book will still be in service well into the 21st Century, the operational requirements governing the development of future combat aircraft are already well defined. Unless there is a dramatic alteration in international relations between east and west, vast sums of money will certainly be spent over the next decade or two in equipping NATO's front-line squadrons with new aircraft that fall into three principal categories: supersonic V/STOL, agile multi-role, and advanced technology ('Stealth').

The resurgence of interest in supersonic V/STOL is beyond dispute. However, although at first sight the operational requirement for such an aircraft seems apparent, doubts have been raised about the benefits it would offer compared to the subsonic Harrier/AV-8 of today.

It is a natural, though incorrect, assumption that the faster a combat aircraft, the more effective it is, and therefore better than slower types. This is not necessarily true, as events in the South Atlantic proved in 1982. At low level, supersonic capability can rarely be used to advantage, and success depends primarily on the quality of the pilot, his aircraft weapon systems and his ordnance. The Sea Harrier/Sidewinder combination proved the best in combat across all three categories. It was outnumbered, slower than many of its opponents, and its small force of pilots was subjected to an enormous workload; nevertheless, the Harrier emerged from its baptism of fire with great credit.

In low-level air combat a supersonic aircraft requires reheat to extricate itself from a disadvantage — and then, paradoxically, is immediately more at risk because of the increased infrared signature and combat fuel usage. At similar performance levels, reheat fuel flow is two or three times that of a 'dry' engine — over 600 lb/min at low level in a typical single-engined fighter. A Harrier in low-level combat, on the other hand, rarely exceeds 220 lb/minute. The protagonist who breaks off a close combat due to concern about his low fuel state, and uses reheat to get away, is inviting a hostile AAM.

Broadly, supersonic speed can be effective only at high altitude, in the specialised interceptor role. In today's low-level combat, or in ground attack operations, a supersonic capability can often hinder rather than help. Although it can aid penetration

to, and escape from, the target area — albeit with a major penalty in fuel consumption — it is of no help over the target itself; target acquisition and attack at speeds in excess of twelve miles per minute presents severe problems, to say the least.

Relative to subsonic V/STOL fighters such as the Harrier, supersonic V/STOL capability allows earlier interception of hostile aircraft — an important asset, as stand-off missile ranges increase — and also offers a better chance of intercepting and destroying such missiles once they have been launched. The same principle applies when intercepting a hostile aircraft engaged on a ground attack mission; rapid reaction, which is already a major factor in the Harrier's operational success story, would be backed up by the ability to intercept the target aircraft before it was able to reach its weapons release point.

Supersonic and subsonic aircraft are distinguished in current thinking by the use of a reheated and unreheated engine respectively. But what if a reheated engine is married to a subsonic airframe? The result is a comparatively light aircraft which has a significantly better performance at low level than supersonic aircraft with the same powerplant. The weight saving includes avionics and general systems, but is mainly due to the use of thicker aerofoil sections in the wing and tail unit; this permits more fuel to be carried in the wing and less in the fuselage, which can then be shortened. An aircraft of this type would be considerably cheaper than current supersonic designs and so could be available in greater numbers, offering a much improved operational flexibility.

A supersonic capability is essential for a modern radar-equipped fighter/interceptor in air-to-air combat. However, an active radar emits a signal which is obviously undesirable in a low-level ground attack role as it advertises the aircraft's presence, as well as its speed, direction and distance from the target, enabling hostile ground defences to be prepared. Apart from this, the radar would also occupy the prime nose area, which is better employed for the laser ranging or FLIR systems required for a fully-effective ground-attack mission. Also, the ground-attack role calls for high penetration speed with reheat off, a high 'g' capability and a good view from the cockpit, together with good self-defence systems.

An ideal mix would be a majority of high-performance subsonic V/STOL aircraft, covered by a minority of supersonic interceptors for the few occasions when beyond visual range (BVR) combat is a viable option. There have been many attempts to bridge this gap with aircraft that are supersonic, multi-role and which possess a very short take-off capability. None of these, however, can recover vertically, which would be essential for true invulnerability to anti-airfield counter-attacks. Only the Harrier has successfully come anywhere near to meeting these requirements. The only asset it lacks is supersonic speed, and this factor is now within the bounds of existing technology. Supersonic capability would enable the Harrier to close with its target in a much shorter time, though it would not then be as flexible in off-base deployments as is the current subsonic Harrier family.

From the original P 1127 project in the early 1960s, the Harrier family has grown to include the RAF's GR 3s, GR 5s and T 4s; the US Marine Corps' AV-8As, AV-8B Harrier IIs and their two-seat variants; the Royal Navy's Sea Harrier FRS 1 and T 4N, with the FRS 2 coming along; the Spanish Navy's AV-8S and TAV-8S, and finally the Indian Navy's Sea Harrier FRS 51 and T 60. This picture shows the growth areas of the V/STOL family, and, looking ahead, it is reasonable to assume that this growth will not cease — but where is it to go now?

Naturally, existing Harrier types will be improved in pace with new technology. An example of this is the Royal Navy's Sea Harriers, which will be undergoing their mid-life update programme towards the end of the 1980s. They are to receive a new Ferranti pulse-Doppler radar for a look-down shoot-down capability, a complete cockpit information databus system, improved radar warning, and will carry single or twin AMRAAM missiles on their outer wing pylons, all of which will bring them up to FRS 2 standard. They will, however, still be subsonic.

Configurations for supersonic Harrier designs have varied over the years, and it is worth remembering that the prototype of a supersonic V/STOL strike aircraft, the Hawker Siddeley P 1154, was well advanced in construction when the project was cancelled in 1965. Its cancellation led directly to the development of the P 1127 (RAF) which first flew eighteen months later and subsequently entered service as the Harrier.

Although the P 1154 was cancelled, a later similar supersonic configuration was studied in 1973 for the US Navy. Designated AV-16S, this project was the product of a joint programme between Hawker Siddeley Aviation and McDonnell Douglas, and stemmed from a US Navy requirement for a supersonic deck-launched aircraft capable of VTOL intercept missions as well as long-radius subsonic strike against surface targets. The AV-16S engine was to have been the larger-diameter Pegasus 15 with PCB (Plenum Chamber Burning, a new type of exhaust boost system). Performance was initially aimed at a Mach 1.7 capability, with a Mach 1.9 potential. The wing design was larger than that of the P 1154 and the main undercarriage units were moved to pods on the wing trailing edge, though the design was still recognisable as a Harrier derivative.

However, the programme never moved beyond the Phase One study stage due to the predicted development costs versus the available budgets in the US Navy. Even the complementary subsonic

project — the AV-16A — was seen as needing almost 1 billion for research, development and testing, of which over half was required for the development of the Pegasus 15 engine in its non-PCB configuration. There was little chance at that time that the USN could be persuaded to spend this sort of money on a weapons system just for the Marine Corps. However, the loss of the AV-16 programme led directly to the development, in 1975-6, of the aircraft we know today as the Harrier II.

From 1975 to 1979, the BAe team at Kingston continued design studies, involving wind tunnel and other testing, which resulted in the constant refinement and updating of the supersonic V/STOL concept. A number of configurations were examined, including some, like the P 1205-11 design to AST 403, with the air intake relocated at the chin position. The design powerplant for the P 1205 was a Rolls-Royce Pegasus PCB, producing about forty per cent more static thrust than the non-PCB engine. However, the engine had its origins in the 1960s, and was therefore somewhat dated for a 1990s application.

Other designs followed. One of them was the P 1214, a forward sweep design which avoided the most damaging effects of the high-energy exhaust on the parts of the aircraft aft of, and close to, the Pegasus nozzles. Affectionately known at Kingston as the 'Star Wars' design, the P 1214 had three vectoring nozzles, the two forward ones with PCB and a single nozzle at the rear. However different it might look, it was still a derivative of the original vectored thrust principle. The P 1214 was the last supersonic V/STOL design revealed by British Aerospace; subsequent studies and developments are very much a reality at Kingston, but they are subject to the constraints of high security.

The second requirement, for an agile multi-role aircraft to equip NATO's combat squadrons into the 21st century, is much closer to fruition. In June 1986, a company known as Eurofighter/Jagdflugzeug GmBH was formed in Germany to manage the new European Fighter Aircraft (EFA) programme. The company is wholly owned by four partner companies — Aeritalia, British Aerospace, CASA and MBB — and is based in Munich, housed in the same building as Panavia. It will use many of the management techniques which have been used so successfully by Panavia in controlling the Tornado programme.

The EFA programme involves about 800 aircraft for the air forces of the Federal Republic of Germany, Great Britain, Italy and Spain. The agreed participation level is United Kingdom 33 per cent, Germany 33 per cent, Italy 21 per cent and Spain 13 per cent. Eight prototypes will be built to flight test the weapon system and produce the necessary flight clearances to enable production aircraft to enter service in 1995. The powerplant for the early prototype aircraft had not been agreed at the time of writing, but later prototypes and the production aircraft will be powered by a new engine to be developed by the engine companies in the partner countries, based on their respective advanced technology programmes. Production arrangements will be similar to those employed on the Tornado programme, with major components built uniquely in the four countries but with each country having an assembly line.

The EFA programme will run well into the 21st century, and the aircraft now being planned may well see more than twenty years of active service in several versions. The aircraft is intended to replace the ageing Jaguar, Phantom, F-104, and Buccaneer tactical aircraft now used in a wide variety of roles in Western European air forces; ultimately it will also replace the F-16, although for some years the two will serve side by side. Many of the aircraft the EFA is designed to replace have been in service for a very long time, so that by the time the EFA itself becomes operational in 1995, those aircraft will not only be elderly, but also outclassed by the new military aircraft under development in the Soviet Union. Eventually, it is anticipated that as many as 800 to 1000 EFAs could be needed in Western Europe, but the design, research, development and production over a period of more than twenty years seems likely to involve sums amounting to £20 billion, if not more.

The EFA is essentially a conventional weapon system, designed for the air superiority role and tactical support. Unlike the Tornado, it will have no interdictor capability, nor is it intended to be nuclear-equipped. The project definition phase of the programme was already well on course in the summer of 1986, with confirmation that the design satisfied the requirements of the four participating Air Staffs to an acceptable level. In addition to the key design parameters already agreed — basic mass empty weight of 9.75 tonnes, two engines each with 90 kN thrust and a wing area of 50 sq m — the Air Staffs have now also reached agreement on the equipment fit of the aircraft, although selection of the actual equipment items has still to be made. This substantial progress in overcoming earlier design problems has come about through increased confidence in fly-by-wire technology and improvement in the aerodynamic shaping of the fuselage, both reducing structural weight, coupled with the introduction of convergent/divergent nozzle technology to the engines to give increased operational performance.

In view of the time-scale involved, it is expected that a new variant of the well-proven Rolls-Royce RB-199 engine will be developed for the prototype EFA, but that eventually a major new fighter engine will be developed for production aircraft, based on the XG-40 programme now in an advanced stage at Rolls-Royce. The latter engine is the only new fighter engine available among the four EFA participating nations, although the French aero-engine company, SNECMA, also has a new engine, the M-88, under development for the rival Rafale venture.

A key factor in the EFA programme is British Aerospace's Experimental Aircraft Programme (EAP). The EAP technology demonstrator made its first flight from Warton Aerodrome on 8 August 1986 in the hands of Dave Eagles, executive director of flight operations. In the course of a flight lasting 1 hour 7 minutes Eagles carried out general handling manoeuvres up to 4g, plus Dutch rolls, and took the aircraft to 30,000 ft and a maximum speed of Mach 1.1.

Only one EAP demonstrator will be built, and the aircraft is not intended as a specific prototype for EFA. Its function is to prove technologies that might be incorporated in the European Fighter Aircraft, and even before it made its first flight it had already taught the countries and companies involved in the airframe, engine and avionics much of what they needed to know for the EFA.

The cost of the EAP is shared between the UK Ministry of Defence, British Aerospace, Aeritalia and other equipment companies in the UK, Italy and West Germany. Continued funding is vital to keep the EAP demonstrator flying until the first EFA prototypes become available later this decade, by which time many of the aeronautical and technological concepts embodied in it — design shape, materials and fly-by-wire flight technique, for example — will have been thoroughly validated.

As far as NATO is concerned, the question is not whether the European Fighter Aircraft will work — that is virtually beyond doubt, given the wealth of experience behind the project — but whether it will be accepted by air forces other than those of the four nations involved in the programme in the face of fierce competition from both the United States and France.

France is the principal challenger, with Dassault-Breguet's Rafale — formerly known as the Avion de Combat Expérimental, or ACX. Rafale A, as the technology demonstrator is known, flew for the first time on 4 July 1986. Powered by two General Electric F404 turbofans, Rafale is a single-seat aircraft with compound-sweep delta wing, all-moving canard, single fin and semi-vented intakes. It incorporates digital fly-by-wire, relaxed stability and an electronic cockpit with voice command. Wide use of composites and aluminium-lithium have resulted in a seven to eight per cent weight saving.

The operational version, to be known as Rafale B, will be externally similar but smaller and lighter, and will replace the Armée de l'Air's Mirages and Jaguars and the Aéronavale's Super Etendards. Six Rafale B prototypes will be built, four for the Air Force and two for the Navy; the first will begin flight testing in 1990 and deliveries will begin in 1995, the production Rafale B being powered by two SNECMA M88 engines.

France's development of the indigenous Rafale was the result of her withdrawal from the EFA project, mainly because of a squabble over design leadership, and in 1986 she was seeking potential Rafale partners among several NATO countries, including Belgium, Denmark, Greece, the Netherlands and Norway. Dassault has also proposed a single-engined Rafale C version to be built jointly with Indonesia, and the aircraft forms the basis of Dassault's submission for a light combat aircraft (LCA) for the Indian Air Force in the 1990s.

Meanwhile, the USAF is proceeding with its enormously expensive Advanced Tactical Fighter programme, which is already seriously behind schedule. The USAF's last fighter, the F-16, entered service in 1979, and since then the Russians have introduced no fewer than five new fighter types. The Su-24 Fencer has an all-weather/low altitude penetration capability that enhances Soviet ability to carry out deep strikes into NATO territory. The Su-25 Frogfoot ground attack aircraft has already proved itself to be an excellent close air support fighter. Then there are the MiG-29 Fulcrum, with capabilities similar to the F-18 Hornet, the Su-27 Flanker, which is comparable to the F-15, and the MiG-31 Foxhound, a vastly improved version of the MiG-25 Foxbat.

The reason for the delay in developing a new USAF fighter is not hard to find. The Americans have set themselves the formidable goal of producing a tactical aircraft that will remain viable for the next quarter of a century — an aircraft that will have a range 50-100 per cent greater than that of the F-15 Eagle, be capable of short take-off and landing on damaged airfields, and be capable of engaging multiple enemy fighters at once, beyond visual range. And it will have to do all that and survive, operated by a single pilot, in an environment filled with people, both in the air and on the ground, whose sole purpose is to destroy it.

Demonstration of the technology that will be applied to the Advanced Tactical Fighter began in the 1970s. Since that time a number of test aircraft have flown, demonstrating advances in aerodynamics, flight control and avionics. They include the YF-16 control-configured vehicle, the HiMAT highly manoeuvrable remotely piloted research vehicle, the integrated flight and fire control F-15, the advanced fighter technology integration F-16, the X-29 forward-sweep demonstrator and the mission-adaptive-wing F-111. Another testbed, the F-15 STOL and manoeuvre technology demonstrator, is due to fly in 1988.

Seven US companies are involved in ATF design work, with Lockheed-California possibly some distance ahead of the rest. Lockheed has the advantage of long experience in former highly secret projects such as the F-104, U-2 and SR-71, and has also been privately developing advanced fighter concepts for the past ten years. Meanwhile, in an effort to push down the aircraft's weight and therefore its overall cost, the USAF has trimmed some of ATF's operational concepts. The weight has been reduced by several thousand pounds through trimming the mission concepts in a number of places, taking the g loading down, and reducing the cruise altitude on some mission profiles. The gross take-off weight of ATF has now stabilised at around 50,000 lb. To put this in context, an F-15C with a centreline tank and eight missiles weighs about 51,000 lb, but ATF will have a range far in excess of the F-15's on internal fuel only for the air-to-air mission.

One of ATF's problems is that it is still only fifth on the USAF's list of priorities. Tactical Air Command alone has about 150 requirements, led by AMRAAM, LANTIRN, the F-15E dual-role fighter, and the procurement of more F-15s and F-16s. Current forecasting is that full-scale development of the ATF will begin in 1988, with the aircraft in service by 1995.

Whatever its eventual format, the ATF will certainly employ so-called 'Stealth' technology, which is the real key to the survival of a combat aircraft in a hostile electronic environment. Two companies, Lockheed and Northrop, have been primarily involved in the most secret of all of the USAF's 'Black Programmes'; Lockheed has already developed the Covert In-Weather Survivable Reconnaissance System (COSINS) which is a deliberately vague acronym to cover its Stealth aircraft, the F-19. Twenty of these aircraft have been built and are assigned under conditions of extreme secrecy to the 9th Strategic Reconnaissance Wing.

In the meantime, Northrop is going ahead with the development of its own Stealth aircraft, the Advanced Technology Bomber, which is a flying-wing design somewhat smaller than Rockwell's B-1B, which it will eventually replace. First flight of the prototype is scheduled for 1987, with an anticipated in-service date of 1992. The ATB is subsonic and powered by unreheated turbofans. The aircraft will be optimised to penetrate Soviet defences and to deliver a warload of free-fall high-accuracy weapons. It will not need to penetrate at low level for radar avoidance, it will be more aerodynamically efficient than an aircraft at sea level and it will need less fuel for an equivalent-range mission flown at low level.

INDEX

145

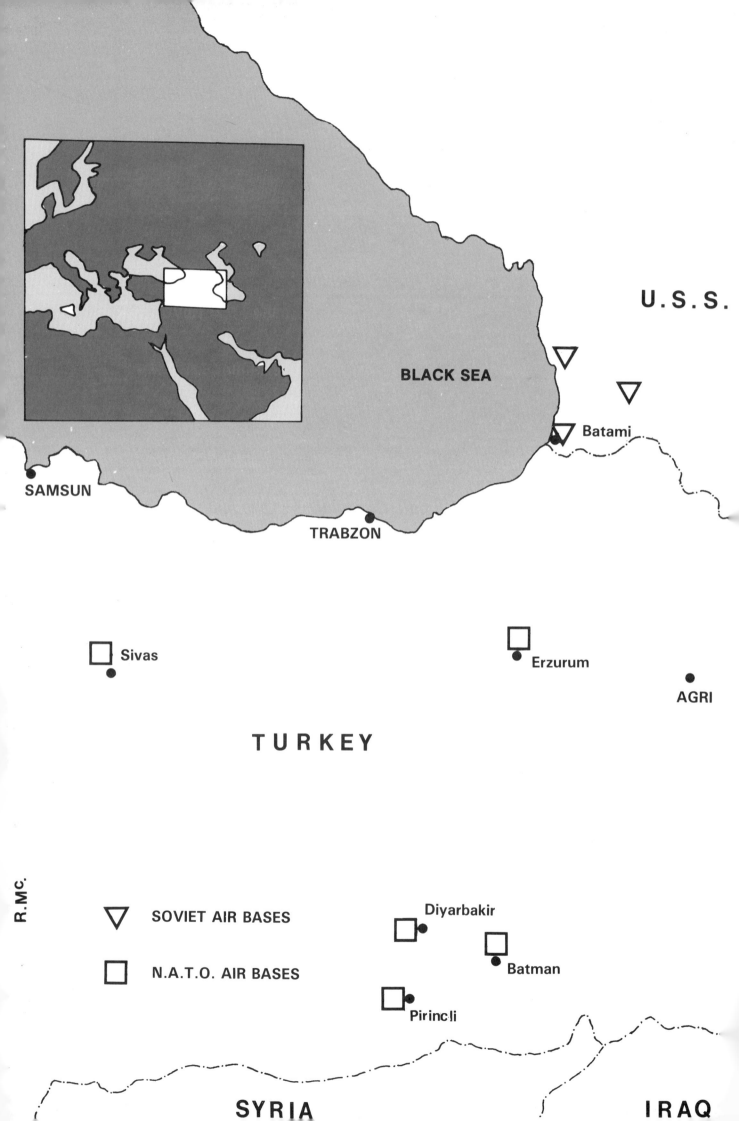

U.S.S.

BLACK SEA

Batami

SAMSUN

TRABZON

Sivas

Erzurum

AGRI

T U R K E Y

Diyarbakir

R.MC.

▽   SOVIET AIR BASES

□   N.A.T.O. AIR BASES

Batman

Pirincli

SYRIA

IRAQ